WordPress for Bussiness Bloggers

Promote and grow your WordPress blog with advanced plugins, analytics, advertising, and SEO

Paul Thewlis

[PACKT]
PUBLISHING

BIRMINGHAM - MUMBAI

WordPress for Bussiness Bloggers

Copyright © 2008 Packt Publishing

First published: August 2008

Production Reference: 1300708

Published by Packt Publishing Ltd.
32 Lincoln Road
Olton
Birmingham, B27 6PA, UK.

ISBN 978-1-847195-32-6

www.packtpub.com

Cover Image by Karl Moore (karl.moore@ukonline.co.uk)

Credits

Author

Paul Thewlis

Reviewers

Lee Jordan

Narayan Bhat

Senior Acquisition Editor

David Barnes

Development Editor

Ved Prakash Jha

Technical Editor

Dhiraj Chandiramani

Editorial Team Leader

Akshara Aware

Project Manager

Abhijeet Deobhakta

Project Coordinator

Rajashree Hamine

Indexer

Monica Ajmera

Proofreader

Chris Smith

Production Coordinator

Shantanu Zagade

Cover Work

Shantanu Zagade

About the Author

Paul Thewlis has worked as a web communications professional in the public and private sectors. He is currently E-Communications Manager for a multi-national transport company, headquartered in the UK. He began his web career as a Technical Editor, working on web design books for a well-known publisher. He has extensive experience of many content management systems and blogging platforms. He is an expert in the use of social media within corporate communications, and blogs about that subject, as well as WordPress and the Web in general, at `http://blog.paulthewlis.com`. Paul lives in Birmingham, England, with his fiancée, Zöe.

I would like to thank Matt Mullenweg and the WordPress development team, as well as all the hard-working members of the wider WordPress community, who created the plugins featured in this book. Scott Wallick and Andy Skelton deserve a special mention for the great work they do on the Sandbox theme. I would also like to thank my parents, Jack and Margaret, for their unending support, and my wonderful fiancée, Zöe, for putting up with so many late nights and lonely weekends during the writing of this book.

About the Reviewers

Lee Jordan is an avid user of Blogger, Twitter, and other useful web applications. She designs interactive customer service portals, enterprise-level websites and other web-based applications and writes web content and user guides. She applies over ten years of experience designing and writing for the Web to developing interactive, user-friendly websites, and writing technical guides to popular web technologies.

Narayan Bhat is passionate about wandering the Internet and blogging. Get Blogger tips from his blogging websites:

Dummies Guide to Google Blogger (Beta)—`http://betabloggerfordummies.blogspot.com/2007/08/hot-tips-on-blogger-profiles.html`

SEO Adsense Tips—`http://seoblogadsense.blogspot.com/`

THE WIDGETS OF BETA BLOGGER—`http://widgetry.blogspot.com`

Tips for Bloggers—`http://tipsforbloggers.blogspot.com`

Table of Contents

Preface

WordPress for Business Bloggers provides advanced strategies and techniques to take your WordPress business blog from average to extraordinary. Whether you already have a blog, or are still in the planning stages, this book will show you how to use WordPress to create a highly successful blog for your business.

The release of version 2.6 has confirmed the status of WordPress as the leading blogging platform. This book has been written for and tested on WordPress 2.6, so all the screenshots and tutorials are accurate for users of that version of the software.

This is a practical, hands-on book based around a fictitious case-study blog, which you will build using a development server on your own computer. The vast majority of tutorials and examples will be applied to the case study blog. The case study grows chapter by chapter, from installing your local development server, right up to the finished blog. You will be installing and configuring a selection of WordPress plugins to improve the functionality of the case-study blog.

You are provided with clear instructions and detailed screenshots, so you can see exactly what to do at each step of the build. When you have completed the case study, you will have the knowledge and confidence to apply all the techniques you have learned to your own WordPress business blog.

The author assumes you have basic experience with WordPress, already know how to set up a self-hosted WordPress blog, and are familiar with the basics: creating posts and pages, configuring blog settings, and so on. By the time you have finished the book you will have moved forward from WordPress novice to an advanced user of the software in a business context.

What This Book Covers

In *Chapter 1* you will examine many different types of business blogs. You will be shown a selection of great business blogs and see what you can learn from them.

In *Chapter 2* you will be introduced to the case study blog, and taken through the process of developing strategic goals and your blog plan. You will learn that the planning process is important, even if your blog is already up and running.

In *Chapter 3* you will learn the basics of blog design. You will work through a brief introduction to HTML and CSS, and see how easy it is to create your own custom design using the Sandbox theme.

In *Chapter 4* you will learn some advanced image and video handling techniques, including setting up an image gallery and using video from third-party sources, such as YouTube and Google Video.

Chapter 5 focuses on different techniques and methods required for creating the best possible content for your business blog.

Chapter 6 covers some of the most important SEO strategies and how to apply them, as well as how to submit your blog to the search engines.

In *Chapter 7* you will learn some advanced blog promotion techniques, including: advanced RSS with FeedBurner; using Internet Explorer 8 Web Slices; submitting to the blog search engines, like Technorati; using social networks, such as Facebook and Twitter; and using social bookmarks, such as Digg and del.icio.us.

In *Chapter 8* you will learn the importance of connecting with other bloggers and playing an active role in the blogosphere to promote your business blog.

In *Chapter 9* you will learn how to analyze your blog's performance using tools such as Google Analytics and WordPress.com Stats.

In *Chapter 10* you will be introduced to a variety of strategies to help you generate revenue from your blog, like using advertising and affiliate programs.

In *Chapter 11* you will learn how to manage the growth of your blog by optimizing it for high traffic and introducing multiple authors by using WordPress MU.

Who is This Book for?

This book is for anybody running or starting a business blog using WordPress. Whether you plan to use your blog for PR and marketing, or want to profit directly from blogging, this book offers you everything you need.

As we want to get into the specifics of business blogging as quickly as possible, we don't cover the WordPress basics. So it's best to have some experience with WordPress before you start with this book.

The book mainly focuses on a self-hosted WordPress installation, but most of the advice also applies to blogs hosted on WordPress.com.

Conventions

In this book, you will find a number styles of text that distinguish between different kinds of information. Here are some examples of these styles, and an explanation of their meaning.

There are three styles for code. Code words in text are shown as follows: "The `<table>` tag was only intended to present data in a tabular format."

A block of code will be set as follows:

```
body
  {
    font-family: Arial, Helvetica, sans-serif;
    margin: 0;
    padding: 0;
    background-color: #CCCCCC;
    color: #000000;
  }
```

When we wish to draw your attention to a particular part of a code block, the relevant lines or items will be made bold:

```
<html>
<head>
 <title>A Simple Web Page</title>
  <style type="text/css">
    h2
      {
        color: #FF0000;
        font-size: 16px;
      }
  </style>
</head>
```

New terms and **important words** are introduced in a bold-type font. Words that you see on the screen, in menus or dialog boxes, for example, appear in our text like this: "clicking the **Next** button moves you to the next screen".

Important notes appear in a box like this.

Tips and tricks appear like this.

Reader Feedback

Feedback from our readers is always welcome. Let us know what you think about this book, what you liked or may have disliked. Reader feedback is important for us to develop titles that you really get the most out of.

To send us general feedback, simply drop an email to feedback@packtpub.com, making sure to mention the book title in the subject of your message.

If there is a book that you need and would like to see us publish, please send us a note in the **SUGGEST A TITLE** form on www.packtpub.com or email suggest@packtpub.com.

If there is a topic that you have expertise in and you are interested in either writing or contributing to a book, see our author guide on www.packtpub.com/authors.

Customer Support

Now that you are the proud owner of a Packt book, we have a number of things to help you to get the most from your purchase.

Downloading the Example Code for the Book

Visit http://www.packtpub.com/files/code/5326_Code.zip to directly download the example code.

The downloadable files contain instructions on how to use them.

Errata

Although we have taken every care to ensure the accuracy of our contents, mistakes do happen. If you find a mistake in one of our books—maybe a mistake in text or code—we would be grateful if you would report this to us. By doing this you can save other readers from frustration, and help to improve subsequent versions of this book. If you find any errata, report them by visiting http://www.packtpub.com/support, selecting your book, clicking on the **let us know** link, and entering the details of your errata. Once your errata are verified, your submission will be accepted and the errata added to the list of existing errata. The existing errata can be viewed by selecting your title from http://www.packtpub.com/support.

Piracy

Piracy of copyright material on the Internet is an ongoing problem across all media. At Packt, we take the protection of our copyright and licenses very seriously. If you come across any illegal copies of our works in any form on the Internet, please provide the location address or the website name immediately, so we can pursue a remedy.

Please contact us at copyright@packtpub.com with a link to the suspected pirated material.

We appreciate your help in protecting our authors, and our ability to bring you valuable content.

Questions

You can contact us at questions@packtpub.com if you are having a problem with some aspect of the book, and we will do our best to address it.

1
A Blog Less Ordinary— What Makes a Great Blog?

Blogging has been part of the web landscape for over a decade now. From personal journals to big corporate marketing, the medium has matured to become a ubiquitous mode of live communication. The power of blogging has been recognized by the business community, and canny marketers view it as a powerful weapon in their digital arsenal.

Done well, blogging can bring myriad benefits to businesses of any size. Done badly, it can cause more harm than good. Central to the success of any business blogger is a thorough understanding of the technology he or she is using. This will give you a competitive advantage by being able to create a more engaging blog. You have wisely chosen **WordPress** as your blogging platform and this book will give you the in-depth knowledge of the software you need to take your blog from ordinary to exceptional.

This is not an introduction to WordPress; that is, we will not be covering the basics such as installation or how to post. Most readers will already have an established WordPress blog or will at least be in the advanced stages of planning one.

In this chapter, we will consider the essence of great blogs and the groundwork that is required to produce one. What separates the mediocre from the marvelous? What should you do to blast through the blogosphere and take your blog to the next level? We will look at some examples of the best blogs out there and see what we can learn from them. The principles outlined here are a jumping-off point for the techniques and methods that we will cover through the rest of the book.

You Can Stand Out from the Crowd

Let's begin with a quick pep talk.

Making a success of your blog can seem like an uphill struggle. It's easy to be disheartened in the early days because success rarely happens overnight. One of the first psychological stumbling blocks for many bloggers is the overwhelming size of the blogosphere. It's easy to feel like a small fish in a very big pond. But, that's not necessarily the case.

It's true, the blogosphere is a crowded place, with millions of blogs out there all clambering for attention.

The statistics are mind-boggling. **Technorati**, the leading blog directory, claims it is tracking in excess of 112 million blogs, with over 175,000 new blogs created daily and 1.6 million new postings per day (see `http://technorati.com/about/` for the latest data, as the figures will almost certainly have increased by the time you read this).

It's actually very difficult to be precise about the number of blogs out there. The 112,000,000 blogs quoted above are just those being tracked by Technorati and not all of them will be active. Putting an exact figure on it is largely an academic exercise (as you'll see from my attempt, below). The point here is that *the blogosphere is big and getting bigger by the second*.

At first this seems a little daunting. You may be wondering how you can stand out in such a crowded arena. With so much live information being constantly updated, is there room for any more? Does the world need another blog? Is the web-surfing public in danger of reaching blog-saturation or information-overload? I believe the answers to these questions are **yes, yes**, and **no**, respectively.

When you break them down, the numbers become a little more reassuring. Many of the 122 million blogs being tracked by Technorati are inactive—we can deduce this from their own statistics. 1.6 million new posts per day works out at just 0.014 postings per blog, per day. If we assume that for a blog to be considered active it needs at least one new post per week, we'd expect that figure to be more like 0.14. In which case, the total number of **active** blogs is around 11.2 million.

OK, that's some pretty rough and ready arithmetic, but it highlights the point that most blogs out there are, in fact, dormant. This effectively thins out the blogosphere and adds weight to blogs like yours, which are regularly updated.

11.2 million is still quite a big number, but when you consider the size and diversity of the global web audience (currently estimated at around 1,250 million), hopefully you can see there is room for you and your blog. Yes, there are a lot of blogs out there, but there are also a lot of web users hungry for information.

As well as being big, the blogosphere is also diverse. However, there are millions of blogs, which cover an enormous spectrum of subjects and genres. The blogosphere can be almost endlessly segmented, which adds even more weight to your activities as a business blogger. You're not competing for audience share against the blogosphere as a whole. Like most bloggers, you'll find your niche and realize success is within your grasp.

Where Do You Fit In?

Blogging began very much as an exercise in personal publishing. It was an evolution of the personal home pages that have been with us since the early days of the Web. It's still true that the majority of blogs take the form of a personal journal, with no implicit business agenda. (However, many 'personal' bloggers have found ways to monetize their activity; there is now a growing breed of 'professional bloggers', who derive much, if not all of their income from blogging.)

It's widely believed that John Barger first used the term **weblog** in December 1997. Peter Merholz shortened it to **blog** in 1999, saying, "I've decided to pronounce the word 'Weblog' as 'wee-blog'. Or 'blog' for short."

It was politics and journalism that brought blogging into the mainstream, particularly in the wake of the 9/11 attacks of 2001. The 2004 US presidential elections marked a watershed as blogging became an increasingly normal part of the media landscape. Journalist, Andrew Sullivan, was a pioneer of the political blog, starting **The Daily Dish** in 2001. The following screenshot is of Andrew Sullivan's blog from September 30, 2001.

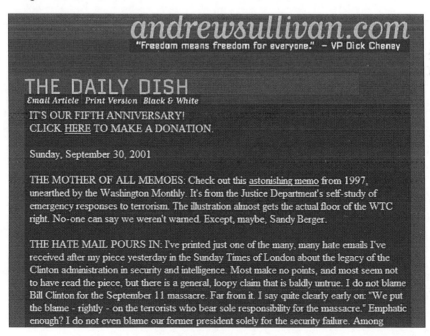

With politicians and influential journalists playing an active role in the blogosphere, it wasn't long until the business community recognized the potential benefits of blogging. Today, business blogging is commonplace with more and more web users expecting to see a 'Blog' link on company home pages.

In this very brief history of blogging we can already see three of the biggest blog genres: Personal Blogs, Political Blogs, and Business Blogs (there are, of course, many others). *Most readers of this book will fall into the 'Business' genre.*

Not All Business Blogs Are the Same

So, you're a business blogger. However, that doesn't say very much about your specific goals and aspirations. All blogs are different. Their reasons for existence vary depending on what the publisher is trying to achieve. Key to the success of your blog is having a clear vision of what you want it to do for you. This is your **blogging strategy**. Once it's clear in your mind, you can start to set concrete **tactical** goals for your blog, which we'll cover in Chapter 2.

For now, consider the 'raison d'être' of your blog. Why are you putting your time, energy, and resources into it? What do you hope to achieve?

[One of the key drivers for many business bloggers is the fact that blogs can be a very inexpensive form of marketing—you can get a lot of value for a relatively small investment.]

Obviously, not all business bloggers are trying to achieve the same things with their blogs, but here are a few of the more common strategic goals of business blogging:

- To increase sales
- To add value to your products and services
- To open a dialog with your customers
- To raise awareness of your company, products, and services
- To demonstrate your knowledge and expertise
- To provide customer service and support
- To improve public relations (for example, media relations, reputation management, crisis management, and so on)
- To drive traffic to your other website(s)
- To give some personality to your corporate image

You may well have several of these strategic goals in mind for your blog. There is no reason why your blog can't achieve a combination of these. Let's take a look at each of the goals in more detail with some examples of blogs that have them. (Not all of the example blogs here are created in WordPress; they're included as they are good illustrations of these strategic goals.)

Increasing Sales

A blog can be a great way of expanding and updating your online and offline sales literature. Posting about the benefits and features of your products or services can be a great way of converting leads into sales. This usually involves a simpler approach rather than a full-on hard sell. Your regular sales brochure, whether online or offline, will probably list your selling points with brief explanations, which for many customers, can seem rather over-hyped. A blog allows you to expand on your selling points and, in doing so, demonstrate that there is more to your products than just sales hype.

A great example of a 'sales' blog is that of GPS manufacturer, Garmin (`http://garmin.blogs.com`). Their blog not only gives background information about the products, it also shows innovative ways in which customers are using their GPS units, going beyond the scope of their regular sales literature. There are also plenty of customer testimonials and images of the products actually being used.

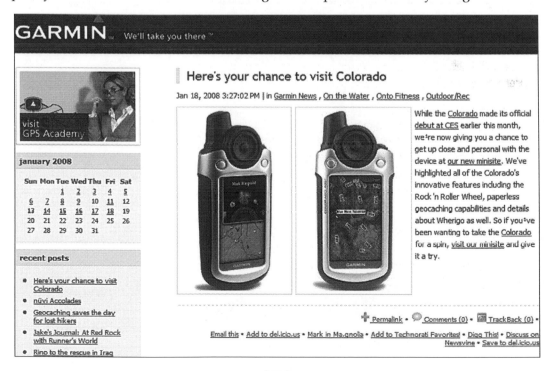

Adding Value

Your blog is a great place to tell customers about extra features and added benefits of your products and services. This is related to the idea of increasing sales, already mentioned, so your blog can probably kill two birds with one stone. Customers who use your products and services can learn ways of getting more out of them. For example, software developers might blog about hidden features that regular users might not otherwise know about.

A good example of this type of blog is the **37signals Product Blog** (`http://productblog.37signals.com/`). The company uses it to educate its customers about features in its range of online productivity software. The following screenshot illustrates this approach — who knew there was a Backpack version optimized for iPhone and iPod? As well as adding value for its existing customers, this kind of information is also sales material for prospective buyers.

A Dialog with Your Customers

Blogs provide the perfect environment for a genuine conversation with your customers. A key feature of any blog is the ability of readers to write comments about posts. Businesses can use this in-built technology to engage in a live conversation with their customers. It can be a great way of receiving feedback and testing opinions about new products and services, as well as finding out what your customers really want.

Obviously, opening up public communication channels with your customers can involve some risk—you may receive damaging comments. How to deal with negative feedback is a delicate issue that we'll look at in more detail in Chapter 8. For this reason, many large businesses do not use comments on their blogs. A notable exception is Boeing, which does allow comments on its blog (http://boeingblogs.com/randy/).

Orders and commitments

Clearly there were two big stories in aviation today, the announcement of Airbus' 2007 results, and Boeing's announcement of 787 delays.

About the 2007 orders story, as you've probably read by now, Airbus had 1,341 net orders last year, compared to Boeing's previously announced year-end total of 1,413 net orders. The Airbus gross total was 1,458 orders and the Boeing gross total was 1,423 orders.

Today's Airbus announcement, combined with Boeing's release earlier this month, provides a really good sense of the orders picture in 2007.

And what I take away from all this is that 2007 was an incredibly strong orders year for our industry. Perhaps that's an understatement. Between our two companies we had more than 2,750 orders. And we've seen our

January 2008

Sun	Mon	Tue	Wed	Thu	Fri	Sat
		1	2	3	4	5
6	7	8	9	10	11	12
13	14	15	16	17	18	19
20	21	22	23	24	25	26
27	28	29	30	31		

Search

Welcome

This is the home page of Randy's Journal, a blog of thoughts and

Raising Awareness

Blogs are a great way to raise awareness for your company and products. The nature of the blogosphere is that bloggers link to each other. This provides a great platform for spreading your message virally. Having your blog linked to and commented on by bloggers across the globe can spread the word quickly. It's a great form of 'buzz marketing' and many start-ups use a blog to create an air of anticipation about their forthcoming launch.

Joost, the web TV Company, used a blog in the lead up to its launch, using the code name 'The Venice Project'. It helped to create a buzz and raised awareness for the company before it launched (`http://blog.joost.com/`).

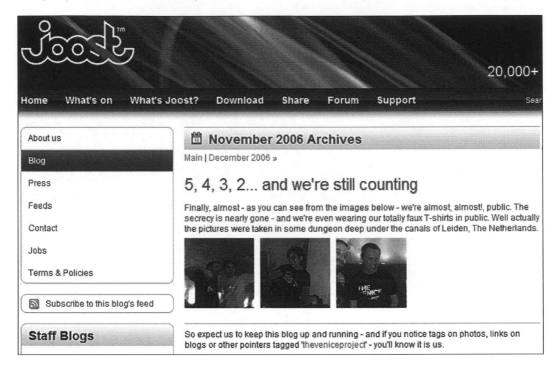

Showing Expertise

Demonstrating your professional knowledge and positioning yourself as an expert in your field is a great way of raising your business profile. This is particularly true for consultants and others who are hired because of their knowledge and experience. Web designers, academics, authors, life coaches, and software developers are just a few examples of the kinds of business people who may wish to demonstrate their expertise. Using a blog is a great way to achieve this because it provides a regularly updated outlet to showcase your professional activities and write about your achievements.

A great WordPress blog that demonstrates this is that of web designer, Jeffrey Zeldman (`http://www.zeldman.com`). He uses his blog to discuss issues in the web design arena and give his comment about what's happening in the industry.

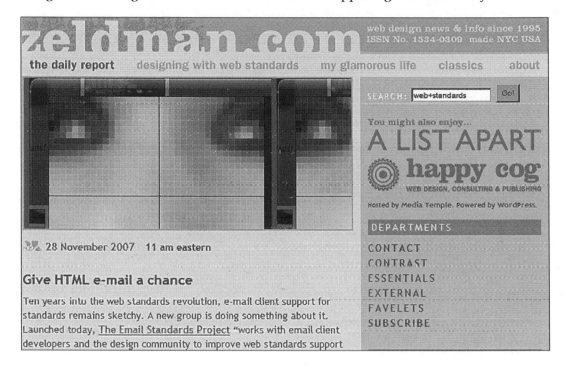

Customer Service

Providing efficient customer service is a cornerstone of most successful businesses. Using a blog as part of your customer service provision can be a great help to both you and your customers. You can use your blog to provide answers to frequently asked customer service questions. Blogs are also great for quickly alerting your customers to product issues as they arise.

A great example of a customer services blog is Dell's **Direct2Dell** (http://direct2dell.com/).

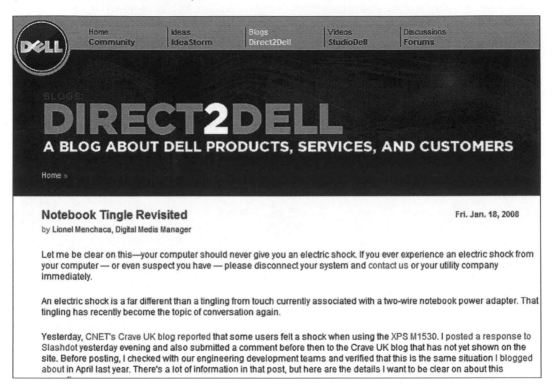

Public Relations

Your blog can provide a great window on your business. It can put a human face on the organization and provide a great way for both the public and media to get an understanding of what you're about. Blogs can also provide a means to transmit your company news, which can complement or maybe even replace the traditional press release. They also provide a forum to discuss and respond to any media coverage you receive, be it good or bad. A blog is also an invaluable tool for crisis management, as it enables you to provide instant updates about any negative situation you may find yourself in. Blogs allow you to control your corporate reputation.

Digg's blog has a strong PR-focus. It provides plenty of good-news stories, such as **awards** the company has picked up and enhancements to its service. It also uses it to respond quickly to any potentially damaging feedback it has received about its service. The blog also gives a good sense of the company's ethos and outlook, which is useful in managing its brand and reputation. All in all, the Digg blog is a great example of a WordPress blog with a PR-focus (`http://blog.digg.com/`).

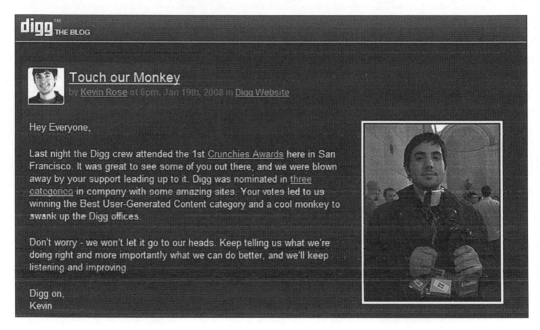

Driving Traffic

Search engines love blogs. A continuous supply of frequently updated content is the key to improving search engine rankings. However, many company websites are updated infrequently, particularly if they are **brochure** style sites. A blog is a great way of bringing dynamic and fresh content into the mix. If you have a relatively lightweight company website that isn't updated too often, you may find you get far better search engine success from a blog. It's basically down to the fact that search engines like fresh content to index.

This strategy would work particularly well if you keep your blog within your site's domain. So, rather than having `www.mycompany.com` and `www.mycompanyblog.com` as separate domains, consider placing your blog at `http://blog.mycompany.com`. This is becoming the standard approach for more and more company websites, who understand the importance of driving traffic from their blog to their main website (or vice versa — it works both ways).

An example of this approach is the blog set up by **HubSpot** (`http://blog.hubspot.com/`). Not only are the blog pages within the main site's domain, they are also well integrated into the design and navigation of the main site. The blog and the main website have similar headers and menu bars.

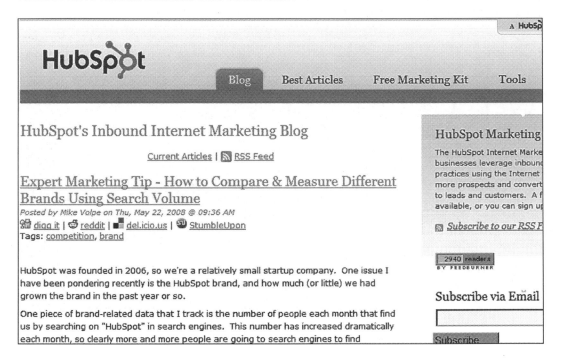

Add Some Personality

Blogging's evolution with its roots in personal journals means many blogs often take on a very conversational style. This lends itself very well to injecting a personal touch or a human face to corporate communications. Many companies use blogs to reveal some of the personalities behind the business. These days, many CEOs and senior executives blog on behalf of their companies. The topics discussed aren't necessarily related to company activities. These bloggers have the opportunity to write about their extra-curricular interests or anything else that takes their fancy.

This approach can be very useful in building a relationship with your customers. People are now far more used to informal communications with the organizations with which they do business. They like to get to know the people behind the corporate façade. But it's still important to gauge the tone correctly. If things get too informal or inappropriate content begins to creep in, you may end up upsetting or alienating some of your customers.

Bill Marriott, Chairman and CEO of Marriott International, maintains a blog at `http://www.blogs.marriott.com/`. The blog contains a mix of his personal musings as well as company news, and remains firmly under the Marriott brand. It's an excellent opportunity for a huge multi-national corporation to give a personal touch to its web communications.

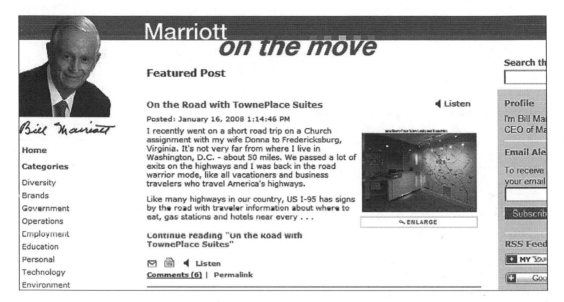

Categorizing Business Blogs

So these are a few of the strategic goals that successful business blogs aspire to. They provide you with one method of analyzing your blog (and the blogs of others).

But we can also look at blogs in terms of their type. Looking around the blogosphere, we see many types or styles of blog. Each of these types of blog is likely to have its own set of strategic goals. By understanding what your strategic goals are, you can probably determine what type of blog you should have. We can measure the success of a blog by looking at its type and deciding whether it achieves the strategic goals for that particular blog type.

Product Blogs

These tend to simply focus on a company's product(s). They provide information on research and development, product features, user guides, where to buy, and anything else directly related to the product or service. They are usually regarded as a straightforward sales channel—their purpose is to close sales. The strategic goals that these blogs are trying to achieve are usually to *increase sales* and *add value*.

Another great example of a product blog is Dopplr — the online service for business travelers (`http://blog.dopplr.com/`). It's built using WordPress.

Corporate or Company Blogs

This is probably the most diverse type of blog as it can fulfill many, if not all, of the strategic goals we highlighted above. The corporate blog can take many forms and has many purposes.

These are at once the easiest kind of business blog to get started and the easiest to get wrong because remaining focused can be a challenge. They provide almost a completely blank canvas, so it's important to identify the strategic goals and stick to them.

General corporate blogs are probably the most common type of business blogs to be found on the Web. They provide a great deal of flexibility and can cover a diverse range of subject matters.

If you have *several strategic goals* in mind for your blog, you will most likely end up with a general corporate blog. A great example of this type of blog, built using WordPress, is Flickr's (`http://blog.flickr.com/en`).

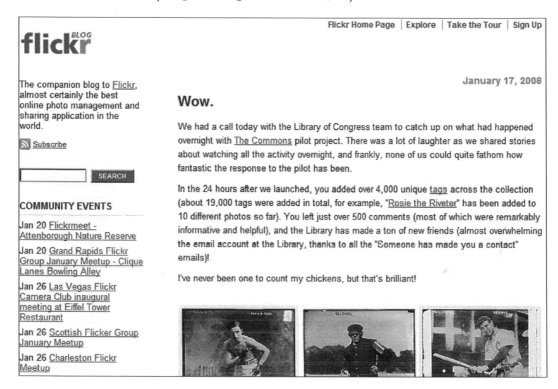

News Blogs

These are a slightly different type of blog as they can be a business in their own right.

They usually provide news coverage for a specific niche and may be run by an expert in that field or a team of experts. Many of the most popular blogs on the Web take this form. A lot of these focus on internet and digital technologies. They are almost like online magazines or newspapers.

Because of the high traffic that these types of blogs can attract, many have become successful independent media businesses by raising revenue from advertising sales and corporate sponsorships.

In terms of the strategic goals behind this type of blog, it tends to be showing expertise and adding personality. However, as many of these are businesses in their own right, they also have the goal of increasing sales, that is, advertising sales.

Two notable blogs in this category are TechCrunch (`http://www.techcrunch.com/`) and GigaOM (`http://gigaom.com/`), both of which use WordPress.

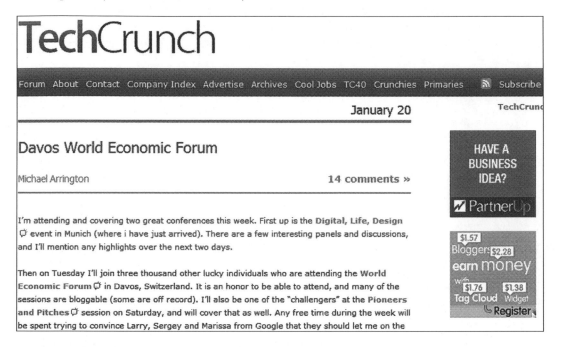

Expert Blogs

These are written by pundits or experts in their field. They are usually aimed at promoting the business activity of the author. The experts behind these blogs may be freelance consultants, professional speakers, authors, or they may run their own companies.

Again, many of the most popular blogs on the Web are of this type. Some expert bloggers derive a good income simply from running their blogs—they can monetize the high traffic they receive by selling advertising space.

The strategic goals behind these blogs are usually *raising awareness* of the expert's business activities, *demonstrating knowledge and expertise,* and *driving traffic* to the expert's other websites.

Expert blogs can also come under the auspices of large corporations who use the reputation of some of their senior employees to improve their company profile.

Some expert blogs have a long history coming directly from the tradition of the 'personal home page', which we have already seen was instrumental in the development of blogging. Famous expert bloggers include Seth Godin (`http://sethgodin.typepad.com/`), Guy Kawasaki (`http://blog.guykawasaki.com/`), and Robert Scoble (`http://www.scobleizer.com/`) who use WordPress to run their blogs.

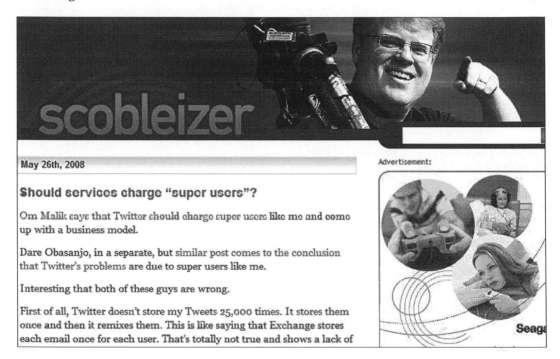

These are just four, rather broad categories. It's easy to see that many blogs will fit into one or another of these types, but some blogs cross over and there are certainly other types of blogs that we haven't covered. The main point to understand is that having a clear idea of the type of blog you want to achieve, based on your strategic goals, is an important first step in making your blog a success.

The WordPress Arsenal

We've seen that successful blogs need clearly defined strategic goals and these goals will often determine the type of blog that will work best.

WordPress is one of the most powerful blogging platforms available, and it makes possible a number of techniques and methods that will help you put your strategic goals into practice. The tools, techniques, and methods you pull out of the WordPress arsenal will depend on your blog's strategic goals.

We'll be covering these techniques in detail throughout the rest of the book, but here are a few of them to give you a taste of what's to come.

Good Design

Whatever your strategic goals may be, design is going to be an important consideration—you must come up with a design that facilitates your strategic goals.

Luckily, WordPress gives you almost unlimited control over the look and feel of your blog. You may have already experimented with ready-made themes, of which there are thousands available from various sources. However, we'll be looking at how to modify WordPress themes so that you can develop a design that is unique and fits your purpose perfectly.

Maximizing Usability

This will be closely linked to the design of your blog. Ensuring that your blog is usable and accessible to everyone is key to its success. Your readers must be able to navigate your blog and find content easily.

WordPress has many built-in features that help to maximize usability. There are also several plugins that can be used to improve this. Throughout the book, we'll be looking at a selection of the best plugins, so that you can see how to choose the ones you really need.

Promoting Your Blog

Again, whichever strategic goals you are aiming for, a key factor to your blog's success will be getting it out to as big an audience as possible.

Promoting blogs is a wide-ranging skill that involves many techniques. For example, **search engine optimization** (**SEO**) is central to any promotion strategy. There are many ways you can use WordPress to improve the **findability** of your site and we will be covering these in detail.

WordPress also enables you to take advantage of social networking and social bookmarking. We will also be looking at syndication and submitting your blog to the various indices, like Technorati. Chapters 6 and 7 will give you all the details on promoting your blog to the search engines and beyond.

Analyzing the Statistics

It is essential to monitor the progress of your blog and WordPress offers many tools that enable you to do this. We will also look at a third-party statistics tool, that is, **Google Analytics**.

We will be looking at the various statistics that are available to you and examining how you can use the data to push your blog forward.

Managing Content

WordPress is a powerful content management system and we will be looking at the ways you can manage all types of content within your blog. Depending on your strategic goals, there may be many different types of content that you need to create. From static pages to image galleries and multimedia content, WordPress gives you the control you need.

We will also be developing the skills you need to create engaging and relevant content, including copywriting techniques, and how to manage categories.

Monetizing Your Blog

WordPress provides you with a variety of options to develop revenue streams from your blog. There are several plugins and widgets that help you to do this.

In Chapter 10, we will be looking at creative methods of generating cash via your blog, which could go a long way towards covering its running costs or even develop into a significant revenue stream for your business.

Measuring Success

To ensure that your blog is a worthwhile use of your resources and is providing benefit to your business, you need to measure its success. It's also useful to be able to assess other blogs against yours and against others within your market sector.

There are several tools that can be used to measure the success of blogs.

Google PageRank

This is an algorithm that Google uses to rank web pages in its index. In very rough terms, the PageRank of a web page is assessed by the number of other pages that link to it. Google gives a numeric weighting from 0-10 for each web page on the Internet. The higher the PageRank, the higher up it appears in Google's search results. So having a high PageRank helps you to achieve a better ranking in Google.

Taken on its own, it is a matter of some debate how important PageRank actually is. But as a general rule of thumb, PageRank is a good indicator of how well a page is doing. You can see the PageRank of any web page by installing the **Google Toolbar** (`http://toolbar.google.com/`).

Alexa Ranking

Alexa (`http://www.alexa.com/`) is a company that measures websites based on the traffic they receive. You can look up any website in Alexa to see how well it ranks. The higher up the list a website appears the more traffic it receives.

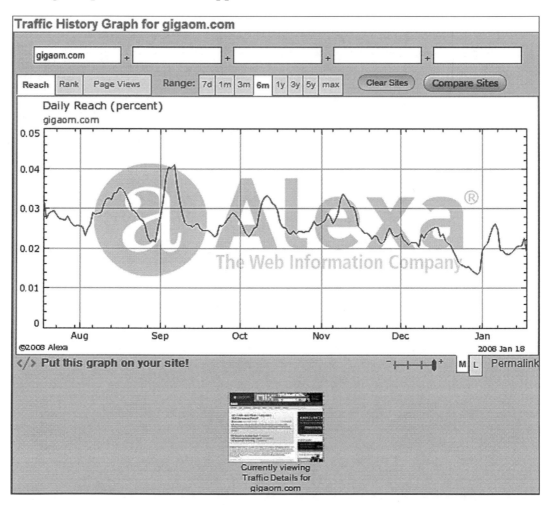

Summary

In this chapter, we have considered what makes a great blog. We have looked at how the success of a blog depends on its strategic goals and how well it fulfils them. We outlined a number of strategic goals that are relevant to business blogs and saw examples of blogs that aspire to those goals.

We have also seen a number of blog types that are derived from the various strategic goals, and introduced some of the tools and features of WordPress that allow bloggers to realize them.

In the next chapter, you'll be introduced to the case study blog we'll be using throughout the book. You'll learn how to identify your own strategic goals and draw up your **blog plan**, by using the case study as an example.

2

Introducing Our Case Study—ChilliGuru

Throughout the book, we'll be using a case study based on a fictitious blog to demonstrate the concepts you'll be learning. It will be the basis for most of the tutorials in the rest of the book. In this chapter, we'll outline what we'll be doing to transform **ChilliGuru** from a mediocre blog into an all-singing all-dancing traffic magnet.

As we discussed in Chapter 1, a successful business blog is achieved by identifying strategic goals and applying these to the type of blog you are publishing. We will work through this process for ChilliGuru to give us a detailed plan of how the blog should be developed. You will then be in a position to apply the planning process to your own blog and identify what needs to be done to improve it.

Even though you may already have a live blog, you should still work through the goal-setting process so that you have a clear roadmap of where your blog is going. This will be your **blog plan**. Think of it in the same way as you would treat your business plan. All businesses should regularly revisit and update their business plans. The same is true for blog plans. No matter how established your blog is, it needs a plan that is updated regularly and responds to your changing demands and business.

ChilliGuru—The Man Behind the Blog

Our (fictitious) eponymous hero is an expert in the world of chilies—what he doesn't know about those spicy little fruits, isn't worth knowing!

If you want to find out a little more about him, take a look at the **About** page on the blog (http://blog.chilliguru.com).

Using a subdomain in your blog URL

Many bloggers use a subdomain in the URL for their blog. This is particularly useful if you have a regular website running alongside your blog. You can have `www.yourdomain.com` pointing to your main home page and `http://blog.yourdomain.com` pointing to your blog.

If you set up a subdomain in your hosting control panel to point to your WordPress directory, remember that you also need to update **WordPress address (URL)** and **Blog address (URL)** on the **General Settings** page in your WordPress admin area:

WordPress address (URL)	`http://blog.chilliguru.com`
Blog address (URL)	`http://blog.chilliguru.com`

Enter the address here if you want your blog homepage <u>to be different from the directory</u> you installed WordPress.

Before and After

If you take a look at the blog now (`http://blog.chilliguru.com`), you'll see the finished version, which is the result of all the work we'll be doing in the chapters that follow.

But ChilliGuru didn't always look like this. Like most new WordPress blogs, ChilliGuru was using a ready-made theme and had very few enhancements like plugins and widgets. What you now see came about by applying the methods and techniques you'll be learning through the rest of the book. The following screenshot shows the 'plain vanilla' version of ChilliGuru before it received its makeover.

You say 'Chili', he says 'Chilli'

Our readers in the USA may notice there are two l's in the word ChilliGuru. This is because ChilliGuru is based in the UK where this is the usual way of spelling the word.

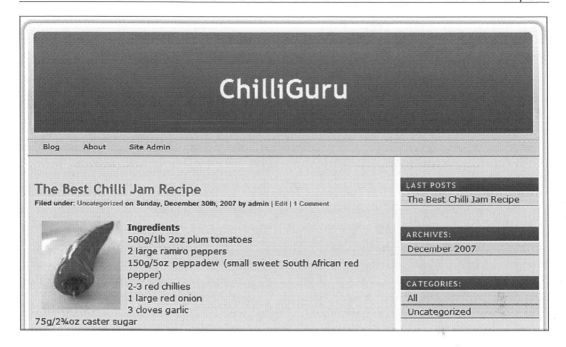

Goals and Planning

Let's now look at ChilliGuru in more detail and see what business objectives he wants to achieve with his blog. We can apply a simple process here that should work with any business blog:

- Consider our business situation
- Decide on our strategic goals
- Come up with ideas based on those goals to give us a blog plan
- Decide how to implement the blog plan

Business Situation

The first step is to stand back and analyze your business situation. ChilliGuru earns his living by writing, speaking at events and shows, appearing on TV, and selling a range of chili products. He is an expert in the world of chili peppers and has amassed a great deal of knowledge through his experience as a chef and traveler.

Thinking back to the blog categories that we outlined in Chapter 1, it seems fairly obvious that ChilliGuru should be an 'Expert Blog'. He checks most of the boxes for that category (that is, demonstrating professional knowledge and positioning himself as an expert).

Strategic Goals

We can now think about the strategic goals that apply to this business situation. What does ChilliGuru want to achieve with his blog? This will probably begin with a brainstorming exercise. Make a list of all the strategic goals you can think of for your blog. For ChilliGuru, this will include things such as:

- Promoting TV appearances
- Selling more books
- Announcing speaking events
- Getting more speaking engagements
- Selling chili sauces
- Building a brand
- Getting freelance writing work

And the list continues…

The following figure is a 'Mind Map' showing all the strategic goals that ChilliGuru would like to achieve.

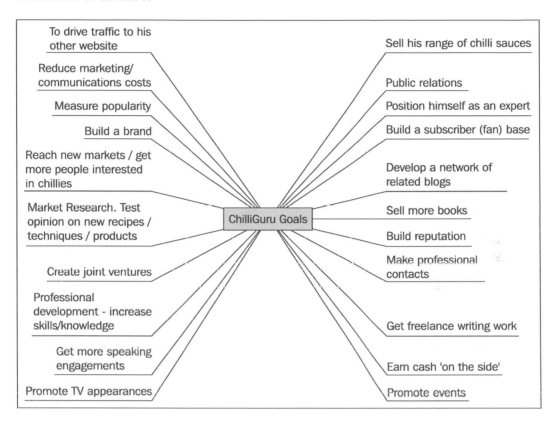

The Blog Plan

Now that we have our strategic goals, it's time to think about how they can be realized. Some of these will be simpler than others. For example, for ChilliGuru to achieve his strategic goal of selling more books he may decide to simply set up a page on his blog that lists the books he has published. However, there may be better solutions that involve a bit more creative thinking. He may decide to add a 'book widget' in his blog sidebar. This will showcase his books right on the main blog page and link directly to Amazon.com.

At this point, it's worth formatting your blog plan into some kind of tabular structure. The blog plan for ChilliGuru is shown overleaf. It has been broken down into three columns, showing each strategic goal, how these goals can be realized, and finally the specific implementation requirements.

Right now you may find it difficult to complete the third column for your own blog as your knowledge of WordPress may not be sufficient. However, as you work through the book and your WordPress skills improve, you will find solutions to your own implementation requirements and add them to your blog plan. Likewise, some of the details you see in the following ChilliGuru plan may not make a lot of sense right now. Don't worry—most items in the ChilliGuru plan will be covered in the rest of the book.

Strategic Goal	How to Realize the Goal	Specific Implementation Requirements
Sell books	Set up a 'books' page	Create a static books page
	Amazon links in sidebar	Book widget
Promote TV appearances	Have a TV category and announce upcoming appearances on the blog	Create a category called 'TV Appearances'
Announce speaking events	Integrate with some kind of calendar?	Events calendar plugin
	Post announcements in the blog	
Get more speaking engagements	Make it easy to contact	Add a contact form
Building buzz to draw in new traffic	Get traffic from social news and bookmarking sites	ShareThis plugin
Build a subscriber base	Encourage readers to subscribe with their email address	Subscribe to comments plugin
		Set up FeedBurner email subscriptions
Sell chili sauces	Make it easy for readers to buy chili sauces	WP e-Commerce plugin
Build a brand	Make an attractive design	Customize the theme with brand colors and images
	Use a logo / favicon	Install a favicon
	Use brand language	Apply a writing style guide
Get a freelance writing work	Make it easy to contact	Add a contact form
	Have a portfolio of published work	Build a portfolio page
Earn cash on the side	Implement AdSense	AdSense manager plugin

Strategic Goal	How to Realize the Goal	Specific Implementation Requirements
	Sell banner ads	Implement a banner rotation script
	Affiliate Marketing	Sign up with an affiliate network (for example, Amazon Associates)
Public relations	Integrate with offline and traditional PR methods	Create a 'Press' page or link to press page on his other website
Build his reputation	Build relationships with movers and shakers in the chili world	Trackbacks to their blogs
		Guest posts from other chili experts
Market research (test opinion on recipes and sauces)	Find out what readers think about new recipes	WP-Polls plugin
		Ask for comments
Position himself as an expert	Demonstrate good knowledge of the chili world	Maintain a blogroll of other experts
	Provide original and top-quality content	Apply copywriting best practice and quality assurance
Make professional contacts	Build relationships with movers and shakers in the chili world	Trackbacks to their blogs
		Guest posts from other chili experts
Measure popularity	Find out visitor numbers	Implement Google Analytics or WordPress.com stats

Tactical Goal	How to Realize the Goal	Specific Implementation Requirements
Increase traffic	Use promotion techniques to drive traffic	Use RSS and FeedBurner
Maintain posting frequency		Plan content ahead
		Get into a routine of posting
Improve search engine rankings		Use good permalinks
		Employ SEO techniques

Tactical Goal	How to Realize the Goal	Specific Implementation Requirements
Maximize usability and accessibility	Maintain best practice in usability and accessibility	Use image alt tags properly
		Have a good category list
		Use tags correctly, (Configurable Tag Cloud widget)
		Use an accessible color scheme
		Don't break WP's valid code with poor quality widgets

Tactical Goals

You will see a section headed **Tactical Goals** at the bottom of the blog plan. These are generic goals that are not linked to any specific business goals. They are things that all blogs should be trying to do no matter what their strategic goals may be. For example, all blogs aim to increase traffic irrespective of what they may be trying to achieve from a business point of view. Even though they aren't specifically related to business objectives, these goals should feature in any good blog plan.

Implementation

Once you have drawn up your blog plan, it's time to begin with the implementation. That's not to say you're done with the plan. You're likely to revisit it frequently as your blog takes shape and make alterations and additions to it. The beauty of any kind of web publishing is that nothing is set in stone. If you find that some aspect of the original plan doesn't look right or doesn't work when you actually place it on your blog, you can always change your mind. Like most Google products, your blog is likely to remain in a state of **perpetual Beta**!

Implementation is the stage where we get our hands dirty and begin the real work of transforming your blog.

An Overview of the ChilliGuru Makeover

Throughout the rest of the book, we will be seeing how the ChilliGuru blog plan is put into action. This will give you the practical skills you need to implement your own blog plan using WordPress.

Design

The first stage of the makeover will be to implement an appropriate design. To achieve this, we will look at some of the principles of good design and how they should be applied to ChilliGuru. We will look at issues related to color schemes, layout, and typography. We will also be paying careful attention to usability and accessibility.

You will be introduced to advanced techniques for editing WordPress themes that will involve manipulating the source code. The following screenshot shows the finished design for ChilliGuru.

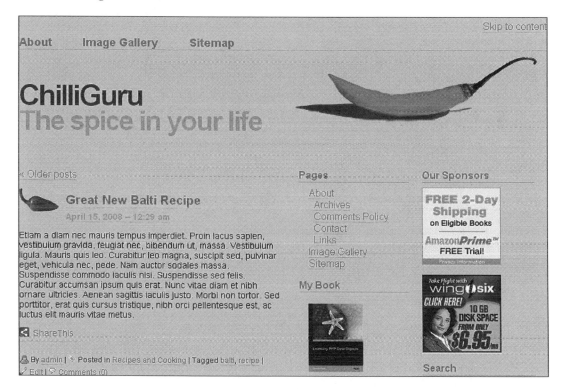

Content

There are two chapters that deal with all aspects of creating content and content management. Images and videos will be an important feature in the ChilliGuru blog and we will also be looking at a range of tools and techniques available in WordPress, which help us to manage this type of content.

There are several plugins that allow us to present content, easily and efficiently, from a third-party website, such as **YouTube**. We will look at how to install and use one of these. ChilliGuru will also feature a photo gallery, as you can see in the following screenshot. Once again this will be achieved by the use of a powerful third-party plugin that makes managing an image gallery a breeze.

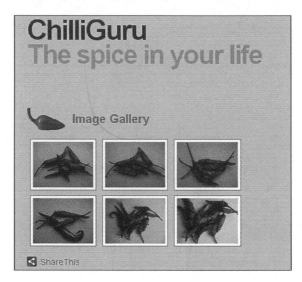

General content issues like copywriting techniques and how to manage tags and categories will also be examined in detail. We will discuss the use of static pages within WordPress and the kinds of static content that might be required in the ChilliGuru blog. The importance of safeguarding content with appropriate back-up procedures will also be demonstrated.

Promotion and Analysis

A key element in the success of ChilliGuru, and indeed any blog, will be effective promotion. This subject will be looked at in detail in Chapters 6 and 7. There is a wide range of techniques and tools to be employed to ensure ChilliGuru's promotional activity is as effective as possible.

We will examine the principles of effective SEO, including how to submit ChilliGuru to the search engines and directories. Understanding keywords and how they relate to SEO will be a fundamental lesson, as will the use of sitemaps and implementing a good permalink structure.

The importance of social networks and other social media will also be examined. We will see how the **ShareThis** plugin can be used to promote the blog via social bookmaking sites.

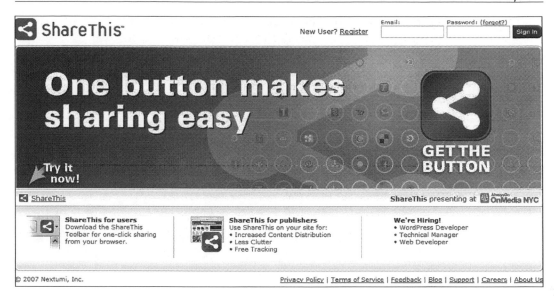

One of the goals laid out in the blog plan is to effectively measure the popularity of ChilliGuru. We will be looking at the tools that enable us to achieve this, including a comparison between WordPress.com stats and Google Analytics, in Chapter 9.

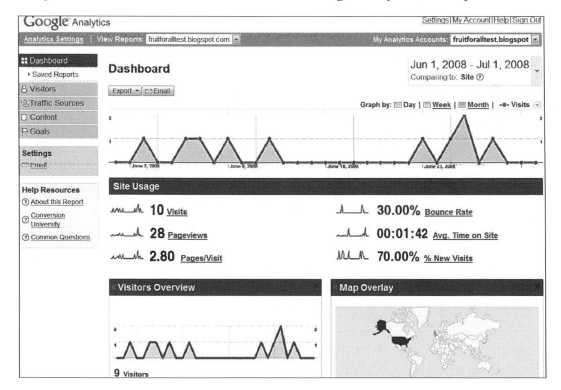

Generating Revenue

Another goal in the ChilliGuru blog plan is to earn some revenue directly from the blog. We will be looking at some methods to achieve this. These include introducing a banner rotation system so that ChilliGuru can sell advertising and sponsorship banners directly. Revenue will also be generated by using advertising networks, like **Google AdSense**.

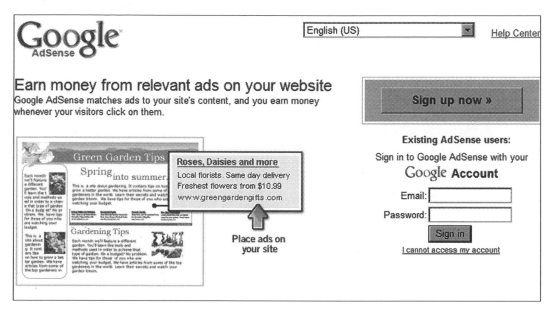

Enabling Growth

We will be looking at how to effectively manage the growth of the ChilliGuru blog. This includes practical considerations like how to ensure smooth server operation when faced with high traffic. We will also examine options for expanding ChilliGuru's blogging activities. For example, we will see how **WordPress MU** can be used as a tool for developing a network of linked blogs.

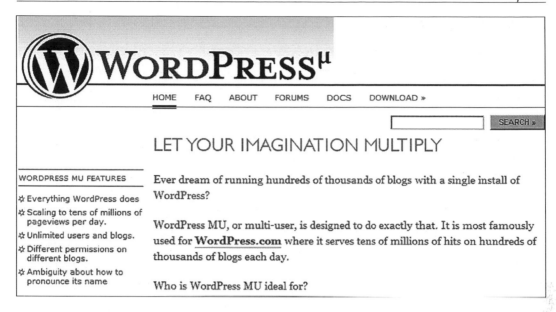

WORDPRESSμ

HOME   FAQ   ABOUT   FORUMS   DOCS   DOWNLOAD »

SEARCH »

LET YOUR IMAGINATION MULTIPLY

WORDPRESS MU FEATURES

✿ Everything WordPress does
✿ Scaling to tens of millions of pageviews per day.
✿ Unlimited users and blogs.
✿ Different permissions on different blogs.
✿ Ambiguity about how to pronounce its name

Ever dream of running hundreds of thousands of blogs with a single install of WordPress?

WordPress MU, or multi-user, is designed to do exactly that. It is most famously used for **WordPress.com** where it serves tens of millions of hits on hundreds of thousands of blogs each day.

Who is WordPress MU ideal for?

Summary

In this chapter, we have introduced our case study blog—ChilliGuru. We have also seen how to develop a detailed **blog plan**. This began by analyzing our business situation and deciding what we want to achieve from our blog. We then identified the specific goals that will enable us to achieve this and how they might be realized by using WordPress. We also saw an overview of how the ChilliGuru blog will be implemented through the rest of the book.

Now is the time to sit down and work on your detailed blog plan before the practical work begins. In the next chapter, you will learn how to redesign the theme of a WordPress blog.

3
Designing Your Blog

In this chapter, we'll look at one of the most important aspects of your blog—design. We'll begin by considering some of the principles of good blog design. We'll then move on to apply some of those design principles to our ChilliGuru case study, based on the strategic goals we outlined in the previous chapters. Even if your blog is already up and running, this chapter will allow you to critically evaluate its design and replace your current theme with a custom-designed one.

Blog Design Principles

Blogs tend to have a fairly simple, minimalist design. This has always been one of their key characteristics. Blogs are all about frequently updated content, so the main purpose of their design is to present that content as efficiently and conveniently as possible. The vast majority of blogs present their most recent content on the page that visitors arrive at, hence the front page contains the latest posts. There's no home page with a verbose welcome message and a long navigation menu to click through to the important stuff. The visitor gets straight into the meat of the blog. By default, this is the structure that WordPress provides. It is possible to set a static page as your blog's front page, but, in the vast majority of cases, I wouldn't recommend it.

So when considering the architecture of a blog, unlike other types of website, we don't have to worry too much about a complex navigation structure. There is a convention that we can follow. Yes, we may want to add some extra static pages, but probably only a few of these. What we are most concerned with in blog design is not a complicated navigation structure and how all the pages link together, but how the actual blog page should look and feel. This can be broken down into four key components, which we will examine one by one:

- Layout
- Color
- Typography
- Usability and Accessibility

Layout

Good design is all about making something easy for people to use. Designers achieve this by employing standards and conventions. For example, cars have a standard design: four wheels, a chassis, a steering wheel, gas pedal, brake, gear shift, and so on. Car designers have stuck to this convention for many years. First, because it works well and second, because it enables us to drive any car we choose. When you sit down in any standard road car, you know how it works. You turn the key in the ignition, select a gear, hit the gas, and off you go. It's certainly not beyond the ken of car designers to come up with new ways of making a car go (a joystick maybe, or a hand-operated brake) but this would make it more difficult for people to drive. Cars work reasonably safely and efficiently as we are all familiar with these conventions.

The layout of blog pages also tends to follow certain conventions. As with cars, this helps people to use blogs efficiently. They know how they work, because they're familiar with the conventions. Most blogs have a header and a footer with the main content arranged into columns. This columnar layout works very well for the type of chronological content presented in blogs.

Because of these conventions, the decisions about our blog layout are fairly simple. It's basically a case of deciding where we want to place all our page elements and content within this standard columnar layout. The set of page elements we have to choose from is also based on fairly well entrenched blogging conventions. The list of things we may want on our page includes:

- Header
- Posts
- Comments
- Static content (for example, the 'About' page)
- Links to static pages (simple navigation)
- RSS feeds
- Search
- Categories
- Archives
- Blogroll
- Widgets and plugins
- Footer

There will be other elements to add to the page as we work through later chapters, but for now these should be enough for us to come up with a page layout. If we look at this list in more detail, we can see that these page elements can be grouped in a sensible way. For example:

- Group 1
  - Header
  - Links to static pages
- Group 2
  - Posts
  - Comments
  - Static content
- Group 3
  - RSS Feeds
  - Search
  - Categories
- Group 4
  - Archives
  - Blogroll
  - Widgets and plugins
- Group 5
  - Footer

This isn't the only possible grouping scheme we might come up with. For example, we may place the items in Groups 3 and 4 into a single larger group, or we may have widgets and plugins in a group on their own. From this grouping, we can see that the type of items in Group 2 are likely to be the main content on our page, with Groups 3 and 4 being placed in **sidebars**.

 Sidebars are areas on the page where we place ancillary content.

Having considered the elements we want on the page and how they might be grouped, we can think about possible layouts. Within the conventional columnar structure of blogs there are quite a few possible layout variations. We'll look at four of the most common. The first is a three-column layout.

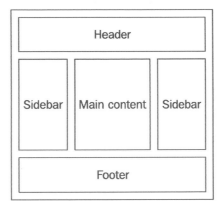

Here, we have two sidebars, one on either side of the main content. Using this type of layout, we would probably place the items in Groups 3 and 4 in the sidebars and Group 2 in the main content area.

A variation on the three-column layout is to have the two sidebars next to each other on one side of the page (usually the right), as shown in the following diagram. This is a popular layout for blogs, not just for aesthetics, but as the search engine spiders encounter the post column first, as that content is at the top of the template. (You'll find out all about search engine spiders in Chapter 6, so if you don't know what they are right now, don't worry.)

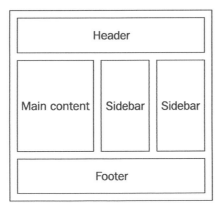

Using two sidebars is useful if you anticipate having a lot of ancillary content on your blog. The list of page elements given earlier is really the bear minimum you would want on your page. However, if you decide to use lots of widgets or have a long blogroll, it's a good idea to spread them across two sidebars. This means that more of your content can be placed 'above the fold'.

> The concept of 'above the fold' in web design applies to content in a web page that is visible without having to scroll down, that is, the stuff in the top part of the page. It's a good idea to place the most important content above the fold so that readers can see it immediately. This is particularly true if you plan to monetize your blog by displaying adverts. Adverts that appear above the fold get the most exposure, and therefore, generate the most revenue (more on this in Chapter 10).

Another popular layout amongst bloggers has just two columns. In this layout, we would place the items in Groups 3 and 4 together in the one sidebar. It doesn't really matter which side of the page the sidebar is placed, but it seems more common to have it on the right. Studies have shown that a web user's eyes are most often focused on the top-left region of a web page, when they first open any page. So it makes sense to place your main content there, with your sidebar on the right. Also, remember that the search engine spiders will find the leftmost content first. You want them to find your main content quickly, which is a good reason for placing your sidebar on the right, out of their way.

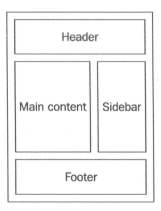

An important benefit of a two-column layout is that it allows more room for your main content area. This may be important, if you intend to use a lot of video or images within your blog posts. The extra room allows you to display this visual content bigger.

Many blogs place some of their ancillary content just above the footer, below the main content. This also has the advantage of leaving more space for the main content, as with the two-column layout. The following diagram shows this type of layout. Here, the content just above the footer isn't strictly speaking about a sidebar, but I've labeled it this way because it's the terminology most often applied to this type of ancillary content.

Wireframing

The layout diagrams we've just seen are referred to as **wireframes** by web designers. They give a simple overview of where the elements of a page should be placed. It would be a good idea for you to create your own wireframe for your blog design. This can be done using most graphic software packages or something like Microsoft Visio, or a simple pen and paper does the job equally well!

Color

This is the next design principle we need to consider. It may be that you already have a corporate color scheme based on your company logo, stationery, or existing website. In this case, you'll probably want to continue that theme through your blog design. Even if you already have your corporate color scheme, this section may still be useful in case you decide to change your blog colors in the future.

The subject of color in design is a large one. Design students spend a great deal of time learning about the psychology and science of colors and techniques for achieving the best color schemes. Obviously, we don't have enough space to go into that kind of detail, but I will try to give you a few pointers.

The first thing to think about is the psychology of color, in particular color associations. This is the idea that different colors evoke different feelings and emotions in the eye of the beholder. To a certain extent this can be rather subjective and it can also depend on cultural influences, but there are some generalities that can be applied. For example, red is often perceived as being exciting, passionate, or dramatic. Yellow is an active and highly visible color, which is why it is used in warning signs. It is also associated with energy and happiness. Blue is sometimes thought of as being 'cold'. It can also be a calming color and may sometimes be seen as corporate or conservative. White, for many people, gives the idea of cleanliness, purity, and perfection. Black can be seen as strong, elegant, and chic. Obviously, these color associations can vary from person to person, so designers don't rely on them solely in their color decisions, but they are certainly useful to bear in mind.

There are more practical considerations regarding color that are probably more relevant than color psychology. For example, we all know that some color combinations don't work well together. There is a great deal of design theory aimed at devising good color combinations, but unless you're a professional designer, it's not really worth going into. Probably the best method for working out good color combinations is trial and error. If you're trying to figure out a background color and text color for your blog, simply test a few out. You could use a graphics package like Photoshop or Microsoft Paint, or one of the many online color tools such as, `http://www.wellstyled.com/tools/colorscheme2/index-en.html` or Adobe's Kuler at `http://kuler.adobe.com`.

When choosing background and text colors you need to think about contrast. For example, yellow text on a white background can be very difficult to read. Some people also find light text on a black background a strain on their eyes.

It's also important not to use too many colors in your design. Try to limit your palette to a maximum of three or four. Sometimes you may only need two colors to make an attractive design.

One method for devising color combinations is to look for examples all around you, particularly in nature. Maybe look at a photograph of a landscape and pick out color combinations you like. Also consider the work of professional designers. Think about websites and blogs you like, and examine the color schemes they have used. You will also find good examples in offline design—pick up a book and see how colors have been used in the cover design.

If you would like to base your blog's color scheme on your company logo, you could use lighter and darker versions of one color from the logo. Use the most vivid color in the logo for emphasis or headings.

Web Color Theory

At this point, it's worth looking at the technical theory behind colors on the Web. Web browsers use something called the **Hexadecimal RGB** color system to render colors in web pages. This is because computer monitors use an RGB color model, which means every pixel is colored using a combination of red, green, and blue light (hence RGB). There are 256 different levels of red light, 256 different levels of green light, and 256 different levels of blue light. These can be combined to create 16,277,216 different colors, which are all available for your web browser.

The hexadecimal system gives us a way of counting from 0 to 255 using numbers and letters, which covers all 256 levels of RGB light. In the hexadecimal scale, 0 is 00 and 255 is FF. A six-character hexadecimal color code specifies the levels of red, green, and blue, which form a particular color. For example, the color **white** combines red, green, and blue at their highest possible levels, that is 255. Remember in hexadecimal 255 is FF, so the color code for white is **FFFFFF** (Red: FF, Green: FF, and Blue: FF). The color code for black is **000000** as the levels of red, green, and blue are set to their lowest or 00 (in hexadecimal). The code for red is **FF0000**, blue is **0000FF**, and yellow is **FFFF00**, and so on.

We can use six-character Hexadecimal RGB codes to define all of the 16,277,216 web colors.

So how do we know the hexadecimal code for a particular color? Well, there are many tools available that define the Hexadecimal RGB codes for the colors you choose. Some are standalone applications for PC or Mac, and others are online. Take a look at `www.colorpicker.com` or do a quick search in Google on "color picker". For more information on web colors, read the article at `http://en.wikipedia.org/wiki/Web_colors`.

Typography

Another important consideration for your blog design is the fonts you use. Your choice of font will have a big impact on the readability of your blog. It's important to bear in mind that although there are literally thousands of fonts to choose from, only a small number of them are practical for web design. This is because a web browser can only display fonts that are already installed on the user's computer. If you choose an obscure font for your blog, the chances are that most users won't have it installed on their computer. If this is the case the web browser will automatically select a substitute font. This may be smaller or far less readable than the font you had in mind. It's always safest to stick to the fonts that are commonly used in web design. These include the following popular web fonts:

- Arial
- Verdana
- Times New Roman
- Georgia

There are two types of font, serif and sans-serif. Serif fonts have little flourishes at the end of the strokes whereas sans-serif fonts don't have this extra decoration. Arial and Verdana are sans-serif fonts whereas Times New Roman and Georgia are serif fonts.

As you'll see later in the chapter, when we look at CSS, fonts are usually specified in groups or families. They are listed in the order of the designer's preference. For example, a designer may specify `font-family:"Georgia, Times New Roman, serif"`. This means when the browser renders the page it will first look for the Georgia font; if it isn't installed, it will look for the Times New Roman font and if that isn't installed, it will look for the computer's default serif font. This method gives the designer more control over the font choices the browser will make.

The size of your font is also an important factor. Generally speaking, the bigger it is, the easier it is to read. Computer displays are getting bigger and bigger but the default screen resolutions are tending to get smaller. In other words, the individual pixels on users' screens are getting smaller. This is a good reason for web designers to choose larger font sizes. This trend can be seen on many 'Web 2.0' sites, which tend to use large and clear fonts as part of their design, for example `http://www.37signals.com`. But be careful not to go too big as this can make your design look messy and a little 'childish'.

Remember that you're not limited to using just one font in your blog design. For example, you may decide to use a different font for your headings. This can be an effective design feature but don't go crazy by using too many fonts, as this will make your design look messy. Probably two, or at the most three, fonts on a page is plenty.

Usability and Accessibility

This is another very important area to consider when designing your blog. Many people, who live with various disabilities, use a range of 'assistive' software to access the Web. For example, people with visual impairments use screen readers, which translate the text in a web browser into audible speech. There are also people who are unable to use a mouse, and instead rely on their keyboard to access web pages. It's the responsibility of web designers to ensure that their websites are accessible for these different methods of browsing. There's no sense in alienating this group of web surfers just because your blog is inaccessible to them.

There are also many other circumstances when your blog might be accessed by means other than a standard web browser, for example, via mobile phones or PDAs. Again, a good designer will ensure that these modes of browsing are catered for. The web design industry has been well aware of these accessibility issues for many years and has come up with guidelines and technologies to help conscientious designers build websites that are **standards compliant**. These **web standards** help ensure best practice and maximize accessibility and usability.

Luckily, WordPress takes care of a lot of the accessibility issues simply by the way it's been developed and built. The code behind WordPress is valid XHTML and CSS, which means, it complies with web standards and is easily accessible. It's important, then, that you don't 'break' the system by allowing bad practice to creep in.

Some of the things to bear in mind relate to a couple of the design principles we've already discussed, for example, using a color scheme and font size that makes your text easy to read. Other issues include keeping the number of navigation links on your page to a minimum—a whole load of useless links can be annoying for people who have to 'tab' through them to get to your main content. One way of overcoming this is to include a 'Skip to content' link at the top of your blog, which is a technique we'll see in the case study later in this chapter.

You should also ensure that any third-party plugins you install are standards compliant and don't throw up any accessibility problems. The same is true if you decide to use a ready-made theme for your blog design. Just make sure it's accessible and satisfies web standards. For more background reading on web standards, you could take a look at http://www.alistapart.com or the **World Wide Web Consortium (W3C)** website at http://www.w3.org.

Implementing Your Blog Design

We've now considered the principles involved in designing our blog. The next thing to decide is how we actually carry out the design work. There are three main options available, each of which involves varying degrees of work. However, they all require knowledge of the design principles we just covered.

The first approach is probably the easiest; it simply involves finding a ready-made theme and installing it in WordPress. By working through the earlier design principles, you should have an idea of what you want your blog to look like and then you simply need to find a theme that matches your vision as closely as possible. A good place to start looking is the official WordPress **Theme Viewer** at http://wordpress.org/extend/themes/. You'll also find many more theme resources by running a search through Google.

There are hundreds of very attractive WordPress themes available for free and many others that you can pay for. However, if you adopt this approach to your blog design, you won't have a unique or original blog. The chances are the theme you choose will also be seen on many other blogs.

At the other end of the scale, in terms of workload, is to design your own theme from scratch. This is a fairly complicated and technical process, and is well beyond the scope of this chapter. In fact, it's a subject that requires its own book. If you intend to build your own theme, I recommend *WordPress Theme Design* by Tessa Blakeley Silver ISBN 978-1-847193-09-4 published by Packt Publishing.

The third approach is to modify a ready-made theme. You could do this with any theme you choose, even the default 'Kubrick' theme that ships with WordPress. However, if you edit a fully developed theme, you spend a lot of time unpicking someone else's design work and you may still be left with elements that are not completely your own. A better method is to start with an 'empty' theme, which has been specially designed to be a 'blank canvas' for your own design. This is the approach we'll use in the case study later in the chapter.

We will be using the **Sandbox** theme designed by Scott Allan Wallick and Andy Skelton at plaintxt.org. Sandbox has been specially developed as a plain vanilla theme to which you can add your own style. The beauty of Sandbox is that you can customize it just by modifying the CSS or style sheet. You don't need to touch the other files that make up the theme, if you don't want to. However, you will need some understanding of CSS to achieve this, so before we begin with the case study, here's a crash course in CSS.

A Brief Introduction to CSS

I would recommend anyone who is involved in web publishing, including all you business bloggers, to learn at least the basics of HTML and CSS. A full CSS tutorial is way beyond the scope of this chapter, in fact, there are many books that are exclusively devoted to the subject. However, I will attempt to give you a very rudimentary grounding in the principles of web design using HTML and CSS. For a more thorough tutorial, you can find many excellent online resources such as http://www.w3schools.com or http://www.cssbasics.com.

The Early Days of the Web

The worldwide web was invented by academics in the early 1990's, who mainly used it to publish research papers via the Internet. Their layout requirements were fairly simple and early web pages usually contained nothing more than text arranged into headings and paragraphs.

 The technology that makes the Web work is **HyperText Markup Language (HTML)**, which tells web browsers, such as Internet Explorer and Mozilla Firefox, how to display content in a web page.

As the web grew in popularity, with more and more individuals and businesses using it to publish different types of content, web designers arrived on the scene and began to experiment with HTML to create more complex web pages. They wanted to create pages with images, lots of different colors, multiple columns, and more interesting layouts. It was possible to achieve this with HTML but it went way beyond what the language was originally intended for.

The main problem was that designers were forced to use the HTML `<table>` tag to create their complex page layouts. The `<table>` tag was only intended to present data in a tabular format. But by creating tables with hundreds of columns and rows, merging cells together, and nesting tables within tables, the designers could build the fancy-looking pages their clients demanded.

This was bad for a number of reasons. These huge complicated tables were slow to download. They were extremely difficult to maintain—making just one small change to a page could 'break' the entire layout table. And, most importantly, they caused accessibility issues.

There was also a deeper 'philosophical' dissatisfaction with using HTML for complicated web design—it simply isn't meant for it. HTML is the wrong tool for the job. The purpose of HTML is just to display content in a web browser, and not to format or style that content.

The W3C decided that something else was needed to handle the formatting and styling of web pages. So, in December 1996 it published the first specification for **Cascading Style Sheets (CSS)**.

Content and Style

The arrival of CSS meant that a web page's **content** could be separated from its **style**. HTML handles the content and CSS takes care of the style. The content of a web page includes things like text, images, and links. The style of the page refers to things such as the colors, the typeface (font), the positioning, and the layout.

The following screenshot shows the content of a web page. No styling has been done—it just uses HTML to mark up the content into headings, links, and paragraphs.

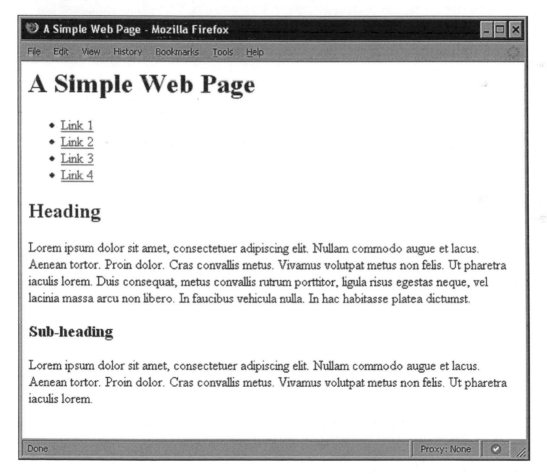

After making this simple page, we could add the following styling:

- Make the page heading white text on a dark gray background.
- Line up the links in a 'navigation bar' under the header and make them bold.
- Give the body of the page a light gray background.
- Change the font to Arial.

In the bad old days, before CSS, all this styling would have been done by using HTML tags and tables. Nowadays, the correct way is to use CSS. The following screenshot shows the page after the CSS was added. *The changes you see have been achieved by just adding CSS to the web page – the HTML hasn't changed at all.*

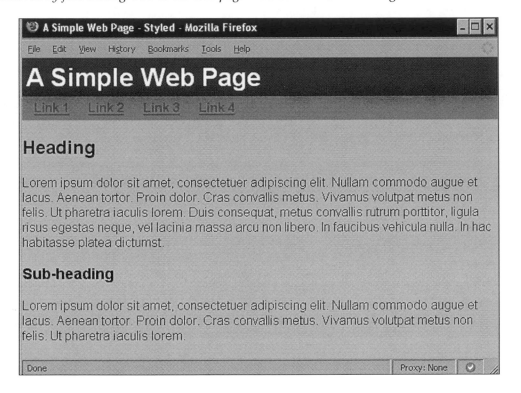

Looking at the Code

OK, let's look at the HTML and CSS used to make these simple web pages. You can download the example files from the Packt website: http://www.packtpub.com/files/code/5326_Code.zip.

First, let's look at the HTML files. Once you've downloaded the code bundle, unzip it, and open the **CSS Example** folder. In it you will see three files: **page.html**, **page_styled.html**, and **style.css**:

Double-click on **page.html** and it should open up in your default web browser. It looks like the first screenshot you saw below the heading *Content and Style*.

To view the HTML code that makes this page, go back to the **CSS Example** folder, right-click on **page.html** and select **Open With | Notepad**.

You will now see the following code in your Notepad window:

```
<html>
<head>
<title>A Simple Web Page</title>
</head>
<body>
<h1>A Simple Web Page</h1>
<ul>
  <li><a href="http://www.packtpub.com">Link 1</a></li>
  <li><a href="http://www.packtpub.com">Link 2</a></li>
  <li><a href="http://www.packtpub.com">Link 3</a></li>
  <li><a href="http://www.packtpub.com">Link 4</a></li>
</ul>
<h2>Heading </h2>
<p>Lorem ipsum dolor sit amet, consectetuer adipiscing elit. Nullam
commodo augue et lacus. Aenean tortor. Proin dolor. Cras convallis
metus. Vivamus volutpat metus non felis. Ut pharetra iaculis lorem.
Duis consequat, metus convallis rutrum porttitor, ligula risus egestas
neque, vel lacinia massa arcu non libero. In faucibus vehicula nulla.
In hac habitasse platea dictumst. </p>
<h3>Sub-heading</h3>
```

```
<p>Lorem ipsum dolor sit amet, consectetuer adipiscing elit. Nullam
commodo augue et lacus. Aenean tortor. Proin dolor. Cras convallis
metus. Vivamus volutpat metus non felis. Ut pharetra iaculis lorem.
</p>
</body>
</html>
```

If you've never seen HTML before, this might look rather confusing. Don't worry, we'll go through it bit by bit.

The first thing you'll notice is lots of angle brackets: < >. These contain the HTML tags. Each HTML tag appears as a pair, with an opening tag < > and a closing tag </ >.

The very first tag you see is the `<html>` tag. This tag encloses the entire HTML document—you'll see the closing `</html>` tag is right at the bottom. The `<html></html>` tag simply tells the browser where the HTML document begins and ends.

All HTML documents are made up of two main parts, the **head** and the **body**. The head, also called the **header**, is contained in the `<head></head>` tag. The header gives information about the HTML document—this is known as **Metadata**. In our simple document the only information included in the header is the page title, which you can see in the `<title></title>` tag. The document title is shown in the title bar of your web browser as in the following screenshot:

Everything in the `<body></body>` tag is the main content of the page, which actually appears in the browser window. Our page begins with an `<h1></h1>` tag, which is a **level 1 heading**—it contains our main page heading. Next comes a `<ul></ul>` tag, which is an **unordered list** or bulleted list. Each item in the unordered list is placed in `<li></li>` tags. These are the four links at the top of the page.

Next you'll notice the `<a href></a>` tags. These are special tags for **hyperlinks**. Let's look at one of these in more detail:

```
<a href="http://www.packtpub.com">Link 1</a>
```

It begins with `<a href=`, which tells the browser that this is a hyperlink. Next, between double quote marks we have the URL to which the link points `"http://www.packtpub.com"`. Then comes an angle bracket > which closes the first part of the tag. Now we have the link text that actually appears in the browser window. In this case, it is `Link 1`. And finally, there is the closing tag `</a>`, which tells the browser it's the end of the hyperlink.

We then have another heading tag, `<h2></h2>`—this time it's a **level 2 heading**, which appears in the browser slightly smaller than a level 1 heading. Next comes a `<p></p>` tag—these hold **paragraph** text. Then we see another heading, this time level 3 `<h3></h3>`, and then another paragraph.

Next, we have the closing body tag—`</body>`, as we have come to the end of our page's content. Finally, there's the closing `</html>` tag, as it's the end of the HTML document.

The Style Sheet

Now, let's look at the CSS, which gives the web page its style; that is the color and size of elements on the page and the layout, or placement of the elements on the page. In the **CSS Example** folder that you downloaded, right-click on the **style.css** file and select **Open With | Notepad**.

What you are now looking at is a **Cascading Style Sheet**. It actually comprises a number of **rules**, which tell web browsers how to display specific types of content structures. Our style sheet contains six **rules**.

Let's examine one of those rules in more detail:

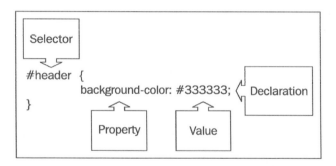

A CSS rule has **two parts**. The first part is the **selector**, which defines the HTML element to which the rule applies. There are various types of selectors, but we won't go into each type in detail as that would be the subject of a full CSS tutorial. Suffice to say that the selector in the preceding diagram is known as an **ID selector**—a # is used to identify this type of selector. I have defined this ID selector as `#header`; I could have chosen any ID that is appropriate and makes sense to me or anyone else who reads the style sheet. Any word can be used to define an ID selector, there is no set vocabulary. `#goofy` or `#sandwich` would both work as ID selectors, but they may not make a lot of sense to someone else reading the style sheet. Another common type of selector is called an **element selector**—these are based on standard HTML elements like `body`, `h1`, or `p`. In our style sheet, the very first rule uses an element selector: `body`. All the other selectors here are ID selectors.

The second part of a CSS rule is known as the **declaration**, which is made up of a **property** and a **value**. The declaration describes the appearance of all the elements that match the selector.

 There are hundreds of CSS properties available to web designers for use in their style sheets. You can see a complete reference guide defining each and every available CSS property at: `http://www.w3.org/TR/REC-CSS2/propidx.html`.

In this example, the **declaration** uses the `background-color` **property**, giving it a **value** of `#333333`. In CSS, the `background-color` property, fairly obviously, defines the background color of the selector. Colors can be defined using the RGB hexadecimal system. In this case, the hexadecimal value is `#333333`, which is a dark gray color.

So, in this example, the CSS rule states that *any HTML elements defined as* `#header` *will have a dark gray background*.

Let's examine another one of our CSS rules:

```
body {
    font-family: Arial, Helvetica, sans-serif;
    margin: 0;
    padding: 0;
    background-color: #CCCCCC;
    color: #000000;
}
```

This rule defines the `body` selector. As we've already seen, the HTML `<body>` element contains all the content for the web page. So, the styles defined here will apply to all the content in our HTML document. The first declaration in this rule refers to the `font-family` property, to which we have given the value, `Arial, Helvetica, sans-serif`. This means that all the text on our web page will appear in the **Arial** font.

The next two declarations deal with `margin` and `padding`. These affect the positioning of text (or other content) on the web page. Basically, by giving these two properties a `0` value, there is no space between the edge of the browser window and the content. Later on, in this chapter, we'll adjust these values and see what happens.

 To fully understand positioning in CSS, you need to know about something called the **CSS Box Model**. Again, it's beyond the scope of this chapter, but you can find excellent discussions on the CSS Box Model at `http://www.brainjar.com/css/positioning/default.asp` and `http://redmelon.net/tstme/box_model/`.

The next declaration uses the `background-color` property. We've seen this property before and here, it sets the background color for the whole page to light gray (#CCCCCC). The final declaration gives the `color` property a value of #000000. The `color` property applies to all the text on the page, making it black.

 As you become more experienced with CSS, you'll notice that different browsers display some CSS declarations in slightly different ways. This is why you should always test your web pages in as many different browsers as possible.

Applying the Style Sheet

So, we've seen the style sheet. Now you're probably wondering how these styles are applied to our HTML document, **page.html**.

There are three ways of adding CSS to an HTML document. The first is known as **Inline Declarations**. This method simply involves adding CSS styles throughout the HTML document as and when they are required. For example, each time we have an `<h2>` heading in our HTML document, we could add a CSS style direct to the `<h2>` tag, like this:

```
<h2 style="color: #FF0000; font-size: 16px;">Level 2 Heading</h2>
```

This would give us a red heading with a size of 16 pixels. The problem with this method is that we would have to add the styling to each and every `<h2>` heading in our document. If we decided at a later date that we wanted our `<h2>` headings to be blue, we would have to go through the document and edit each and every `<h2>` style.

The next method of adding CSS to our HTML is known as **Embedded CSS**. This involves placing the CSS in the **header** of our HTML document, for example:

```
<html>
<head>
<title>A Simple Web Page</title>
<style type="text/css">
h2 {
    color: #FF0000;
    font-size: 16px;
}
</style>
</head>
```

This would also make all `<h2>` headings in our HTML document red with a size of 16 pixels. This is a slightly better approach because we only have to define our `<h2>` heading style once and it is automatically applied to every `<h2>` heading in the document. The downside with this approach is that the CSS has to be added to every page in our website—there might be dozens or hundreds of pages that need the CSS added to their headers. Once again, if we wanted to make our `<h2>` headings blue throughout the website, we would have to edit the **Embedded CSS** on every page.

The third approach is widely regarded as the best. It is called **External CSS**. This involves keeping your CSS in a completely separate file from your web page, for example, **style.css**. You then add a **link** to your CSS file in the header of each web page that requires those styles. The benefit here is that you just need to maintain one CSS file. If you want to change your `<h2>` headings to blue, you just make one change to the **style.css** file and the new style is automatically applied to every page in your website.

This is the approach we'll use in our simple web page example. So, let's work through the steps that will apply the style sheet to our HTML document.

Go back to the **page.html** file and open it in Notepad. The first step is to link our style sheet to the HTML document. To do this, add the following line to the header just after the `<title>A Simple Web Page</title>` line:

```
<link rel="stylesheet" type="text/css" href="style.css" />
```

Your header should now look like this:

```
<html>
<head>
<title>A Simple Web Page - Styled</title>
<link rel="stylesheet" type="text/css" href="style.css" />
</head>
```

The link tag tells the browser that it needs to use an external style sheet for this web page. The location of the style sheet is specified by `href="style.css"`. In this case, **style.css** is in the same directory as our HTML document, so we just need the file name for the link to work. However, you can link to any **.css** file, which may be in another directory or on another web server. So, you could have a link like this: `href="http://www.anotherwebsite.com/style/style.css"`.

At this point let's take a look at the page. Save the file in Notepad, using **File | Save**. If you already have the page open in your browser, refresh or reload it. If it's not already open, go back to the **CSS Example** folder and double-click on **page.html**.

You'll see that the background color and font have already changed.

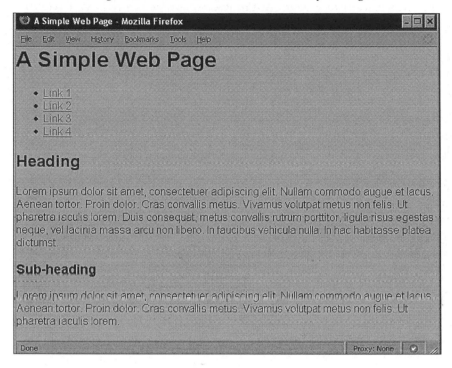

The web browser has already applied the first CSS rule in our style sheet, because it's based on an **element selector**. Remember, these types of selectors apply to standard HTML elements and as we already have a <body></body> element in our document, the style for body has been applied.

The other rules in our style sheet use **ID selectors**, so we need to tell the web browser which elements of our HTML we want these selectors to apply to. We do this by using **<div>** tags.

> <div> tags enable us to define **divisions** or regions of an HTML document.

Let's begin by defining the #header element and, in so doing, tell the browser where we want the header style to be applied.

Back in **page.html** in Notepad, add the following line immediately after the opening <body> tag:

```
<div id="header">
```

Now add a closing `</div>` tag after the `<h1>A Simple Web Page</h1>` heading. This section of code should now look like this:

```
<body>
<div id="header">
<h1>A Simple Web Page</h1>
</div>
```

What we've done is, tell the browser that everything within the `<div id="header"></div>` tag should be styled using the `#header` rule. Save the file again, go back to the page in your browser and refresh it. You'll see that the `header` styles have now been applied:

There are actually two rules from our style sheet being applied here:

```
#header {
    background-color: #333333;
}
```

and:

```
#header h1 {
    padding: 5px;
    margin: 0;
    color: #FFFFFF;
}
```

We have already looked at the first rule—it simply applies the dark gray background. The other rule uses a special kind of ID selector, known as a **descendent selector**. This **specifies** a rule for all `<h1>` elements that come within the `#header` ID. In this case, all `<h1>` elements within `#header` are white (#FFFFFF), with a `padding` of 5 pixels and a `margin` of 0.

Just to demonstrate that this only affects `<h1>` tags within `#header`, add this line immediately after the closing `</div>` tag:

```
<h1>Another H1 Heading</h1>
```

Now save **page.html** and refresh your browser. You will see another `<h1>` heading but it isn't styled the same as the heading in `#header`:

 You can delete the line we just added — it was only for demonstration.

Now we'll style the links to create the navigation bar. Once again, we need to create a `<div>` to tell the browser where to apply our nav styling. Add the following line just after the closing `</div>` tag for the `#header` element:

```
<div id="nav">
```

And then add a closing `</div>` tag straight after the closing `</ul>` tag. This section of code should now look like this:

```
<body>
<div id="header">
<h1>A Simple Web Page</h1>
</div>
<div id="nav">
<ul>
  <li><a href="http://www.packtpub.com">Link 1</a></li>
  <li><a href="http://www.packtpub.com">Link 2</a></li>
  <li><a href="http://www.packtpub.com">Link 3</a></li>
  <li><a href="http://www.packtpub.com">Link 4</a></li>
</ul>
</div>
```

Save **page.html** and refresh your browser. You should see the navigation bar just below the header. The browser has applied these three CSS rules to the `#nav` element:

```
#nav {
  font-weight: bold;
  background-color: #999999;
  padding: 5px;
}
#nav ul{
  margin: 0;
  padding: 0;
}
#nav li{
  display: inline;
  margin: 0;
  padding: 10;
}
```

Hopefully, these CSS rules are starting to make a bit more sense now. You should be able to see what's going on in the first `#nav` rule above. You may also have noticed that the other two contain more examples of **descendent selectors**. This time we're specifying styles that only apply to `<ul>` and `<li>` elements within `#nav`. If you added another unordered list (`<ul>`) elsewhere on the page, it would appear as a regular bulleted list.

In the `#nav li` rule, it's interesting to note the `display: inline;` declaration. This is what tells the browser to display the list items horizontally rather than in a vertical list.

That's our simple web page. I've included the finished HTML document (**page-styled.html**) in the **CSS Example** folder.

Tweaking the Styles

The last stage in this very brief introduction to CSS is to see what happens if we make some changes to the style sheet. Go back to **style.css** in Notepad. First, let's see what happens if we change the values for `margin` and `padding` in the `body` rule. Change it to this:

```
body {
  font-family: Arial, Helvetica, sans-serif;
  margin: 10px;
  padding: 10px;
  background-color: #CCCCCC;
  color: #000000;
}
```

Save **style.css** and refresh your browser. You should see some extra space around the edge of the browser window. This is the 10 pixels `margin` and `padding` we just added.

Now let's add a rule to change the styling of our `<h2>` heading. Add the following at the end of the style sheet:

```
h2 {
    font-family: Courier New, Courier, mono;
    color: #0000FF;
}
```

After you've saved **style.css** and refreshed your browser, you'll see that our `<h2>` heading is now in Courier font and colored blue. This style will also apply to any other `<h2>` headings we add to the document.

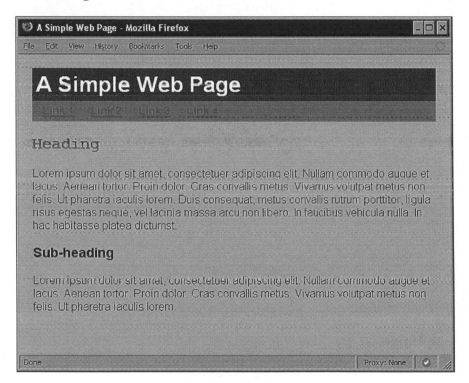

That was a very brief introduction to HTML and CSS and you'll probably want to supplement it with some further reading. It's a large subject and there is no way you could become an expert after such a short introduction. The aim of this brief tutorial was to teach you what HTML and CSS code looks like and how the two technologies work together to create web pages. Admittedly, much of the detail has been glossed over. However, this overview should enable you to follow the work we'll be doing in the case study as it involves editing the style sheet for the WordPress theme (I will provide all the CSS; to see it working, you just need to paste it into the case study style sheet). But before we move on to that you may want to set up an environment on your own computer that allows you to run WordPress locally.

Setting Up a Local Development Environment

If you are considering making big changes to your blog, particularly ones that require editing the WordPress source files, it's worth considering setting up a development environment on your local computer. This has a number of benefits. First, if you mess up and cause irreparable damage to the WordPress files, you haven't broken your live blog. Second, you don't have to take your blog offline while you're playing around 'under the hood'. Third, you don't have to keep FTPing files to your remote server to view the changes.

Admittedly, most of the editing we'll be doing in the rest of this chapter could be done using the Theme Editor in the WordPress administration area. If you follow through the case study example at the end of this chapter, it will probably only take half an hour or so. However, if you do decide to design your own theme the chances are it could take several hours or even days. Much of the work will involve trial and error—saving your changes and then previewing them.

WordPress 2.6 has made tweaking a theme a lot easier, thanks to the new Theme Previewer, which allows you to view a theme as it would actually appear with your content, before you install it. However, using the WordPress Theme Editor to do a lot of editing work is not ideal. The editor is not as user-friendly as a desktop text editor (it's really only meant for minor changes) and using the Theme Previewer repeatedly during the design process is not as easy as just refreshing your browser window. This is why it's well worth using a local development environment. You may also find your development environment useful in future web projects.

To run WordPress you need a **web server**, **PHP**, and **MySQL**. For the web server I recommend **Apache** as it's widely regarded as the best. It's also open-source (as are PHP and MySQL), so it's free to download and use. These are the components we will install to set up our development environment.

It is possible to download Apache, PHP, and MySQL as separate components and then install and configure them one by one. However, this can be quite a complicated process that requires a fair amount of technical knowledge. Luckily there are a number of open-source Apache distributions that come bundled with PHP and MySQL pre-configured. They also include an installer, which makes setting up your server a breeze. One of the best is **XAMPP**, from Apache Friends, and it's the one we'll be using for our development environment. XAMPP is available for the most popular desktop operating systems including Windows, MAC OS X, Linux, and Solaris.

 XAMPP stands for: X (any of the four operating systems supported), A (Apache), M (MySQL), P (PHP), and P (Perl).

Installing XAMPP

We will now run through the process of installing XAMPP on your computer.

1. Go to `http://www.apachefriends.org/en/xampp.html` and click on the link for your operating system. We'll be working through the installation for Windows, but there are installation instructions for the other operating systems on the Apache Friends website.

2. On the **XAMPP for Windows** page choose to download the latest stable release of the **XAMPP Installer** and save it to your desktop. The file is about 37MB, so this may take some time depending on the speed of your connection.

XAMPP for Windows 1.6.5, 2007/12/24

Version	Size	Content
XAMPP Windows 1.6.5 [Basic package]		Apache HTTPD 2.2.6, MySQL 5.0.51, PHP 5.2.5 + 4.4.7 + PEAR + Switch, MiniPerl 5.8.7, Openssl 0.9.8g, PHPMyAdmin 2.11.3, XAMPP Control Panel 2.5, Webalizer 2.01-10, Mercury Mail Transport System v4.52, FileZilla FTP Server 0.9.24, SQLite 2.8.15, ADODB 4.96, Zend Optimizer 3.3.0, XAMPP Security, Ming. For Windows 98, 2000, XP. See also ☑ README
☑ Installer	37 MB	Installer MD5 checksum: 9ad46876110d81e62f6945083c34c71f
☑ ZIP	82 MB	ZIP archive MD5 checksum: d673b8fe1315e853589c4f0cf64d7e25
☑ EXE (7-zip)	32 MB	Selfextracting 7-ZIP archive MD5 checksum: 965b66b8c8012875d2ee3e79dec98000

3. Click on the XAMPP Installer icon on your desktop and when prompted, choose your preferred language. The **XAMPP Setup Wizard** will now begin.

4. Click **Next** and then choose the location for your XAMPP installation. I recommend using **c:\xampp**. Click **Next**.

5. On the next screen, I recommend you stick with the defaults. Do not install the components as services. (If they are installed as services, they will start automatically every time you turn on your computer.) Click **Install** and wait for the various packages to be extracted and installed. If the Command Prompt window opens, don't touch it, just let it run.

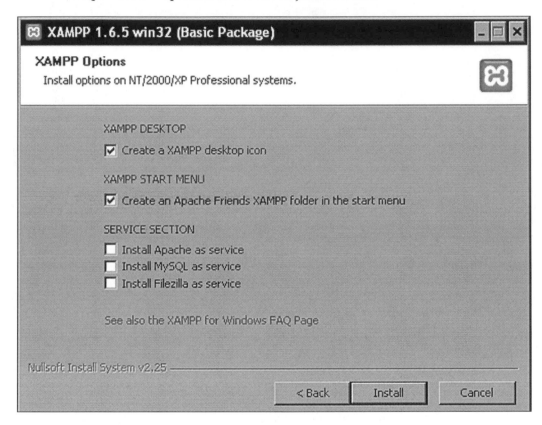

6. Click **Finish** and select **Yes** to start the **XAMPP Control Panel**.

7. Start the servers by clicking the **Start** buttons next to Apache and MySQL in the Control Panel.

8. Open your web browser and enter the address `http://localhost/`. If your installation has worked properly, XAMPP should now be visible in your browser. If you can't see XAMPP, refer to the FAQs and help on the Apache Friends website.

Congratulations you now have an Apache / MySQL / PHP web server running on your computer!

Setting the 'root' Password for MySQL

By default, when you install XAMPP there is no password set for the 'root' MySQL user. This isn't a major security problem, when you're only running a local server, but we'll fix it anyway.

1. Open your web browser and go to `http://localhost/`. From the XAMPP welcome page, select **phpMyAdmin** under **Tools** in the left hand menu. You'll now see the phpMyAdmin home page.

phpMyAdmin is a browser-based administration tool for MySQL. It allows you to create and drop (delete) tables and databases, and run SQL statements right from your browser.

2. Click on the **Privileges** link. You will be presented with the **User overview**:

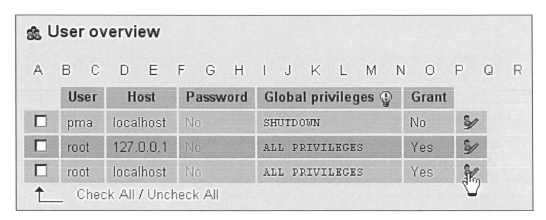

3. Click on the **Edit privileges** icon for 'root' on 'localhost'. On the next page, scroll down to **Change password**, enter a password and click **Go**:

4. You've now set a password for the 'root' MySQL user. However, in order to continue using phpMyAdmin, we need to set this password in the phpMyAdmin configuration file. Without it, phpMyAdmin won't be able to connect to the MySQL server. Click on the **Home** icon in the top left hand corner of your browser window under the phpMyAdmin logo. You'll see the following error message:

Welcome to phpMyAdmin 2.11.3

phpMyAdmin tried to connect to the MySQL server, and the server rejected the connection. You should check the host, username and password in your configuration and make sure that they correspond to the information given by the administrator of the MySQL server.

Error

 MySQL said: ⑦

```
#1045 - Access denied for user 'root'@'localhost' (using password: NO)
```

5. Don't close the browser window, just minimize it.
6. To fix the above error, go to the XAMPP directory on your computer. This should be **c:\xampp** (or wherever you installed it).
7. Open the **phpMyAdmin** folder and locate the **config.inc** file. Open the file in any text editor (Windows Notepad should be fine). Find the line that begins with:

```
$cfg['Servers'][$i]['password']       = '';
```

[You may want to use **Edit | Find...** in Notepad to locate the line more easily.]

8. Insert the MySQL password (the one we set in step 3, above) between the quote marks just before the semi-colon, so the line now reads:

```
$cfg['Servers'][$i]['password']       = 'yourpassword';
```

9. Now save the **config.inc** file and close it.

10. Return to your web browser that still has phpMyAdmin running. Refresh the page and you should now see the phpMyAdmin home page.

11. Click **Privileges** again. In the **User overview** click the **Edit Privileges** icon for 'root' on '127.0.0.1'. In the same way as we did before, enter the password (the same one you used above) and click **Go**.

We're now ready to install WordPress.

Installing WordPress Locally

You've probably installed WordPress at least once on a remote server and the principle is exactly the same for installing it on your local server.

1. First, let's create a MySQL database for your WordPress installation. Back on the phpMyAdmin home page (`http://localhost/phpmyadmin/`), locate **Create new database** and enter a name for your database in the input box. Click **Create**.

2. Download the latest stable release of WordPress from `http://wordpress.org/download/` and unzip it to the **htdocs** folder in your XAMPP directory. This should be at **c:\xampp\htdocs**.

 The **htdocs** folder in XAMPP is the same as the 'www', 'httpdocs', or 'htdocs' directory on your remote web server. It's where you must place all the files you want to 'publish' so that you can view them as web pages in your browser.

3. In the **wordpress** folder, open the **wp-config-sample.php** file using Windows Notepad or any other text editor. Edit the configuration details for the MySQL database we created earlier. These should be:
   - DB_NAME = 'wordpress'
   - DB_USER = 'root'
   - DB_PASSWORD = 'yourpassword' (This is the MySQL password we set for the 'root' user earlier).

   You can leave the other configuration settings as they are.

4. Save the file as **wp-config.php**. If you're using Notepad, in the **Save As** dialog box, remember to set **Save as type** to **All Files**.

5. Point your web browser to `http://localhost/wordpress/` and you will
    see the familiar WordPress installation screen. Enter your blog title (call it
    ChilliGuru), email address, and click **Install WordPress**.

    You now have a fully functional copy of WordPress on your own computer.

Note that the email functions in WordPress won't work with your local
server. This is because we haven't configured a mail server and we would
need one for PHP to handle outgoing mail. Setting up an outgoing mail
server is complicated and for many people it's impossible because
their ISP won't allow them to run an SMTP server over their standard
internet connection.

Not having the mail function in WordPress shouldn't be too much of
a problem for the majority of things you're likely to be doing locally.
*However, do ensure that you don't lose or forget your password as WordPress
won't be able to email a reminder to you!*

Case Study—ChilliGuru Design

As I mentioned earlier, we'll be using the **Sandbox** theme from `plaintxt.org` to apply a custom design to the ChilliGuru blog. All the design work we'll be doing will only require changes to the theme's style sheet.

To begin, download the **Sandbox** theme and maybe take a look at the brief introduction to the theme over at `http://www.plaintxt.org/themes/sandbox/`.

Now, we'll install the theme in your local copy of WordPress. Unzip the Sandbox directory you just downloaded and place the entire folder in the themes directory in your local WordPress. If you followed the XAMPP installation exactly as it appeared earlier, this should be at **C:\xampp\htdocs\wordpress\wp-content\themes**.

If you log in to the admin area and click on the **Design** tab, you will see Sandbox listed under **Available Themes**. If you clicked on it, you would see it in the Theme Previewer, and if you clicked Activate **Sandbox** (in the top right-hand corner of the Theme Previewer), the theme would be installed, but don't do it right now as we're going to create our own theme.

Actually, we're not creating a complete theme from scratch. The beauty of Sandbox is that it allows us to change the design of the theme just by editing one file: **style.css**. We don't need to change any of the template files in the original theme.

Go back to the themes folder in your WordPress directory **C:\xampp\htdocs\ wordpress\wp-content\themes**. Create a new folder called **chilliguru**. Now go into the **sandbox** folder within the **themes** folder, copy the file called **style.css** and paste it into the **chilliguru** folder you just created. Open up the code archive you downloaded from Packt and copy the folder called **images**; then paste it into the **chilliguru** folder. Your new **chilliguru** folder should now contain the **style.css** file and a folder called **images**.

Before we go ahead and edit **style.css**, there are a couple more housekeeping tasks we could do to make the job a little easier. The first is to load some dummy content into our rather empty blog. Your default installation of WordPress contains very little content; just a 'Hello World!' post, a comment, and a short 'About' page. When you're working on a theme design, it's useful to have plenty of content to see how your style sheet affects the many different elements available in WordPress. Scott Wallick, co-creator of the Sandbox theme, made some dummy content for the 2007 Sandbox Design Competition (`http://www.sndbx.org`), and he's given kind permission for us to use it here. The steps to install it are as follows:

1. In the WordPress admin area, click on the **Comments** tab. Delete the comment that accompanies the 'Hello World!' post.

2. Now delete the 'Hello World!' post itself from **Manage | Posts**.

Important: You must work in this order; delete the comment first, then the post itself.

3. Delete the sample 'About' page from **Manage | Pages**.

4. In the code bundle you downloaded from Packt, locate the file called **dummy_content.xml** and remember where it is on your computer.

5. Go back to the WordPress admin area and select **Manage | Import**. Select **WordPress** (at the bottom of the list), click **Browse...**, and navigate to the **dummy_content.xml** file you just located on your computer. Click **Upload file and import**.

6. On the next screen, choose **admin** from the **map to existing** drop-down box as shown in the following screenshot. Leave the default settings for the author, **Susan Flowerpot**. Under **Import Attachments**, check **Download and import file attachments**. Click **Submit**.

7. The import process should now run successfully. Once it is complete, click **Visit site** and you will see the dummy content.

 After importing the dummy content, you should check whether the Page parents are set up correctly. You can do this by going to **Manage | Pages**. Open the **Archives** page. Under **Advanced Options** select the **Page Parent** menu then from the drop-down box choose **About** and **Save** the page. You can do the same for the **Links** page.

The second housekeeping task is to download and install a decent text editor. A good text editor makes it far easier to work with code files like **style.css**, which we'll be editing shortly. In our brief introduction to CSS we used Notepad to edit the CSS documents. That was fine with such small files, but now we'll be working on more complex CSS, Notepad is not ideal. You may already have another text editor or a fully-blown HTML editor like Dreamweaver; if so, use that. Otherwise, for Windows, I recommend **Crimson Editor**, which is a good open-source option (`http://www.crimsoneditor.com/english/download.html`). Once downloaded, install it on your PC. For Mac OS X or Linux, try **Emacs** (`http://www.gnu.org/software/emacs/`).

OK, now we've installed Sandbox, created the folder for our new theme design, imported some dummy content, and installed a good text editor. We can now roll our sleeves up and get stuck in to the CSS.

The Style Sheet Header

In WordPress themes, the style sheet has a header, which gives WordPress some meta-information about the theme. This includes things like the theme's author, version number, and most importantly for Sandbox themes, the name of the theme template. This is the first part of the style sheet we'll edit.

Fire up your new text editor (Crimson Editor) and open the **style.css** file in the **chilliguru** theme folder (**C:\xampp\htdocs\wordpress\wp-content\themes\ chilliguru**).

It's a good idea to show the line numbers in your text editor, for easy reference. In Crimson Editor, select **View | Line Numbers**. You may also find it easier with Word Wrap switched on. This breaks long lines of code so you don't have to scroll horizontally to read them; select **View | Word Wrap**.

Lines 1-9 in **style.css** provide the meta-information for our new **chilliguru** theme. Each line is fairly self-explanatory. Edit the section similar to the following code (if you like, you can replace my name and website with your own):

```
/*
THEME NAME: ChilliGuru
THEME URI: http://blog.chilliguru.com
DESCRIPTION: A spicy theme for the ChilliGuru blog
VERSION: 1.0
AUTHOR: Paul Thewlis
AUTHOR URI: http://blog.paulthewlis.com
TAGS: sandbox, microformats, hcard, hatom, xoxo, widgets, blank slate,
starter theme, minimalist, developer
*/
```

You may be wondering what Tags are. We'll discuss them in detail in Chapter 5. Don't worry right now; they're not important for our theme design.

Now, we'll tell WordPress where to find the template file for our theme. As this is a Sandbox design, it will be using the Sandbox template. Insert another line after the TAGS that reads TEMPLATE: sandbox, like so:

```
/*
THEME NAME: ChilliGuru
THEME URI: http://blog.chilliguru.com
DESCRIPTION: A spicy theme for the ChilliGuru blog
VERSION: 1.0
AUTHOR: Paul Thewlis
AUTHOR URI: http://blog.paulthewlis.com
TAGS: sandbox, microformats, hcard, hatom, xoxo, widgets, blank slate,
starter theme, minimalist, developer
TEMPLATE: sandbox
*/
```

Save **style.css**.

We can now install our new theme. Go to your admin area and select the **Design** tab (if you were already in **Design**, you'll need to refresh your browser). You should now see **ChilliGuru** listed under **Available Themes**. Click on **ChilliGuru** and it will open in the Theme Previewer. Click on the **Activate "ChilliGuru"** link in the top right-hand corner of the Theme Previewer to install it.

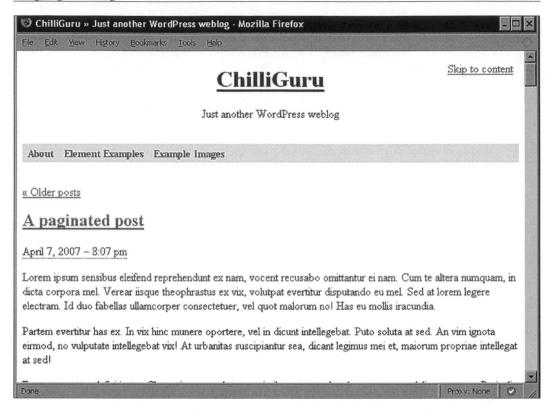

Now view the blog and you will see the default Sandbox design.

 Now, we have the theme installed, we can view the progress of our design as we continue to work on **style.css**.

The Page Layout

We're now getting into the meat of the CSS and the code will begin to get a little more complicated. Once again, a detailed explanation of the code would be in the realm of a more complete CSS tutorial, but I will give a summary explanation of the various sections in our style sheet. As you edit the style sheet, you should see how the chunks of code affect the design of the blog; even if you don't fully understand the intricacies of the CSS.

All the CSS selectors we'll be using are already coded into the template files for the Sandbox theme—open up **index.php** in your text editor and you will see some of the elements that the selectors refer to.

You can either type out the code as it appears in the following pages, or copy and paste it from **style_copy.txt** included in the code bundle you downloaded from Packt. The code in **style_copy.txt** is split up into chunks that correspond to the sections you'll be working through here.

The next stage is to give some structure to the blog page by designing the layout. Having considered ChilliGuru and its strategic goals, I think there may be quite a lot of content to go in the sidebar. This is largely as it is a demonstration blog and we'll be adding lots of functionality throughout the rest of the book. Because of the quantity of sidebar content, I think we need two sidebars and they should go on the right-hand side of the page, for the reasons we discussed earlier in the chapter (as it's best to have the main content on the left, because that's where people's eyes are likely to be drawn when they first open the page, and the search engine spiders will find it first). Out of the four wireframes we looked at earlier, the one that we'll apply to ChilliGuru is this:

You will have noticed that the code in **style.css** is spaced differently to the code we saw in our brief introduction to CSS earlier in the chapter. For example:

```
div#header{text-align:center;margin-bottom:2em;}
```

could be written like this:

```
div#header {
text-align:center;
margin-bottom:2em;
}
```

Both ways of lining up the code are correct and a web browser will read and display each of them in exactly the same way. It's basically a matter of personal choice. Some designers like to space their CSS rules out with each declaration on a separate line and the closing brace on its own line. Others keep the whole rule on one line. The advantage of one rule per line is that it takes up less space in your text editor window, making more of the style sheet visible at once. It also makes the code more compact if you are working on it from within the text editor in the WordPress administration area. This is probably why the authors of Sandox have laid out their code like this. We'll stick to their structure.

Back in your text editor, look at Line 12 (this is a **comment**):

```
/* Two-column with sidebar on left from the /examples/ folder */
```

Comments are enclosed within an opening comment tag /* and a closing comment tag */. They are ignored by web browsers and can only be read by humans. They are most often used to notate CSS code so that other people reading it can follow the original author's thoughts. You can type anything you like within comment tags; it won't affect the way the web browser displays the CSS.

Now look at Line 13:

```
@import url('examples/2c-l.css');
```

Sandbox includes a selection of example layouts, each of which is kept in its own **.css** file in a folder called **examples**. Line 13 uses the @import rule to link **style.css** to an external file called **2c-l.css**. In effect, this combines the styles from both files into the overall style of the blog.

However, we're not going to use any external CSS files—we'll confine everything to **style.css**. Let's begin by deleting all of the existing code from Line 12 onwards. Yes, it sounds extreme, but you need to select and then delete everything from Line 12 downwards. (If you save **style.css** and preview the blog now, it looks even plainer than the default Sandbox theme!)

Now type the following code, starting at Line 12 (or paste it from **style_copy.txt**):

```
/* The Page Layout */
div#wrapper {width: 850px; margin-left: auto; margin-right:
auto;position: relative;}
div#container {float: left;width: 100%;}
div#content {margin: 0 430px 0 0;}
div.sidebar {float: left;overflow: hidden;width: 180px;}
div#primary {margin: 0 0 0 -400px;}
div#secondary {margin: 0 0 0 -200px;}
div#footer {clear: left;width: 100%}
```

As you can see, we've used our own comment here, which tells anyone reading the style sheet that this section handles our page layout. We won't go through the CSS in detail, but you can see the affect it has had by saving **style.css** and previewing the blog in your web browser. We now have a three-column layout with two sidebars on the right-hand side of the page. (The header looks a bit odd at this stage, but it will be fixed soon.)

The layout has a fixed width of 850px, which is defined in the div#wrapper rule. This is a good width for screen resolutions of at least **1024x768**, which is the minimum resolution of most modern computer displays (around 80% of web users have a screen resolution of at least 1024x768). The div#primary and div#secondary rules define the two sidebars.

Colors and Fonts

Based on the subject matter of ChilliGuru, I decided on a color scheme that uses earthy brown and red tones. I knew that I wanted to use images of red chili peppers in the design and this color scheme works well with them. I chose a simple Arial font, as it is readable and gives the design a clean, contemporary look.

Back in your text editor add this CSS rule after the page layout:

```
/* Colors and Font */
body {font-family:Arial, Helvetica, sans-serif;
     background-color:#F8DC9E;}
```

Save **style.css** and preview the blog in your browser (remember to refresh or reload). This rule has set the font family and background color for the entire blog. We'll add the text color later.

The Header

In keeping with the clean contemporary look I was aiming for, I decided to go with a simple header. It contains a large image of a red chili pepper with the blog title and description in a fairly large font size, all set against the body background color. To achieve this, add the following five CSS rules to **style.css**:

```
/* The Header */
div#header{text-align:left;margin-bottom:1em; padding-
top:6.5em;height: 120px;background:#F8DC9E url('images/background.
jpg') no-repeat center;}
div#header h1{font-size: 46px;text-decoration: none;color:
#800000;font-weight:bold;letter-spacing:-2px;line-height:36px;margin:0
5px 0 0; }
div#header h1 a{font-size: 46px;text-decoration: none;color:
#800000;font-weight:bold;letter-spacing:-2px;line-height:36px;margin:0
5px 0 0;}
#header h1 a:hover{color: #F5AD61;}
div#header div#blog-description{font-size:44px;color:#F5AD61;font-
weight: bold;letter-spacing:-2px;line-height:46px; }
```

You should also log in to the WordPress admin area and under **Settings**, change the **Tagline** to **The spice in your life**. Remember to click the **Save Changes** button.

The header is designed to work with this fairly short Tagline, so that it does not overlap the chili pepper image.

In this section of CSS, the most interesting part to note is the `div#header` rule. The `background` property places our chili pepper image in the header. You can see the header image in the **images** folder for the ChilliGuru theme. The other rules in this section set the font-size and font-color for the header. Save the style sheet and preview the blog to see our progress. The header should now look like this:

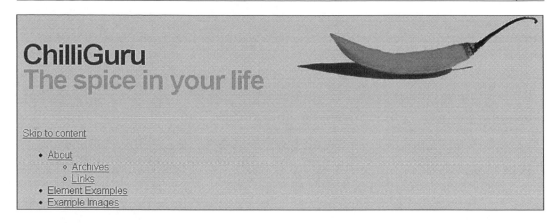

The Menu

I wanted to keep the same background color throughout the design, including the header. However, this would make it difficult to delineate a horizontal menu if it was to be placed below the header. So, I placed the menu at the top of the page, above the header. Back in your text editor, add the following 12 CSS rules to **style.css**:

```
/* The Menu */
div#access div.skip-link{padding: 0; position: absolute; right: 0;
text-align: right; top: 0; border-bottom: 1px dotted #F5AD61;}
div#access a{color:#DF5E37;text-decoration: none; }
div#menu{font-size:0.9em;height:1.5em;padding-top:0.3em;background:#F8
DC9E;width:100%;border-bottom: 1px dotted #F5AD61;position: absolute;
top: 1.5em}
div#menu ul a{font-weight:700;text-decoration:none; }
div#menu ul,div#menu ul ul,div#menu ul li{list-style:none;margin:0;pa
dding:0;}
div#menu ul li{float:left;}
div#menu ul li a{background:#F8DC9E;padding-right:50px;font-
size:18px;}
div#menu ul ul{display:none;}
div#menu ul ul li{float:none;}
div#menu ul ul li a{margin:0;padding:0;}
div#menu ul li:hover ul{display:block;font-size:0.9em;padding-
top:0.5em;position:absolute;}
div#menu ul li:hover ul li a{background:#f5f5f5;border:none;display:
block;padding:0.1em;width:10em;}
```

In this section of code, we have used the `position` and `top` properties to place the menu at the top of the page. This section also applies font-size and font-color to the menu and places the dotted line underneath it. The `div#access` rules apply the style to our **Skip to content** link in the top right-hand corner of the page. Remember, this link is an important accessibility feature, which allows users of screen readers and other non-standard browsers to skip the menu and get straight to the page content.

Save **style.css** and refresh or reload the blog in your browser. At this point, the blog should look like this:

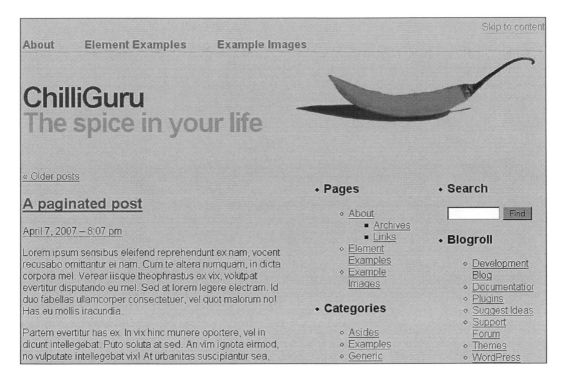

The Main Content Area

We'll now turn our attention to the main content area. The first elements to style here are the post title and the post date. So far the design has been fairly simple, so I wanted to add a red chili pepper 'icon' to the post title to give a bit of impact. Once again, we'll use the `background` property to add the image.

Add the following five CSS rules to the style sheet:

```
/* The Main Content Area */
div.hentry{border-bottom: 1px solid #F5AD61; padding: 0 0 20px 0;
margin: 10px 0 60px 0:}
```

```
.entry-title{clear:both;background-image:url(images/redchilli.jpg);
background-repeat: no-repeat;line-height:38px; margin:10px 0 0 0;}
h2.entry-title{font-size: 20px; padding:0  0 0 75px;}
h3.entry-title{font-size: 20px; padding:0  0 0 75px;}
.entry-date{padding: 0 0 0 75px; font-size: 14px;font-weight:
bold;color: #F5AD61;display: inline;}
```

Once again, save **style.css** and preview the blog (remember to refresh or reload your browser). You'll see that the red chili icon has been added, and the post title and the post date have been partially styled.

Next, we'll work on the post meta-information. This comprises the links at the bottom of each post that show the author, the categories the post is in, and also allow you to add comments and edit the post (when logged in). I'm going to add icons for 'author', 'categories', 'comments', and 'edit'. Once again this will be achieved using the background property. I'm using the free 'Silk' icon set by **FamFamFam** released under the Creative Commons License (http://www.famfamfam.com/lab/icons/silk/). However, you could make the design even more unique by designing your own 'chili' icons—unfortunately, my artistic talents don't stretch that far! You can see the four icons that I'm going to use from the images folder. We'll also be styling the page link, which is used for paginated posts.

Add the following six rules:

```
.page-link{color: #800000;font-size: 14px;line-height: 20px;padding-
top:10px;}
.entry-meta{color: #800000;font-size: 12px;line-height: 20px;padding-
top:10px;}
.entry-meta .author{background: url(images/author.gif) 0 0 no-
repeat;padding-left:18px;}
.entry-meta .cat-links{background: url(images/category.png) 0 0 no-
repeat;padding-left: 16px;}
.entry-meta .edit-link{background: url(images/edit.png) 0 0 no-
repeat;padding-left: 16px;}
.entry-meta .comments-link{background: url(images/comment.png) 0 0 no-
repeat;padding-left: 16px;}
```

Save **style.css** and preview the blog in your browser. You should now see the styled meta-information for each post:

And lastly for the main content section, add the following 16 CSS rules:

```
div#container,div.sidebar{margin-top:0;}
div#content p{font-size: 14px;}
div#content a{color: #DF5E37;text-decoration: none;border-bottom: 1px
dotted #F5AD61;}
div#content h2{color: #DF5E37;}
div#nav-above,div#nav-below{width:100%;height:1em;}
div#nav-above{margin-bottom:1em;}
div#nav-below{margin-top:1em;}
.alignleft,div.nav-previous{float: left;}
.alignright,div.nav-next{float: right;}
form#commentform .form-label{margin:1em 0 0;}
form#commentform span.required{background:#F8DC9E;color:red;}
form#commentform,form#commentform p{padding:0;}
input#author,input#email,input#url{width:50%;}
input#author,input#email,input#url,textarea#comment{padding:0.2em;}
div.comments ol li{margin:0 0 3.5em;}
textarea#comment{height:13em;margin:0 0 0.5em;overflow:
auto;width:66%;}
```

Preview the blog again and you'll see that the most noticeable change we applied here was the styling for links in the main content—their font-color and the dotted line underneath them. We've also changed the main font size to 14px, which is a good readable size. Most of the section is minor layout styling that improves the spacing between some elements on the page. The last few rules in this section apply to the comment form, which we haven't altered from the original Sandbox styling. This could be something for you to work on later.

The Sidebars

The first thing to do here is apply link styling that matches the rest of the design and remove the bullets from the lists in the sidebars.

Add these nine rules to the style sheet:

```
/* The Sidebars */
div.sidebar div,div.sidebar h3,div.sidebar ul,div.sidebar
li{margin:0;padding:0;}
div.sidebar h3{font-size: 16px;color: #DF5E37;font-weight:
bold;margin: 0 0 8px 0;border-bottom: 1px solid #F5AD61;}
div.sidebar li{list-style:none;margin:0 0 1em;}
div.sidebar li form{margin:0.2em 0 0;padding:0;}
div.sidebar ul ul{margin:0 0 0 1em;}
div.sidebar ul ul a{color: #DF5E37;text-decoration: none;border-
bottom: 1px dotted #F5AD61;}
div.sidebar ul ul li{list-style:none;margin:0;}
div.sidebar ul ul ul{margin:0 0 0 0.5em;}
div.sidebar ul ul ul li{list-style:none;}
```

Preview the blog to see the changes. Now we'll add a feed icon to the
RSS Feeds heading:

```
li#rss-links h3 { background:url(images/feed.png);background-repeat:
no-repeat;padding-left:20px; }
```

The next four rules apply some nice styling to the **Search** input box and **Find** button
(notice how the colors change when you hover your cursor over them):

```
div.sidebar input#s{width: 100px;border: 1px solid #F5AD61;color:
#800000;}
div.sidebar input#s:focus,div.sidebar input#s:hover{border: 1px solid
#DF5E37;}
input.button{background: #F5AD61;border: 1px solid #DF5E37;padding: 0
0.4em 0 0.4em;margin-left: 0.4em;color: #DF5E37;font-weight: bold;}
input.button:focus, input.button:hover{background: #800000;border: 1px
solid #F5AD61;color: #F5AD61;font-weight: bold;}
```

Save the style sheet and preview the changes.

The Footer

Finally, we'll add some styling to the page footer. Add these rules at the bottom of
the style sheet:

```
/* The Footer */
div#footer{margin:30px 0 0 0;text-align:right;border-top: 1px solid
#F5AD61;padding: 10px 0 0 0;color: #000;font-size: 10px;}
div#footer a{color: #DF5E37;text-decoration: none;border-bottom: 2px
dotted #DF5E37;}
```

The content of the footer is rather minimal so we need to add our own. This is one
change that we can't do via the style sheet. Go to the **sandbox** folder in your themes
directory (**C:\xampp\htdocs\wordpress\wp-content\themes\sandbox**) and open
up the **footer.php** file (you can use Notepad or Crimson Editor). Delete everything
between the `<div id="footer">` and `</div>` tags and replace it with this (you can
paste it from the **footer.txt** file included in the code bundle for this chapter. I've also
included the edited **footer.php** file, for reference):

```
&copy; Copyright 2008 <a href="http://blog.chilliguru.
com">ChilliGuru</a>   |   Powered by <a href="http://
wordpress.org">WordPress</a>   |   Designed with <a
href="http://www.plaintxt.org/themes/sandbox/">The Sandbox</a>
```

Save **footer.php**.

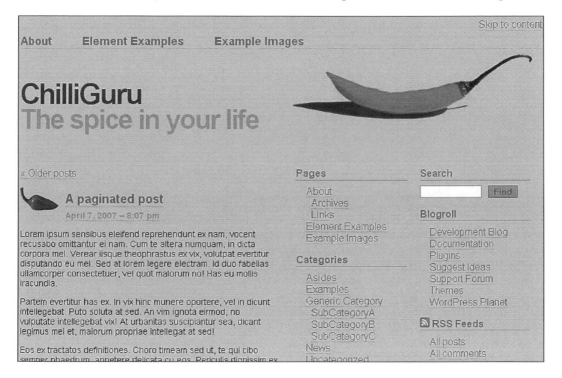

Now save and close **style.css** in Crimson Editor and preview the finished design:

If you take a look in your **chilliguru** theme folder (**C:\xampp\htdocs\wordpress\wp-content\themes\chilliguru**), you now have a completed style sheet and an images folder. This is almost everything you need for a complete Sandbox-designed theme. All that's missing is a screenshot. I've included a screenshot in the code bundle—copy it into the **chilliguru** theme folder and now log in to your WordPress admin area. Click on the **Design** tab and you'll see the screenshot on the **Themes** page.

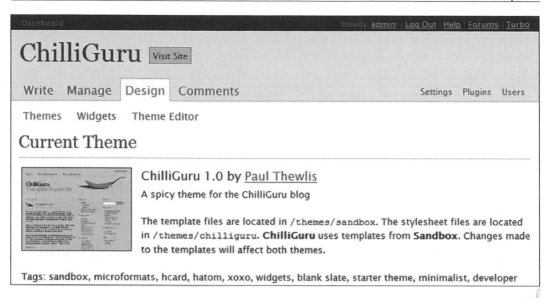

Summary

We've covered a lot of ground in this chapter. You should now know about some of the design principles to consider when working on your blog theme. These should give you the confidence to critically evaluate your existing blog design and maybe make some improvements.

We also went through a very brief introduction about HTML and CSS before setting up a local development environment. Finally, we worked through the process of applying a completely new design for our case study blog by using the Sandbox theme. We saw how an attractive design can be achieved by just editing the Sandbox style sheet.

At this point you may wish to do some further experimenting with the style sheet. Try changing a few of the values and see what happens — it's not called the Sandbox for nothing! Get in there and play around.

In the next chapter, we will be looking at a variety of options for adding images and videos to our WordPress blog.

4
Images and Videos

In this chapter, we are going to look at some advanced image handling techniques to ensure the images you use in your blog are displayed consistently and are easy to manage. We'll begin with a little bit of image theory and move on to look at image editing. We'll see how to alter the size and styling of thumbnails and images within posts. The second half of the chapter will demonstrate how to create an image gallery in WordPress. We'll also learn how to incorporate videos from third-party sites such as YouTube and Google Video, before adding a favicon to our blog.

Image Theory Basics

The most common formats for web images are JPEG, GIF, and PNG. These are the three formats you're most likely to come across. JPEG and GIF have been around for a long time, while PNG is a relative newcomer. PNG is a far more versatile format than GIF and JPEG but you should be aware that some browsers (such as Internet Explorer 6 and older) have problems rendering PNG images correctly, particularly ones with transparent backgrounds.

Whichever format you use, there are three important image measurements you need to be aware of. They are **dimensions**, **resolution**, and **file size**.

Dimensions

This is simply the width and height of an image. Most image editing software allows you to express the dimensions of an image in a variety of units (for example centimeters, inches, or pixels). The most common and most useful unit in web design is pixels. Most computer monitors have a screen size (or resolution) of about 1024 by 768 pixels, so there is little point in setting the dimensions of an image any higher than this, unless you want people to be able to print them at a reasonably high quality. Images intended for print should be placed in a separate folder for downloading.

Resolution

The resolution of an image is measured in **pixels per inch** (**ppi**). This is how much data is contained in each square inch of an image. The higher the ppi, the sharper the image will appear. However, computer monitors can only display around 72-100 pixels per inch so there's little point in having a resolution of more than 72ppi for images on the Web. The only time when a higher resolution is necessary is when an image is intended to be printed, in which case, around 300ppi is recommended.

File Size

The file size of an image is the amount of space it takes up on a hard disk and is measured in **kilobytes** (**KB**), **megabytes** (**MB**), or **gigabytes** (**GB**). Crucially, the larger the dimensions and resolution of an image are, the bigger the file size. Large images take longer to download for your end user (which makes a web page slow to load), and they eat up the bandwidth allowance allocated by your web host. It's important to keep the dimensions and resolution of your images to the absolute minimum so that the file size is as small as possible. This is known as **optimization**.

Optimization

To maximize usability and efficiency in terms of bandwidth, images for the Web need to be optimized. This simply means setting the resolution to 72ppi and making sure that the dimensions are no larger than the area of the screen you want the images to occupy. Optimization is done using image editing software; there are many products available. The industry standard for design and web professionals is Adobe Photoshop, however, it's very expensive and if you're only using it to optimize images for the Web, it's probably not worth the expense. There are cheaper alternatives but they don't come close to Photoshop in terms of features and performance. Luckily, there is an open-source product, which does provide a viable alternative to Photoshop. It's called **The GIMP** (**The GNU Image Manipulation Program**) and many designers prefer it to Photoshop, not just for the economic advantage it offers (The GIMP is free, of course), but because of its impressive feature set.

We'll be using The GIMP to optimize our images later in this chapter, so let's download and install it now.

Installing 'The GIMP'

Go to `http://www.gimp.org/downloads/` and download the GIMP installer for Windows 2000 and above (there are also versions available for Linux and Mac OS X). Run the installer and when it is finished, launch The GIMP.

Images in WordPress Posts

WordPress does a pretty good job of handling images that you upload via the Posts Editor in the admin area. For example, when you upload an image, WordPress automatically creates a thumbnail of the image. To get the best results from this feature, there are a few things to bear in mind.

Thumbnail Creation

First, you should note that even though WordPress creates a thumbnail of the image, the original full-size image will still be stored on your server. If the original image is particularly large (for example, wider than 1024 pixels), you need to decide whether you want your readers to be able to view it. If you do allow your readers to click the thumbnail and see the full-size image, it could be costly for you in terms of bandwidth and disk space. We will see how to prevent your readers from being able to open the full-size image shortly. But first, let's assume that you do want your readers to be able to see lager versions of the thumbnails.

Remember that most computer monitors have a viewable size of about 1024 x 768 pixels (admittedly, monitors are getting bigger all the time, but this size is still the most common). Therefore, I recommend optimizing your images *before* you upload them to WordPress, so that they are no bigger than this maximum monitor size. Let's try this out on the ChilliGuru case study.

In the code bundle for this chapter, you'll find an image called **dried_chillies.jpg**. Unzip it somewhere locally.

Now open up The GIMP and use **File | Open** to open **dried_chillies.jpg**. You'll notice that the image opens in a separate window. In the image window, select **Image | Scale Image**. In the **Scale Image** dialog, you'll see that the image dimensions (**Image Size**) are **3072 x 2304** pixels:

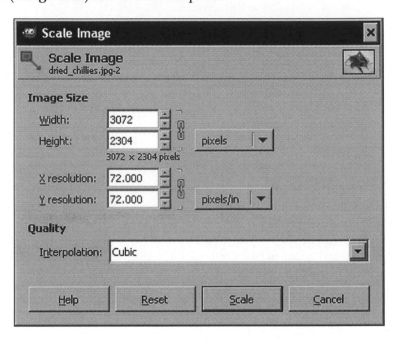

We need to make the width 1024 so that it fits nicely into our presumed maximum monitor size. Place your cursor in the **Width** box, delete **3072** and type **1024**.You can see that the resolution is already set to 72ppi, which is perfect for web images. Click the **Scale** button and save the image (**File | Save**). In the **Save as JPEG** dialog box, move the **Quality** slider all the way to the right so that the number in the box is **100** then click **Save**. Having resized the image, the file size has reduced to about 550KB—a nice improvement for download speeds and bandwidth economy.

The **Quality** slider is a useful optimization tool in The GIMP. If you have a very large JPEG image with a high resolution, you can reduce the quality to maybe 60 or 75. This helps to reduce the file size. Here our image is 72ppi and we've just reduced the dimensions, so we can set the quality to 100 without affecting the file size too much. This is a feature you should experiment with and see how different quality settings affect the sharpness and file size of JPEG images. You're always looking for a trade-off between quality and file size.

Now let's upload the image to our test blog. You should already have the ChilliGuru blog we created in Chapter 3 on your local test server. Open the XAMPP control panel and start the servers (Apache and MySQL). In your web browser, go to `http://localhost/wordpress/wp-login.php` and log in.

1. Create a new post and add a few paragraphs of 'Lorem ipsum' dummy text (you can get it for free at `http://www.lipsum.com/`). Place the cursor on a new line and click the **Add an Image** icon:

2. The file upload window will open. Click the **Choose files to upload** button:

3. Locate the **dried_chillies.jpg** image on your computer and upload it. Give the image a suitable **Title**, **Caption**, and **Description**:

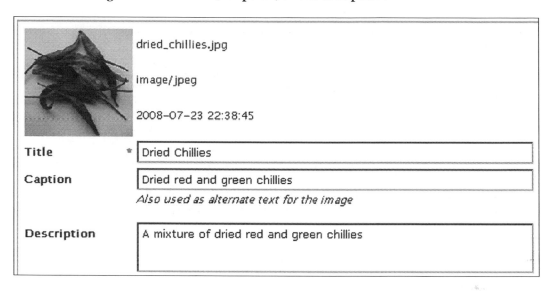

4. For **Link URL** select **Post URL**, for **Alignment** select **None**, and for **Size** select **Thumbnail**. Then click the **Insert into Post** button:

 If you want to prevent your readers from being able to view the original full-size image file, you have to select **None** for **Link URL**.

5. Now place another paragraph of dummy text below the image and publish the post. Notice that the caption is displayed below the image—this is a new feature in WordPress 2.6.

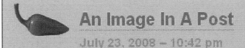

An Image In A Post

July 23, 2008 – 10:42 pm

Lorem ipsum dolor sit amet, consectetuer adipiscing elit. Sed sed purus. Donec luctus sem sit amet nisi. Donec quis elit eget arcu dictum porttitor. Cum sociis natoque penatibus et magnis dis parturient montes, nascetur ridiculus mus. Vivamus felis urna, pulvinar ullamcorper, varius a, interdum sed, neque. Mauris porttitor est eu nibh. Duis adipiscing orci at ante.

Dried red and green chillies

Sed eget augue. Proin varius quam ut augue. Nunc vehicula eros eget sapien. Nam vitae velit sed eros mattis venenatis. Donec id pede et eros imperdiet mattis. Sed nunc leo, ornare pretium, euismod ac, fermentum non, diam. Quisque tortor est, ullamcorper vel, ornare id, eleifend eu, odio.

So, that's how we ensure that our images are optimized for WordPress. Use image editing software to scale the image width to 1024 pixels before uploading it to WordPress.

Thumbnail Size

As you can see from the previous exercise the thumbnail image is rather small. By default WordPress creates thumbnails that are 150 x 150 pixels. That may be fine for your blog design. Some people align their images so that paragraph text wraps around them, in which case, 150 pixels is quite a good size. However, I prefer to place images between paragraphs and for this, I think larger images look better. We can achieve this by changing a couple of settings in WordPress.

In the WordPress admin area, select **Settings | Miscellaneous**. In the **Image sizes** section, change the dimensions for **Medium size** to **400** and then click **Save Changes**:

Image sizes

The sizes listed below determine the maximum dimensions to use when inserting an image into the body of a post.

Thumbnail size	Width 150	Height 150
	☑ Crop thumbnail to exact dimensions (normally thumbnails are proportional)	

Medium size	Max Width 400	Max Height 400

The change we just made won't affect images that we have already uploaded, as WordPress has already resized the images using the old setting of 150 pixels. So, open up the post we created earlier and delete the image we placed there. (To avoid confusion, you could also go to **Manage | Media Library** and delete the original **Dried Chillies** image.)

Once again, position your cursor between the two paragraphs of dummy text and click the **Add an Image** icon. Repeat the process of uploading the **dried_chillies.jpg** image, but this time, for **Size**, select **Medium** instead of **Thumbnail**:

Title	*	Dried Chillies
Caption		Dried red and green chillies
		Also used as alternate text for the image
Description		A mixture of dried red and green chillies
Link URL		http://localhost/wordpress26/?attachment_id=38
		None File URL Post URL
		Enter a link URL or click above for presets.
Alignment		⊙ ▪ None ○ ▬ Left ○ ▬ Center ○ ▬ Right
Size		○ Thumbnail ⊙ Medium ○ Full size
		Insert into Post Delete

Save all changes

Even in the post editor, you'll notice that the image appears larger. When you view the blog, see how the medium thumbnail now fits nicely between the two paragraphs:

Attachment Size

Recall that when we uploaded the image we chose **Post URL** for the **Link URL** menu. In WordPress, the page that this URL links to is known as an **Attachment Page** and the image is an **Attachment**. Click on the thumbnail in the blog and you will be taken to the attachment Page. You'll notice there are a couple of things wrong here. First, the image is way too big. It extends past the main content area and into the first sidebar. The image is also too close to the image title. We can fix both these problems via the style sheet.

Also notice on the attachment page that the image description appears below the image and there is a comment form. Readers can leave comments that relate specifically to the image. If you click on the image, the actual image file will open in your browser.

We only need to make a small change to the style sheet so we can use the Theme Editor within the WordPress admin area. Go back to the admin area, select the **Design** tab and then **Theme Editor**. Our style sheet (**style.css**) will be available for editing in the text editor. Scroll down to the very bottom of the style sheet, and add the following comment and CSS rule:

```
/* Images */
div.entry-attachment img{max-width:400px;margin-top:20px;}
```

Click **Update File** and view the attachment page in the blog (you may need to refresh your browser to see the changes). We've used CSS to set the maximum width for Attachment images to 400 pixels and added a margin of 20 pixels at the top of Attachments.

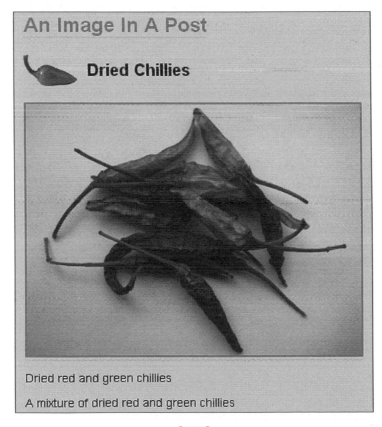

Styling Images

We just changed the size of an image and placed a margin by adding a rule to the style sheet. So you've probably figured out that we can apply a whole load of other styles to our images. We'll run through a couple of simple examples to show how we can style images to enhance our blog design.

Let's begin by changing the border around images on Attachment Pages. Go back to the **Theme Editor** and locate the new CSS rule we just added. Change it to this:

```
div.entry-attachment img{max-width:400px;margin-top:20px;border:solid
#F5AD61 2px}
```

Update the file, and view the attachment page and you'll see that the image now has a border color to match the search box border.

We can apply a different border style to the image within the post. Try adding the following rule:

```
div.entry-content img{border:solid black 1px;padding:5px;}
```

Update the file and view the post we created and you'll see the new border:

Dried red and green chillies

These are fairly simple examples of image styles, but as you build your CSS knowledge, you'll discover more intricate styling that can be applied to images.

Setting Up an Image Gallery

We've looked at some advanced techniques for managing images within posts. However, if you would like to use a lot of images in your blog, you should consider using a standalone image gallery. Placing lots of images in a single post is not ideal. They can take up lots of space and the reader will be forced to do a lot of vertical scrolling to view the entire post. A better approach is to add a link within your post to a dedicated gallery page. A stand alone gallery also allows you to categorize and group your images more efficiently.

Since version 2.5, WordPress includes a simple gallery feature. However, the functionality is very basic and you can achieve far better results using a gallery plugin, which is the approach we will use here. If you are interested in the gallery feature in WordPress, take a look at http://codex.wordpress.org/Using_the_gallery_shortcode.

NextGEN Gallery

One of the best third-party plugins for WordPress is **NextGEN Gallery**. It offers an easy-to-use gallery with lots of features. We'll install NextGEN Gallery for our ChilliGuru case study and take a look at some of the basic features.

Begin by downloading the plugin from http://wordpress.org/extend/plugins/ nextgen-gallery/ (you can also see a list of the main features on this page). Unzip the file and rename the extracted folder **nggallery**. Now place the **nggallery** folder into the **plugins** directory of your local WordPress installation (**C:\xampp\htdocs\ wordpress\wp-content\plugins**).

Log in to the administration area in WordPress, click on the **Plugins** tab, and activate **NextGEN Gallery**.

We're now ready to start using the gallery but you'll need some images. For this demonstration, we'll set up two galleries and place them within an album (the difference between 'gallery' and 'album' will make sense shortly). For convenience, I've included two ZIP files in the code bundle (**gallery_imgs_1.zip** and **gallery_imgs_2.zip**) that contain some copyright-free images that you can use. Of course, any images you have will do just as well.

Images Sources

There are now dozens of great stock image libraries on the Web. Some provide images completely free of charge, others charge a fee. A couple of good ones are **stock.xchng** (`http://www.sxc.hu/`), which offers free images and **Fotolia** (`http://www.fotolia.com`), which has paid-for images starting from just $1. These sites are great if you're looking for images to illustrate you blog-posts. However, always be sure to check the license conditions for each image you download—use of some is restricted.

Now you've activated the plugin, you will see a **Gallery** tab in the admin area. Click on it and then select the **Add Gallery** sub-tab.

A Gallery is simply a collection of images. You can use just one gallery and place all of your images in it, but if you want to keep you images in some kind of order, it makes sense to set up several galleries, each containing related images. Groups of Galleries like this make up an Album.

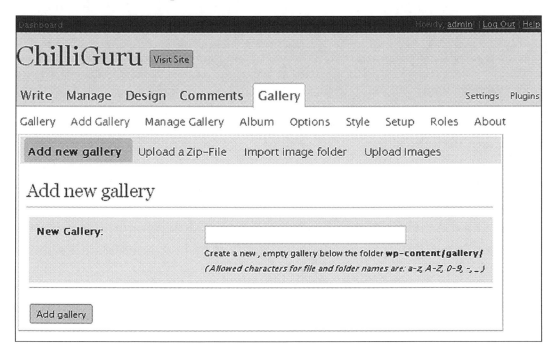

Type **Dried Chillies** in the **New Gallery** box and click **Add gallery**. You should see the following message:

Gallery 1 : **dried-chillies** successfully created!
You can show this gallery with the tag **[gallery=1]**

Now we can import some images to the **Dried Chillies** gallery. There are several options available here. The first is to upload an entire ZIP file of images. The second is to use your FTP client to upload a folder of images to the gallery. And the third is to upload images one by one. We will use the first option, which should be the quickest. Click on the **Upload a Zip-File** tab. Use the browse button to locate **gallery_imgs_1.zip**, which you downloaded with the code for this chapter. From the **in to** drop-down box, select the **dried-chillies | Dried Chillies** gallery. You can leave the **Add Metadata** box checked. Click on **Start Upload**.

Once again, you should see a success message:

Now click the **Manage Gallery** tab. You should see our **Dried Chillies** gallery in the **Gallery Overview** list. Click on **Edit**.

The page you are now looking at allows you to change the settings for the gallery. If you scroll down, you will also see the images we just uploaded into this gallery. There are several enhancements we can make to our gallery. The first thing we need to do is link the gallery to a page in our blog. Click the arrow on the left of the **Gallery settings** heading tab to expand the settings area:

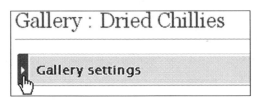

We need to add a description and assign a preview image for the gallery (you'll see the preview image in use when we place the gallery into an album). First click the **Add Page** button. Now type a suitable description in the **Description** box and in the **Preview image** drop-down box, select any one of the images. Click **Save Changes**.

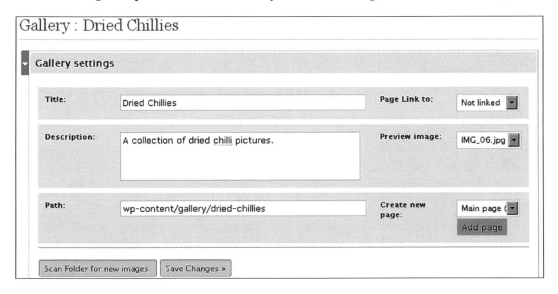

In the bottom half of the **Manage Gallery** page we can change the settings for each image. For the time being, we'll just give the images some more meaningful titles. The title for each image appears in its **Alt tag**.

 It's important to have sensible Alt tags for images to ensure maximum usability and accessibility for our readers. People who use screen readers and can't see the images rely on the Alt tags to make sense and understand the context of a web page. This is a basic principle of good usability and you should be sure to apply it in all your websites. Alt tags are also good for search engine optimization.

In the **Alt & Title Text** column, enter a meaningful title for each image and then click **Save Changes**.

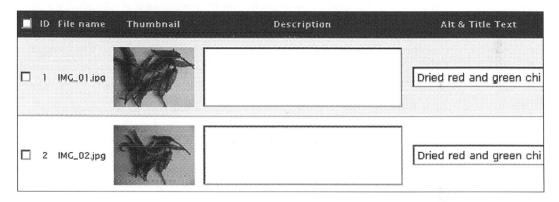

You could also add a description for each image, but for now we're done editing this gallery. We'll create our second gallery.

Click the **Add Gallery** tab. Enter a name for the gallery—call it **Colorful Shapes**. Click the **Add Gallery** button. Use the **Upload a Zip-File** feature to upload the images in the **gallery_imgs_2.zip** archive, which came with this chapter's code. (Remember to select **colorful-shapes | Colorful Shapes** in the drop-down box.)

Go back to the **Manage Gallery** tab and choose to **edit** our new gallery. Under **Gallery settings**, first click the **Add Page** button. Now give the gallery a description and choose a preview image, then click **Save Changes**.

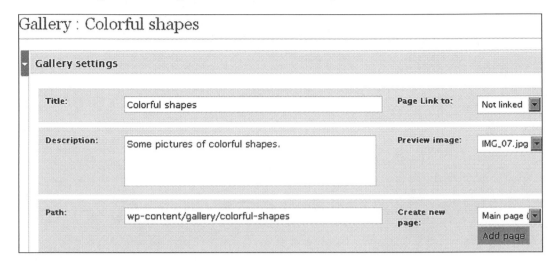

Give each image a new title. Save all your changes.

If you preview the blog now you'll see two new links in the main menu. These are the two pages that NextGEN gallery created to link our galleries to.

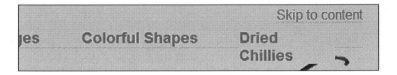

Go ahead and click on one of these links and you'll see a gallery page:

If you click on the thumbnails the full-size image will appear as an overlay in your browser window. You can also see the images as a slideshow.

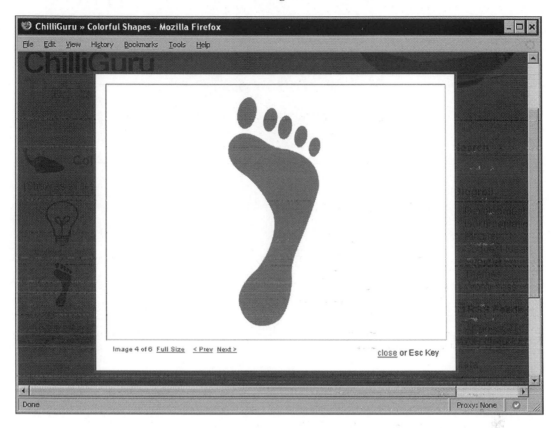

Pretty cool! But we don't want links of each gallery to appear in the main menu of our blog. A better option would be to have an **Image Gallery** link that takes us to a page that lists all of our galleries. We can set this up easily.

Creating an Image Gallery Page

Go back to WordPress admin. Click the **Manage** tab and then the **Pages** tab. You should see the two gallery pages in the list. Click on the page title to edit one of them. In the **Publish Status** menu on the right-hand side, check the **Keep this page private** box and then **Save** the page. Do the same for the other gallery page.

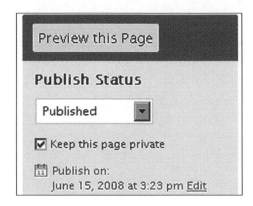

By setting both pages to **Private**, we have removed them from the blog's main menu.

Click on the **Gallery** tab and then the **Album** sub-tab. In the **Add new album** box type **Image Gallery** and click **Update**. You just created a new Album called 'Image Gallery'.

Now choose **Image Gallery** from the **Select album** drop-down box. We want to place our **Dried Chillies** and **Colorful Shapes** galleries into the 'Image Gallery' album we just created. You can see the two galleries listed in the **Select Gallery** box (notice the preview images you selected earlier). If you place your cursor over one of the galleries, the cursor will become a cross-hair and you can drag the gallery into the Album box on the left-hand side. Drag both galleries over and click **Update**.

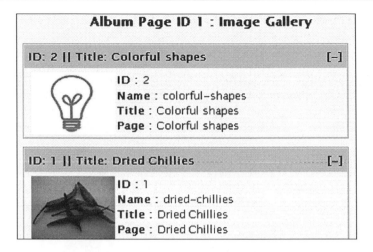

Now we need to create a page for our album and have it appear in the main menu for the blog. Make a note of the Album Page ID (in this case '1'). In the top admin menu click the **Write** tab, then choose the **Page** sub-tab. Enter **Image Gallery** as the page title and type this tag in the **Page** content area:

```
[album=1,extend]
```

Publish the new page. Now view the blog and you'll see the **Image Gallery** link in the main menu. Follow this link and you will see our two albums:

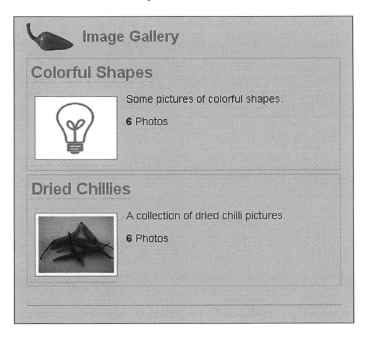

I think you'll agree that NextGEN Gallery is a pretty powerful plugin that allows you to easily create a gallery page. We've really only scratched the surface in terms of its functionality. Now you have the basics, it's up to you to experiment and see what it can do. There are support forums available at `http://alexrabe.boelinger.com/forums/` and a full list of the NextGEN Gallery tags here: `http://wordpress.org/extend/plugins/nextgen-gallery/faq/`.

NextGEN Gallery also has its own style sheet (see the **Style** sub-tab in the gallery admin area), so you can use CSS to change things like the border colors and spacing between thumbnails.

Just one last exercise before we move on. Back in the gallery admin area, click the **Options** sub-tab and then the **Gallery** tab. In the **Number of images per page** box, type **4** and uncheck the **Integrate slideshow** box. Save your changes and view one of the gallery pages in the blog. You'll notice there are now a maximum of four thumbnails per page and the **Show as slideshow** option has gone. This is just one example of the many ways you can customize your new image galleries.

Using Video

As well as images, video is a great way to make your blog more interesting. You may want to shoot your own videos or use ones made by other people. If you have your own videos, it's possible to host them on your own web space and embed a media player in your blog posts to show them. However, this could be quite costly in terms of the bandwidth allowance from your web hosts as video files can be very large.

It's probably better to upload your videos to a video sharing service like **YouTube** or **Google Video** and use a plugin to display them in your blog posts. This has a couple of benefits over hosting videos on your own web space. First, it saves your bandwidth. Second, it makes your videos available to a wider audience. Not only will your blog readers have access to them, but they will also be available to YouTube users. This could turn out to be a useful promotional tool for your blog as it may bring in new traffic from YouTube.

EasyTube

We'll now install another third-party plugin called **EasyTube**, which allows you to display YouTube and Google Video content with just one simple tag in your blog posts.

Go to `http://wordpress.org/extend/plugins/easytube/` and download the plugin. Unzip it and place the entire **easytube** folder in your **plugins** directory (**C:\xampp\htdocs\wordpress\wp-content\plugins**). Go to the WordPress admin area, select **Plugins,** and activate **Easy Tube**.

Create a new post; you can add some dummy 'Lorem ipsum' text if you want. Now go over to YouTube and find a video you want to use (maybe your own).

There are two simple tags you can use to insert video—one for YouTube and one for Google Video (just replace 'URL' with the actual URL of the video):

```
[youtube:URL]
```

```
[googlevideo:URL]
```

Place the tag at the point in the post where you want the video to appear. This is an example of a tag:

```
[youtube:http://www.youtube.com/watch?v=KdGkf0wU5l8]
```

You can also adjust the dimensions of the video player by adding the desired width and height at the end of the tag:

```
[youtube:http://www.youtube.com/watch?v=KdGkf0wU5l8 400 300]
```

Publish the new post.

Adding a Favicon

The final image technique we'll look at will give your blog a really professional touch. It involves a special kind of image known as a **favicon**. This is the icon that you see in your browser address bar on many websites you visit. If a website is using a favicon, it will also be displayed in your browser's favorites folder next to the website link (hence the name, *favicon*).

We'll go through the procedure for adding a favicon to your live blog, as there is little point in having one on your local development server (you may have noticed that XAMPP comes with its own favicon, anyway).

A favicon must be a square image of 16 pixels (that is, 16 x 16). You may be able to use your website logo or create a special square version of it. Another option is to make a completely new image—maybe using the initial letters of your blog (for example, I could have made a 'CG' icon for ChilliGuru, much like the WordPress 'W'). I decided to use a red chili, in keeping with the theme design. (I've included the ChilliGuru favicon in this chapter's code bundle.)

[You may wish to use a free favicon generator tool. There is a good one at
`http://tools.dynamicdrive.com/favicon/`.]

Once I had scaled the chili image down to 16 x 16 using The GIMP, I saved it as **favicon.ico** (note the special file extension). Next I used my FTP client to upload it into the **root directory** of my website (the root will be something like **/public-html**, **/www**, or **/htdocs**). It must be in the root, which is not necessarily the directory where you'll have WordPress installed. I then used my FTP client to download the **header.php** file from the Sandbox theme folder within **/wp-content/themes/**. I then edited the file locally, adding the following line just before the closing `</head>` tag:

```
<link rel="shortcut icon" href="http://www.chilliguru.com/
favicon.ico" />
```

Having saved **header.php**, I FTPed it back to the Sandbox theme folder, overwriting the old version. And that's it—the favicon is now visible.

Summary

In this chapter, we've looked at some advanced multimedia techniques. You now know how to prepare images for uploading them to your blog using an image editor like The GIMP. You also know how to ensure that a thumbnail will be generated for every image you upload. We learned how to resize thumbnails so they fit our post area and how to add styles to images in WordPress using CSS.

We also installed a third-party gallery plugin—NextGEN Gallery, which we can use to create great-looking galleries containing multiple categories of images. We installed another plugin that displays videos within posts. Finally, we looked at the process of adding a favicon to our blog to give it that professional look.

Although the majority of the work in this chapter was done in our local development environment, the techniques can be applied in exactly the same way on a live blog.

In the next chapter, we will focus on the content of your blog. We will discuss some copywriting tips to ensure that your content is engaging and keeps your readers coming back for more. We will also look at creating static pages and how to keep a backup of your content.

5
Content Is King

The title may seem like rather an old cliché now, but it still rings true—content *is* king. In this chapter, we will look at issues surrounding content creation, and discuss some techniques and methods to help you produce the best content you can. We've already looked at visual content, in the form of images and videos, but still for many web users, blogging is all about text—that's what we'll be focusing on here.

We will begin with some general writing tips for bloggers. Although you may be familiar with some of these already, it's as well to re-focus your attention on them and ensure that you are applying them as part of your blogging routine. We then look at ways of organizing your content in a user-friendly way by using categories and tags. We will examine the apparently subtle differences between the two and ensure that you're using them correctly. We move on to apply categories and tags to the ChilliGuru case study.

Next, we will look at one of the most important pieces of 'static' content on your blog—the 'About' page. It's vital to get this right as it is so often the first port of call for new visitors to your blog. We will add an 'About' page to ChilliGuru. Finally, we underline the importance of protecting your precious content by carrying out regular backups. You will learn how to back up both your WordPress site files and the all-important MySQL database, which drives your blog.

Blog Writing Tips

The first thing to look at regarding content is the quality of your writing itself. Good writing takes practice. The best way to learn is to study the work of other good writers and bloggers, and by doing so, develop an ear for a good sentence. However, there are guidelines to bear in mind that apply specifically to blogs, and we'll look at some of these here.

Killer Headlines

Ask any newspaper sub-editor and he or she will tell you that writing good headlines is an art to be mastered. This is equally true for blogs. Your headlines are the post titles and it's very important to get them right.

Your headlines should be concise and to the point. You should try to convey the essence of the post in its title. Remember that blogs are often consumed quickly, and readers will use your post titles to decide if they want to carry on reading. People tend to scan through blogs, so the titles play a big part in helping them pick which posts they might be interested in.

Your post titles also have a part to play in search engine optimization (SEO will be covered in detail in the next chapter). Many search engines will use them to index your posts.

As more and more people are using RSS feeds to subscribe to blogs it becomes even more important to make your post titles as descriptive and informative as possible. Many RSS readers and aggregators only display the post title, so it's essential that you convey as much information as possible whilst keeping it short and snappy. For example, **The World's Best Salsa Recipe** is a better post title than, **A new recipe**.

Length of Posts

Try to keep your posts manageable in terms of their word count. It's difficult to be prescriptive about post lengths. There's no *one size fits all* rule in blogging. You need to gauge the length of your posts based on your subject matter and target audience. There may be an element of experimentation to see how posts of different lengths are received by your readership. As with headlines, bear in mind that most people tend to read blogs fairly quickly and they may be put off by an overly long post. WordPress 2.6 includes a useful word count feature:

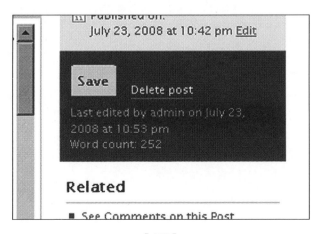

An important factor in controlling the length of your posts is your writing skills. You will find that as you improve as a writer, you will be able to get your points across using fewer words. Good writing is all about making your point as quickly and concisely as possible. Inexperienced writers often feel the urge to embellish their sentences and use long, complicated phrases. This is usually unnecessary and when you read back that long sentence, you might see a few words that can be cut.

Editing your posts is an important process. At the very least you should always proofread them before clicking the **Publish** button. Better still; try to get into the habit of actively editing everything you write. If you know someone who is willing to act as an editor for you, that's great. It's always useful to get some feedback on your writing.

If, after re-reading and editing your post, it still seems very long, it might be an idea to split the post in two and publish the second installment a few days later.

Post Frequency

Again, there are no rules set in stone about how frequently you should post. You will probably know from your own experience of other blogs that this varies tremendously from blogger to blogger. Some bloggers post several times a day and others just once a week or less.

Figuring out the correct frequency of your posts is likely to take some trial and error. It will depend on your subject matter and how much you have to say about it. The length of your posts may also have a bearing on this. If you like to write short posts that make just one main point, you may find yourself posting quite regularly. Or, your may prefer to save up your thoughts and get them down in one longer post.

As a general rule of thumb, try to post at least once per week. Any less than this and there is a danger your readers will lose interest in your blog. However, it's extremely important not to post just for the sake of it. This is likely to annoy readers and they may very well delete your feed from their news reader. As with many issues in blogging, post frequency is a personal thing. You should aim to strike a balance between posting once in a blue moon and subjecting your readers to 'verbal diarrhea'.

Almost as important as getting the post frequency right is fine-tuning the timing of your posts, that is, the time you publish them. Once again, you can achieve this by knowing your target audience. Who are they, and when are they most likely to sit down in front of their computers and read your blog? If most of your readers are office workers, then it makes sense to have your new posts ready for them when they switch on their workstations in the morning. Maybe your blog is aimed at stay-at-home moms, in which case a good time to post might be mid-morning when the kids have been dropped off at school, the supermarket run is over, and the first round of chores are done. If you blog about gigs, bars, and nightclubs in your local area, the readers may well include twenty-something professionals who access your blog on their iPhones whilst riding the subway home—a good time to post for them might be late afternoon.

Links to Other Blogs

We'll examine this in more detail in Chapter 8, but it's worth flagging up here, also. Links to other bloggers and websites are an important part of your content. Not only are they great for your blog's search engine findability, they also help to establish your place in the blogosphere. Blogging is all about linking to others and the resulting 'conversations'.

Try to avoid over-using popular links that appear all over the Web, and instead introduce your readers to new websites and blogs that they may not have heard of. Admittedly, this is difficult nowadays with so many bloggers linking to each other's posts, but the more original you can be, the better. This may take quite a bit of research and trawling through the lower-ranked pages on search engines and indices, but it could be time well spent if your readers come to appreciate you as a source of new content beyond your own blog. Try to focus on finding blogs in your niche or key topic areas.

Establishing Your Tone and Voice

Tone and **voice** are two concepts that professional writers are constantly aware of and are attempting to improve. An in-depth discussion isn't necessary here, but it's worth being aware of them. The concept of 'tone' can seem rather esoteric to the non-professional writer but as you write more and more, it's something you will become increasingly aware of.

For our purposes, we could say the 'tone' of a blog post is all about the way it *feels* or the way the blogger has pitched it. Some posts may seem very informal; others may be straight-laced, or appear overly complex and technical. Some may seem quite simplistic, while others come across as advanced material. These are all matters of tone. It can be quite subtle, but as far as most bloggers are concerned, it's usually a matter of **formal** or **informal**. How you pitch your writing boils down to understanding your target audience. Will they appreciate informal, first-person prose or should you keep it strictly third person, with no slang or casual language? On blogs, a conversational tone is often the most appropriate.

With regards to 'voice', this is what makes your writing distinctly *yours*. Writers who develop a distinct voice become instantly recognizable to readers who know them. It takes a lot of practice to develop and is not something you can consciously aim for; it just happens as you gain more experience. The only thing you can do to help it along is step back from your writing and ask yourself if any of your habits stand in the way of clarity.

While you read back your blog posts imagine yourself as one of your target readers and consider whether they would appreciate the language and style you've used. Employing tone and voice well is all about getting inside their heads and producing content they can relate to.

Developing a distinctive voice can also be an important aspect of your company's brand identity. Your marketing department may already have brand guidelines, which allude to the tone and voice that should be used while producing written communications. Or you may wish to develop guidelines (such as this) yourself as a way of focusing your use of tone and voice.

The Structure of a Post

This may not apply to very short posts that don't go further than a couple of brief paragraphs, but for anything longer, it's worth thinking about a structure. The classic form is 'beginning, middle, and end'. Consider what your main point or argument is, and get it down in the first paragraph. In the middle section expand on it and back it up with secondary arguments. At the end reinforce it, and leave no doubt in the reader's mind what it is you've been trying to say.

As we've already mentioned, blogs are often read quickly or even just scanned through. Using this kind of structure, which most people are sub-consciously aware of, can help them extract your main points quickly and easily.

End with a Question

You may have already applied the 'beginning, middle, and end' structure, but that's not necessarily the best place to end a post. Many bloggers finish with a question. This is a great way of soliciting comments. If it's an interesting or provocative question, it may persuade those readers who only scanned quickly through your post to go back and digest it in more detail, so that they can give an answer to your question and join the debate.

A Quick Check List

Based on the writing tips we've looked at, there are a few common themes that keep popping up. This check list will help you to keep them in mind:

- Know your target audience and try to get inside their heads.
- Ask yourself if each post is truly relevant to your audience.
- Are you posting frequently enough (or too frequently)?
- Are your posts too long?
- Make sure you include plenty of links to other blogs and websites (but try to restrict this to 100 outgoing links per page, for SEO reasons).
- Consider whether your tone and voice are appropriate for your target audience and how they could apply to your brand identity.
- Have you applied a structure to your post?
- Could you add a question at the end of your post?

Remember that the art of blog writing requires plenty of practice, but the points we have covered should help to get you on your way. The key is to constantly analyze your writing and ask yourself how it can be improved.

A Note about Keywords

We'll discuss the whole topic of SEO in the next chapter. But it's worth noting here that your writing has a big impact on search engine findability. This is what adds an extra dimension to writing for the Web. As well as all the usual considerations of style, tone, content, and so on, you also need to optimize your content for the search engines. This largely comes down to identifying your **keywords** and ensuring they're used with the right frequency — we'll discuss this in detail in Chapter 6. In the meantime, hold this thought.

Categories and Tags

It's very important to organize your content in a usable and logical way. Your readers will be frustrated if they cannot find what they're looking for. Their overall experience of your blog is greatly enhanced if you use clear signposts to your content. Luckily, WordPress makes this easy with the use of **Categories** and **Tags** (in version 2.3 and higher).

The Difference between Categories and Tags

There can be some confusion about the differences between categories and tags, which can lead to them being used incorrectly. This is partly due to the fact that different bloggers use them in different ways. There is some debate about how they should be used, and some may argue that there are no hard and fast rules. However, I think it's important to establish in your mind some distinction between categories and tags; what follows is my method for using them.

Categories should be thought of as being part of the hierarchy of your blog's navigation. In a way, they are a bit like a filing system for your blog. Each post is 'filed' in a category, giving your blog a hierarchical structure. Some people also think of categories as being the 'table of contents' for a blog.

Tags supplement categories but they should not really be thought of as part of your blog's navigation. They are rather like an index in a book. You use an index to look up a keyword and it gives you a list of page references for that word. Similarly, when a reader clicks on one of your tags, they are given a list of references for that tag. Tags can also be thought of as keywords or search terms that readers (or potential readers) might associate with your posts.

Categories are a high-level way of organizing content, while tags are more granular or low-level. A category will contain many posts, whereas a tag may point to far fewer.

Using Categories

Bearing in mind that categories are a high-level method for organizing your content, you should keep the number of categories to a minimum. I would recommend not going above 12 categories, and in fact, for many blogs far fewer will be sufficient.

Remember that we are also using categories as part of our blog's navigation; they are not just a way of labeling posts. Your category list should be clearly displayed on each page of your blog so that it can be used as a navigation menu.

Each post should be placed in just one category. This is a controversial point, and you will see some bloggers place their posts in more than one category. However, this detracts from the idea of using categories as a navigational aid on your site or as a table of contents. A section in a book only appears under one chapter heading; it only occurs once within the book, so it is only listed once in the table of contents.

 You can set up your permalinks so that the category is part of the URL. For example: `http://blog.chilliguru.com/recipes/2007/04/01/the-worlds-best-salsa-recipe/`. It's rather like the directory structure used in static HTML sites, where content is organized by placing each page in the relevant folder. *This is an important reason for placing your posts in just one category*. We will apply this to the ChilliGuru case study later in the chapter.

Avoid the use of sub-categories. If you keep the number of categories small, you shouldn't need any sub-categories. You must also constantly monitor your categories and how you are using them. If it turns out that one of your categories is only getting a few posts while all the others have dozens, you should consider merging the underused category into one (or more) of the others. A category with just one or two posts that reflects badly on you, and many of your readers may doubt your expertise or enthusiasm.

Using Tags

We've mentioned that tags are a more granular way of organizing your content. You may only have a few categories, but you should use lots of tags. However, just because there are lots of them, you shouldn't be cavalier in the way you use them. Always use meaningful tags but try to keep them as short as possible. The best tags are just one word, although sometimes you will have to use more.

The whole point of tags is to use the same ones over and over. Do not create more than one tag with the same meaning. For example, if you were frequently writing about architecture you could have the tags such as, 'building', 'construction', 'development', or a whole host of variations. The problem is that they are all too similar. It would be far better to use just one of these tags for posts on that subject. You should also be aware of any ambiguities in your tags, for example, 'building' can mean 'a structure of bricks and mortar' or 'the act of constructing'. If you were to use it as a tag, you would need to be consistent and use it in just one meaning.

You can give more than one tag for a post, in fact, you will usually find you have to. The whole point of tagging is that readers can use it to find related posts, and this may be best achieved by using several tags per post.

Applying Tags and Categories to ChilliGuru

Now, let's look at how we can apply this to our case-study blog. First, we'll consider the categories that are needed for the blog. Based on the subject matter of ChilliGuru, we can come up with a few broad topics that will be our categories:

- Recipes and Cooking
- Planting and Growing
- Chilli Culture
- Chilli History
- Speaking and Events
- TV Appearances

This looks like a good list of categories to begin with—we can always add more, later. Now, start up your local development server and log in to the admin area of the ChilliGuru blog (`http://localhost/wordpress/wp-login.php`). Select **Manage | Categories**. Begin by deleting all the old categories and then add the new ones.

Some of the category names contain several words, but you may wish to use just one word for the category slug. The slugs will be used by our permalinks, once we've re-configured them.

Add Category

Category Name	Recipes and Cooking
	The name is used to identify the category almost everywhere, for example under the post or in the category widget.

Category Slug	recipes
	The "slug" is the URL-friendly version of the name. It is usually all lowercase and contains only letters, numbers, and hyphens.

For the time being, leave the **Uncategorized** category—you can set one of the new ones as **Default** later.

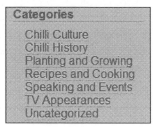

Next, you need to go through each of the posts and assign them to a new category—remember, only one category per post. At the same time add a few tags for each post. Tags are placed in the box immediately below the main post editor. Since, we're only using dummy content, it doesn't really matter which categories and tags you use for each post.

 Tags work in WordPress 2.3 and higher. If you have been following the ChilliGuru case study since the beginning of the book, you will have installed at least version 2.6.

The Sandbox theme, which we used for ChilliGuru, displays tags within the meta-information at the end of each post:

However, it's also useful to display your tags in a **tag cloud** within your sidebar. WordPress comes with its own tag cloud widget, but it's not very flexible. So, we'll use a third-party plugin, called **Configurable Tag Cloud** (CTC) developed by Keith Solomon of `http://reciprocity.be`.

Go to `http://wordpress.org/extend/plugins/configurable-tag-cloud-widget/` and download the plugin. Unzip the file and place **tag-cloud.php** in your **plugins** folder (**C:\xampp\htdocs\wordpress\wp-content\plugins**). Go back to the admin area and activate it.

Click on the **Design** tab and then **Widgets**. So far, we've been using the default sidebar settings. We'll place the CTC widget in **Sidebar 1**. The available widgets are listed on the right-hand side of the page (the Configurable Tag Cloud widget is shown as **CTC**). On the left-hand side under **Current Widgets**, make sure that **Sidebar 1** is selected from the drop-down box. Now click the **Add** link next to the following widgets: **Pages**, **Categories**, **CTC**, and **Archives** (in that order).

Now click on the **Edit** link next to **CTC**.

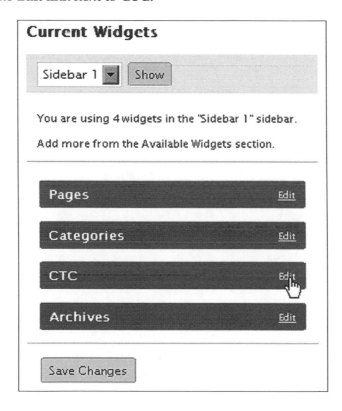

Here we can change a few settings for the tag cloud. I've changed the title to **Site Tags**; set the **Number of Tags to Display** to **100**; set the **Smallest Font Size** to **10** pixels; the **Min. Tag Color** to **#DF5E37**; and the **Max. Tag Color** to **#800000**. Click the **Change** button and then **Save Changes**.

Now, we'll add a quick CSS rule to the style sheet. Select the **Theme Editor**. In **style. css**, add the following rule on the line below /* The Sidebars */:

```
.ctc a{text-decoration:none; border-bottom:1px dotted #F5AD61;}
```

Click **Update File**. If you view the blog, you should see the tag cloud in the first sidebar. Notice that the most-used tags appear larger, in the **#800000** color; there is a sliding scale of font sizes down to the least used tags, which are colored **#DF5E37**. Also notice the dotted 'border' we added at the bottom of each tag using the CSS rule, which also removed the default underlining for hyperlinks. Clicking on one of the tags will show a list of all the posts that have been tagged with it.

 You will see that there is a 'recipe' tag as well as a 'Recipes and Cooking' category. This is because ChilliGuru knows that many of his readers visit the blog primarily to read his recipes. This makes it is as easy as possible to locate all his recipes. Readers can either select the tag or the category. The 'recipe' tag shows just the recipes, while the 'Recipes and Cooking' category contains all the posts that are on the general topic of cooking, for example, techniques, utensils, tips, and so on.

Finally, we will update the permalinks so that the relevant category appears in the URL for each post. Whether you decide to implement this on your own blog is up to you. It has advantages and drawbacks. The advantage is that your category structure is reinforced in your post URLs and the drawback is that the URLs are slightly longer.

Select **Settings | Permalinks**. Under **Common settings**, select the **Custom Structure** radio button, and enter `/%category%/%year%/%monthnum%/%day%/%postname%/` as shown in the following screenshot:

⊙ **Custom Structure**	`/%category%/%year%/%monthnum%/%day%/%postname%/`

Click **Save Changes**. Your permalinks will now be structured like this: `http://blog.chilliguru.com/recipes/2007/04/01/the-worlds-best-salsa-recipe/`.

Now, as we've dealt with categories and tags, we'll look at some of the static content you may wish to include in your blog.

The 'About' Page

Your 'About' page will be one of the very first points of contact with most new readers of your blog, so it's important to get it right. It's your chance to explain who you are and what you're doing with your blog. There are no hard and fast rules for writing the 'About' page. A cursory visit to a random selection of blogs will reveal that there is no standard, as 'About' pages come in all shapes and formats. However, there are a few similarities between most of them, and you would be well advised to include the following as a bare minimum.

About You

This is the place for your potted résumé. Keep it brief and to the point, outlining the skills and experience that make you qualified to write your blog. Readers are more likely to trust what you write and come back for more, if they know it's the words of someone 'in the know'. This might not necessarily include degrees and diplomas. Depending on your blog's subject matter and your own life experiences, you might not hold any relevant paper qualifications, but simply be a knowledgeable and committed 'amateur'. As long as you can demonstrate that knowledge and commitment (both on your 'About' page and in your posts), it should be enough to convince readers of your credentials.

It's also fairly common to include a photograph of yourself. If you do, try to pick a good one or even spend some money on getting your portrait taken professionally. Sometimes bloggers use an 'alternative' image to represent themselves; maybe something like a gaming avatar, a caricature or a graphic portrait. For a good example, you can visit the 'About' page at GigaOm at `http://gigaom.com/about`. There is also a more traditional author image of Om Malik at `http://gigaom.com/about-om/`.

FOUNDER & SENIOR WRITER

 Om Malik, Founder and Senior Writer. Before launching his own publishing venture, Om was a senior writer for Business 2.0 magazine covering **telecom and broadband stories.** For more info on Om, see the **Om Malik extended bio.**

If you have multiple authors on your blog, you should ensure that there is some information for all of them on your 'About' page.

About Your Blog

You should also give some information about what your blog is about. Of course, this would be apparent from reading a few of your posts, but for new readers who may be in a hurry, it's worth including something on your 'About' page. Think of this as being like the cover 'blurb' on the back of a book. In effect, you're trying to sell your blog in a few short paragraphs. Try to stay focused on the blog's aims and think about how to get them across in as concise a way as possible.

This would also be a good place to include any complimentary reviews or quotes, from other experts in your field, who have praised your blog. Maybe you could place a couple of these in block quotes on your 'About' page.

Anything to Declare

Your 'About' page is also a good place to declare any interests you have that might be viewed by some readers as compromising the objectivity of your blog. There's nothing wrong with using your blog to relentlessly promote your products or services, as long as you don't present it in a way that might mislead readers into thinking it's an independent, non-biased recommendation. If you blog about any professional or business interests make sure that your readers are clear that you have a stake in them. The same is true if you regularly blog about potentially partisan subjects such as politics or religion. Make sure your readers know where you're coming from and never pose as an impartial commentator if you have a vested interest in your subject matter.

The ChilliGuru 'About' Page

Now let's work through building the 'About' page for ChilliGuru. We need to add a CSS rule to the style sheet so that our block quotes really stand out. Log into the admin area of the ChilliGuru blog on your development server (`http://localhost/ wordpress/wp-login.php`).

Click on the **Design** tab, followed by **Theme Editor**. Make sure that **style.css** is open for editing in the WordPress text editor. Add the following CSS rule just after `/* The Main Content Area */`:

```
blockquote {color:#800000; font-family:"Times New
         Roman",Times,serif;}
```

Click on **Update File**.

Now, we can add the content to our 'About' page. Select **Manage | Pages**. Choose to edit the existing **About** page. Delete all the existing text and replace it with something new (I've included the ChilliGuru 'about' text in the **about.txt** file in the code bundle for this chapter; if you want to use that, you may). Tidy up the formatting by inserting the bullets and making the headings Level 3 (see `http://blog.chilliguru.com/about/`). You can also upload an image, if you like.

To place the two quotes inside block quotes, highlight the text that belongs in the block quote, and click the **Blockquote** button in the toolbar:

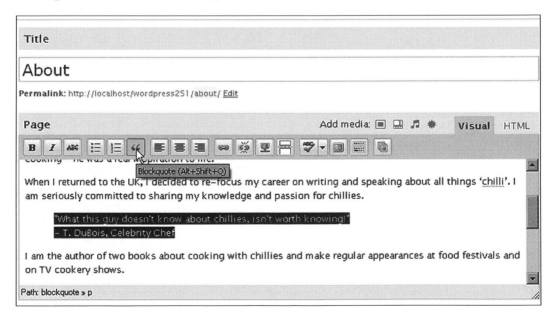

Enter a line break before the name of the quote speaker and make it bold:

> writing and speaking about all things 'chilli'. I am seriously committed to sharing my knowledge and passion for chillies.
>
> "What this guy doesn't know about chillies, isn't worth knowing!"
> **- T. DuBois, celebrity chef**
>
> I am the author of two books about cooking with chillies and make regular appearances at food festivals and on TV cookery shows

Most bloggers don't allow comments on their 'About' page. You can turn comments off by unchecking the **Comments** box under the **Discussion** menu for the page:

Comments & Pings

☐ Allow Comments

☑ Allow Pings

These settings apply to this page only. "Ping

Other Static Content

Besides the 'About' page there may be other static content that you should add to your blog. If you have another website along with your blog, ask yourself whether you could bring that content into WordPress, so that all your web content is together in one place.

There are many other static pages that you may wish to add. For example, designers, photographers, and artists often have a portfolio page to display their work. Or you may wish to set up a page to showcase a handful of your bestselling products. If you've written a book you could add a book page with some blurb and a link to Amazon. As you know, WordPress is more than capable of handling static content alongside your dynamic blog posts.

Backing Up

Now you've put so much time and effort into creating great content, you need to make sure it's protected. To ensure your content is safe, you must back up your blog on a regular basis.

The frequency of your backups will depend on how often you post to your blog, but as a general rule of thumb it's a good idea to back up at least once a week. You never know when something might go wrong and when it does, it's usually beyond your control.

When considering your backup routine, remember there are two groups of data that make up your blog: the **site files** and the **database**. Both of these need to be backed up, but it may be that the site files don't need to be backed up as frequently as the database. The site files are basically everything from your original WordPress core installation. Much of this you won't have changed, so as long as you keep a copy of your version of WordPress somewhere on your PC, you should be able to use that as your backup site (just remember to back up your PC regularly, too!).

For most WordPress users, the only site files that change on a regular basis are the theme, plugins, and uploads, all of which are contained in the **wp-content** directory. The only file outside of this directory that you need to back up is **wp-config.php**. The **wp-config.php** file is unlikely to change after your blog has been installed, so it is probably only necessary to back up this file once, shortly after you first install your blog. So, regarding your site files, all you need to back up regularly is the **wp-content** directory.

Backing up wp-content

Your web host will probably back up all the files on its servers on a daily basis. But you shouldn't rely on them. It's always quicker and easier to access your own backups than having to ask your web host for them. The safest way of backing up your site files is to use your FTP program to download the **wp-content** directory to a safe location on your computer. The following screenshot shows the backup process for the ChilliGuru **wp-content** files using CuteFTP:

Backing up the Database Using phpMyAdmin

While it's important to back up your site files, you'll only need that backup if you suffer a complete loss of data on your server. Thankfully, a complete data loss is fairly rare. If you should experience a data loss, it's far more common that it will involve the MySQL database that drives your blog. Remember, the database contains all the posts, pages, comments, and links from your blog.

Probably the easiest way of backing up your database is to use **phpMyAdmin**, so we'll run through this process here. This example uses version 2.11.3 of phpMyAdmin (other versions may vary).

Connect to phpMyAdmin on your server (if you're not sure how to do this, your web host will be able to give you instructions).

Select the database for your WordPress installation. The quickest way is to use the **Database** drop-down menu on the left-hand side of the main phpMyAdmin page.

You will now see a page that lists all the tables in your WordPress installation.

Click on the **Export** tab at the top of this page.

On the next screen, select all the WordPress tables in the database. If WordPress is the only application using this database, you can just click **Select All**. If WordPress is sharing the database with other applications, you will need to go through the list and just select the WordPress tables. These will be the tables beginning with **wp_** (or whatever table prefixes you chose when you installed WordPress). Ensure the **SQL** radio button (below the table list) is selected.

In the **Options** section, select the following:

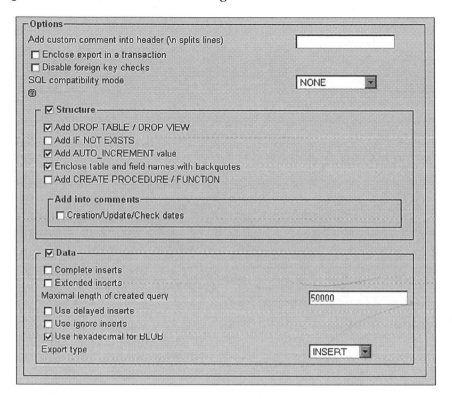

Choose to save the files as **gzipped**:

Click the **Go** button and choose to save the compressed file to disk. Save it using the default filename given by phpMyAdmin. The following screenshot is using Firefox; other browsers will vary slightly:

You now have a backed up copy of your database stored on your local computer.

Restoring the Database from a Backup File

The circumstances that might surround a real-life data loss are many and varied. However, there are a couple of scenarios that are most common. First, the entire database is lost. In this case, when you log in to phpMyAdmin, your WordPress database will no longer appear in the list of databases. Second, one or more of the tables in your WordPress database has been lost or corrupted. In this case, the database will still appear in the database list within phpMyAdmin.

If you suspect the second scenario is the reason for your trouble and you cannot repair the tables or even identify which table is lost or corrupted, it's probably a good idea to remove the entire database and start again using your backup file. To remove the database, select it from the list in phpMyAdmin and then click the **Drop** tab.

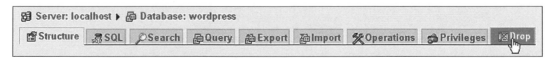

At this point, whichever data loss scenario may have occurred, we're in the same situation. Your WordPress database no longer exists. The good news is you have a copy of all these tables.

The first step to restoring those tables is to create a new database to hold them. From the phpMyAdmin home page, create a new database, with exactly the same name as your old one.

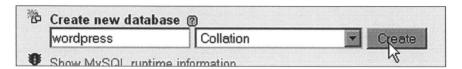

Once you've clicked **Create**, you'll be taken to your new database's phpMyAdmin home page. Click on the **Import** tab.

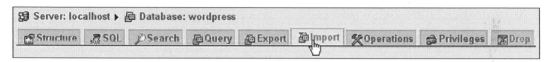

On the import page, click the **Browse** button and locate your database backup file on your computer. Leave all the other settings as they are and click the **Go** button at the bottom of the page. Depending on the size of your backup file, it will take a few minutes to upload. You should then see a success message.

You have now restored your database as it was when you made the backup file and your blog should be working again.

As you can see the process of backing up your WordPress database is fairly straightforward. However, to ensure you don't leave anything to chance, you might want to run through the procedure using the ChilliGuru blog on your local test server so you'll be completely comfortable, should the worst happen to your live blog.

Summary

In this chapter, we've looked at all kinds of written content. We began with some general tips for writing your blog posts. We then looked at how to organize your content in a logical and usable way using categories and tags. We went through the process of setting up the categories and tags for ChilliGuru. We considered the importance of having a good 'About' page. Finally, we saw how to protect your content by performing regular backups.

In the next chapter, we will look at the related subject of search engine optimization. You will see how content plays an important part in making your blog more visible to the search engines.

Search Engine Optimization

6

Having put so much time and effort into making your blog look pretty and creating fabulous content, you would want people to find it. The most common way for this to happen is via search engines. For many people, a typical web browsing session begins with a visit to their favorite search engine, so you want to be sure your blog appears high up in the rankings. Unfortunately, having a great-looking blog with lots of interesting posts isn't enough. To get a good place in the rankings takes time, perseverance, and no small amount of knowledge.

The good news is that search engines love blogs. This fact, coupled with the techniques covered in this chapter, will go a long way to making your blog as findable as possible. **Search engine optimization (SEO)** is the art and science of getting your blog noticed by the search engines and ranked as high as possible. This chapter outlines the most important SEO strategies and how to apply them. We'll also discuss how to submit your blog to the search engines as well as looking at some SEO software and tools, which could save you time and improve your results.

The Principles of SEO

SEO is a huge subject. There are thousands of professionals all over the world who earn their living by providing SEO services to website owners. The good SEO pros spend huge amounts of time and resources learning the skills of effective optimization. This goes to show that you could easily spend your entire life boning up on SEO—there's so much to learn. Obviously, you won't have anything like this amount of time to spend on your own SEO education. However, you can still do a lot to improve your blog's performance with the major search engines. The option to bring in a professional to really rocket through the rankings is there, if your marketing budget allows. If you do decide to hire a professional, make sure you choose a reputable one who does not use unscrupulous tactics, which could harm you more than help you.

The good news is that WordPress has been made with SEO in mind. The software comes with many built-in SEO features. For example, you don't need to worry too much about the validity of the XHTML on your blog. The WordPress developers have ensured their code is valid. This is a big help as search engines will rank sites with valid code higher than those that have been poorly put together. There is plenty of other stuff going on behind the scenes in your WordPress installation that will aid your search engine **findability**—the WordPress developers have been very thoughtful. We'll be considering the aspects of SEO that are your responsibility. But first, a quick '101' on how search engines work.

How Search Engines Find Stuff

Search engines use special programs called **robots** that automatically **crawl** the Web and send back information about the web pages to the search engines' servers. They navigate the Web by following all the links they find. This is how a search engine collects the data for its **index**. The index is a huge database of entries cross-referenced between keywords and relevant website pages. The search engines use special algorithms to determine the rank of the web pages held in their index. When a web user enters a search query, the engine returns a list of results. The order of the search results depends on the rank of the pages, as determined by the algorithm.

These algorithms are closely guarded secrets and the search engine companies are constantly updating them. The aim of the updates is to improve the relevancy of the search results. Because of the secrecy of the algorithms and the constant changes, it is very difficult for website owners to figure out the exact criteria used to rank pages. This prevents website owners from unfairly influencing the search rankings. However, by subscribing to the blogs or feeds of the major search engines, and using tools such as Google's Webmaster tools (more on this later), you can keep abreast of major changes.

SEO professionals spend their lives trying to second-guess the search algorithms, but the search engine companies usually remain one step ahead. It's a game of cat and mouse, with the odds strongly skewed in favor of the search engines—they make the rules and can change them whenever they want.

Despite the ever-changing algorithms, there are certain principles of SEO that stay constant. These are what we will look at in this chapter.

 For the purposes of this chapter, we will be concentrating on techniques for the 'traditional' search engines such as Google, MSN, Yahoo, and Ask. We will look at some of the blog-specific search engines, such as Technorati, in the next chapter.

Keywords

Keywords are the search terms that people type into a search engine when they are looking for something on the Web. They can be single words or several words that make up a phrase. It's essential to know the keywords being used by people who are looking for the type of content on your blog. You then need to ensure that you're using those keywords correctly. Let's look at a few strategies for finding and using keywords effectively.

Choosing Your Keywords

You should spend some time building up a list of your blog's keywords. The first step is to be clear in your mind about what your blog's content is about. What are the main themes you are writing about? If you worked through the planning exercises in Chapter 2, you should already have a fairly good idea of this.

Once you are clear about the main theme(s) of your blog, try a quick brainstorming exercise. You can do this alone or enlist the help of colleagues and friends. Put yourself in the shoes of someone looking for the kind of information you publish on your blog. What words or phrases are they likely to type into a search engine? We could run this exercise for ChilliGuru.com. People looking for the kind of content on ChilliGuru, may use the following keywords:

- Chilli (UK spelling)
- Chili (US spelling)
- Spicy food
- Growing chilies
- Chili recipe
- Mexican food
- Indian food
- Thai food
- Birds eye chilies
- Jalapeno
- Scotch bonnet
- Cook chilies

OK, that's just a small handful of the more obvious keywords that took me about 60 seconds to come up with. If I spent longer, I'm sure I could come up with a list of 50 or more words and phrases. The more people you enlist into your keyword brainstorming, the more you are likely to come up with.

Once you have a fairly good list, you can use keyword software to help you find even more. There are literally hundreds of keyword tools out there. Some are free, some are paid for, and they have a range of features. Later in this chapter, in the section on search engine submissions, we will introduce some software called **Web CEO**, which includes a good keyword tool. In the meantime, you can start with some of the tools provided by the search engines themselves. For example, Google provides a keyword selector tool for its advertising (AdWords) customers, but you can use it to research your keywords. Go to `https://adwords.google.com/ select/KeywordToolExternal` and enter a keyword or phrase into the search box. Keep the **Use synonyms** box checked.

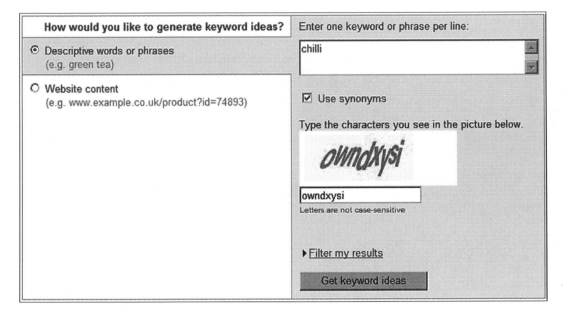

Enter the security code and click **Get keyword ideas** and you will be presented with a list of related keywords:

Keywords	Advertiser Competition ⑦	Search Volume: February ⑦	Avg Search Volume ⑦	Match Type: ⑦ Broad ▾
chilli	▰▰▰▱	▰▰▱▱	▰▰▱▱	Add ⹀
chilli pepper	▰▰▰▱	▰▰▱▱	▰▰▱▱	Add ⹀
chillis	▰▰▱▱	▰▰▱▱	▰▰▱▱	Add ⹀
red hot chilli peppers	▰▰▰▰	▰▰▱▱	▰▰▱▱	Add ⹀
chilli chicken	▰▱▱▱	▰▰▱▱	▰▰▱▱	Add ⹀
chilli vanilla	▱▱▱▱	▰▰▱▱	▰▰▱▱	Add ⹀
red hot chili peppers	▰▰▰▰	▰▰▰▱	▰▰▰▱	Add ⹀
red hot chilli peppers lyrics	▰▰▱▱	▰▰▱▱	▰▰▱▱	Add ⹀
chilli recipe	▰▰▱▱	▰▰▱▱	▰▰▱▱	Add ⹀
chilli sauce	▰▰▱▱	▰▰▱▱	▰▰▱▱	Add ⹀

OK, so it's a pretty long list; not all of the keywords will be relevant to your blog. For example, for ChilliGuru we could ignore 'red hot chilli peppers lyrics' and any other references to the band, *The Red Hot Chilli Peppers*.

The preceding screenshot shows just the first few suggestions for one keyword, 'chilli' (the whole list runs into dozens). So you can see that if you were to use this tool for all the keywords in your original brainstorming list, you could easily end up with a very long list. This might seem like a good idea, but when we discuss using your keywords, shortly, you'll see that you don't actually want too many. When you're working on your list, try to be selective and keep the list manageable. Use your judgment to pick the important keywords and also look at the **Avg Search Volume** column in the Google list. This tells you how often each keyword is actually being used. Focus on the most popular ones.

There's no point in my giving you a recommended number of keywords for your list, as this will depend on the type of content in your blog. If your blog covers a fairly narrow subject area, then you won't need as many keywords as if your blog covers a wide subject or even a range of subjects. Once you've read the next section on using keywords, you'll also have a better idea of how many you need.

Using Your Keywords

Once you've drawn up your list of keywords you need to make sure you're using them correctly. This basically boils down to the number of times you place keywords in each post. This is known as **keyword density**. As with many other aspects of SEO they are no definitive rules. You will see lots of varied advice from different web experts. The fact of the matter is, no one can be certain about the optimum keyword density, because the search algorithms are kept secret. Many SEO experts have used trial and error in an attempt to gauge the best keyword density. Some have arrived at what are probably fairly arbitrary figures. It would be pointless for me to recommend a specific keyword density. Instead, here are a few general tips for using your keywords.

1. Be selective with your keywords. You'll never be able to include your entire keyword list in each and every post you publish. Try to focus on two or three keywords or keyword phrases, which seem most relevant for each post you write.

2. Whenever possible, try to include at least one keyword in the post title.

3. Try to repeat a couple of the most relevant keywords twice in the first two paragraphs of the post. From then on, aim at using a keyword at least once in every paragraph.

4. Keywords aren't just for your posts. Try to use a selection of your most relevant keywords in your 'About' pages and any other static pages in your blog.

5. If you can, use keywords in your image **Alt Tags**. The Alt Tag is the **Title** of your image. Search engines index these Alt Tags; this gives you another way to provide them with more keyword-rich content.

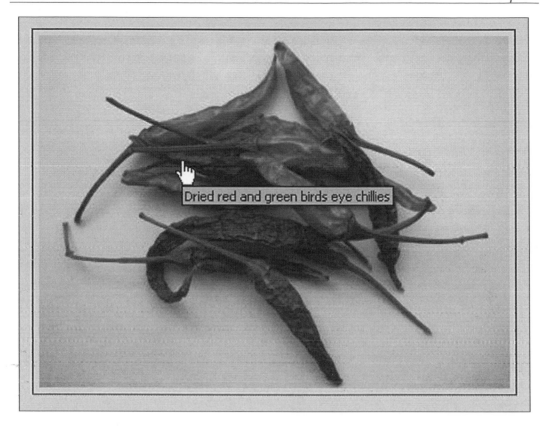

Dried red and green birds eye chillies

Permalinks

We looked at permalinks briefly in the last chapter with regards to structuring your URLs to reflect your blog's categories. Permalinks are also very important for SEO. The default permalink structure in WordPress is `http://blog.chilliguru.com/?p=123`. This format isn't very search engine friendly. It's far better to have the post title appear in the permalink URL. Again, this is another way of getting more of your keywords into the search engine's index. In Chapter 5, we discussed changing the permalink structure to something like `http://blog.chilliguru.com/recipes/2007/04/01/the-worlds-best-salsa-recipe/`. This is better as it includes the post title. However, the optimal permalink structure, in terms of SEO, has the post title as close to your blog's domain name as possible, for example, `http://blog.chilliguru.com/the-worlds-best-salsa-recipe/`.

This structure is the very best for SEO, but it can sometimes cause problems when you try to access some of the WordPress admin pages. If you're really keen on SEO, and are happy to work around any problems accessing admin pages, then go with this structure. However, I would prefer to use a second-best SEO structure, which includes the post's category: `http://blog.chilliguru.com/recipes/the-worlds-best-salsa-recipe/`. This is still a good permalink structure for SEO and avoids any possible pitfalls in accessing your admin pages.

Changing your permalink structure can have a detrimental impact on SEO, unless your blog is very new. If you have a well established blog, the search engines will already have indexed your pages using your old permalink URLs. These URLs will remain in the index for quite some time, so until the index is updated all your links on search engine results pages will be broken. This will also be true for any of your links that appear on other websites or as browser bookmarks. Luckily, there is a third-party plugin that solves this problem. It applies what is known as a **Permanent Redirection**, which will ensure you continue to receive traffic from your old links. We will install it now before changing our permalink structure. The plugin is called **Dean's Permalink Migration**, and was written by Dean Lee (`http://www.deanlee.cn/`).

Installing Dean's Permalink Migration Plugin

Let's go through the process of installing it on the live ChilliGuru blog, as there is no point installing it on your local development server. Go to `http://wordpress.org/extend/plugins/permalinks-migration-plugin-for-wordpress/` and download the plugin. Upload it to the `plugins` folder on your live blog, then go to the admin area and activate it in the usual way. You do not need to do any further configuration as the plugin automatically detects your current permalink structure. You can check it out in your admin area at **Settings | PermalinksMigration**.

We can now go ahead and change our permalink structure, safe in the knowledge that our old URLs will still work.

Under the main **Settings** tab, select **Permalinks** and change to our search engine friendly structure (/%category%/%postname%/) using the **Custom structure** box, then click **Save Changes**.

You can test if the plugin is working by entering one of your old URLs into your browser. You should be redirected to the relevant page and the new URL will appear in your browser's address bar.

Title Tags

Many experts claim that `<Title>` tags are one of the most important aspects of SEO. The `<Title>` tag is displayed in the browser title bar, but it is also one of the first things a search engine sees when it indexes your blog. The `<Title>` tag on your home page is particularly important for SEO.

It's worth spending some time considering your `<Title>` tags and ensuring they are as search engine friendly as possible. Here are a few guidelines to bear in mind about `<Title>` tags:

1. Ensure they include keywords that are relevant to the post.
2. Ensure the keyword or keyword phrase is as close to the start of the tag as possible.
3. Try to keep your home page `<Title>` tag at around 50-60 characters in length
4. Capitalize the first letter in each word of the tag.
5. Don't use the keyword phrase more than once in your title.
6. Include the blog title in the `<Title>` tag on each page.

As you may have noticed the default `<Title>` tags in WordPress are not perfect for SEO — the preceding screenshot shows that the default ChilliGuru title is not using all the guidelines I just outlined. However, there is an excellent plugin we can use to customize our titles (so they are working as hard as possible for SEO). The plugin is **All in One SEO Pack** from `http://wp.uberdose.com/`. We'll work through installing the plugin for our ChilliGuru cas study.

Go to `http://wordpress.org/extend/plugins/all-in-one-seo-pack/` and download the plugin. Start up your local development server. Unzip the plugin and place the entire folder into your `plugins` directory (**C:\xampp\htdocs\wordpress\wp-content\plugins**). Log in to the admin area and activate the plugin.

We'll begin by optimizing the home page title. As you can see, by default, WordPress uses the blog title followed by the blog description in the home page `<Title>` tag. The blog title and description are great for our blog's branding. *The spice in your life* is a good tag line for the blog and it looks nice in the blog header. You may have a company slogan or tag line that you want to keep in your header, which is great for your branding but not necessarily so great for SEO. We can fix this using our new plugin.

Under **Settings**, select **All in One SEO**. Here, we can make the necessary changes to our page titles. First, we need to come up with a good home page title using the guidelines I outlined earlier. How about:

Chili Recipes Plus Growing And Cooking Tips | ChilliGuru.com

This seems to follow our guidelines: It's the right length (52 characters); each word begins with a capital letter; the keywords are close to the start. So, we can insert this in the **Home Title** box. I've also added a brief site description (keep it short; I recommend no more than two lines as they appear in the box) and some of my main generic keywords (again, be brief here, no more than 10 of your most popular keywords). Click the **Update Options** button when you're done.

All in One SEO Plugin Options

This is version 1.4.6.8 Should I upgrade? | FAQ | Feedback | Translations

One Click Upgrade » (Remember: Backup early, backup often!)

Click on option titles to get help!

| Home Title: | Chili Recipes Plus Growing And Cooking Tips | ChilliGuru.com |

| Home Description: | All you need to know about cooking and growing chili peppers from one of the world's leading experts. |

| Home Keywords (comma separated): | chilli, chili, growing chilies, chili recipe, mexican food, indian food, thai food, birds eye chilies, jalapeno, cook chilies |

A Note About Meta Tags

The **Home Description** and **Home Keywords** will be added to your blog's **Meta Tags**. These appear within the `<header></header>` tags on the home page of your blog (view the source of the page in your browser and you will see them). They are not visible on the page but they can be read by the search engines. Ten years ago, these were extremely important to search engines and getting your Meta Tags right was the key to a good search engine ranking. Nowadays, it's widely accepted that search engines place very little importance on Meta Tags. In fact, some experts claim they are completely ignored. However, there is no evidence that they harm your rankings, so we may as well include them.

We now have a search engine friendly home page title…

…whilst keeping the blog title and blog description in our header, for branding purposes:

We'll now turn our attention to the titles on our post pages. By default, they look something like this:

Again, this isn't great for SEO, but it's easy to fix with our plugin. You should already be using keywords in your post title, so it's fine to carry on using post titles for our `<Title>` tags. It may not always be possible to keep within the 50-60 characters length with your post titles, but as long as you are using your keywords wisely, it should be fine. One thing to remember is to use a capital letter at the start of each word in your post title.

Back on the plugin page I've changed the **Post Title Format**, as shown in the following screenshot (remember to click the **Update Options** button):

which gives us this for our post page titles:

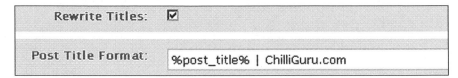

As for the remaining page titles, I've used the following formats. The main change is that I have replaced **%blog_title%** with **ChilliGuru.com** and the **Page Title Format** is now **Chili Recipes Plus Growing And Cooking Tips | %page_title% | ChilliGuru.com** (once again, remember to click the **Update Options** button):

Rewrite Titles: ☑	
Post Title Format:	%post_title%	ChilliGuru.com
Page Title Format:	Chili Recipes Plus Growing And Cooking Tips	%page_title%	Ch
Category Title Format:	%category_title%	ChilliGuru.com
Archive Title Format:	%date%	ChilliGuru.com
Tag Title Format:	%tag%	ChilliGuru.com
Search Title Format:	%search%	ChilliGuru.com
Description Format:	%description%
404 Title Format:	Nothing found for %request_words%
Paged Format:	- Part %page%

So, the title for our 'About' page now looks like this:

So, with the help of the **All in One SEO Pack** plugin, you now have search engine friendly titles for all the pages in your blog. We'll now look at another important element of SEO, which is **Sitemaps**.

Sitemaps

A sitemap is an overview of all the posts and pages in your blog laid out on a single page. Not only is it great for improving your blog's usability, it is also good for SEO. When the search engine robots are crawling your site they will use the sitemap to find all your pages. By providing a sitemap you are making it easier for them to crawl your blog because there will always be a link pointing to each of your posts. Again, we will use a third-party plugin to create a sitemap for ChilliGuru.

The plugin is called **DDSitemapGen**. Go to `http://www.dagondesign.com/articles/sitemap-generator-plugin-for-wordpress/` and download the latest version. Unzip it and place the entire folder in your `plugins` directory, then activate the plugin as usual. Under the main **Settings** tab select **DDSitemapGen**. The configuration settings are fairly straightforward (the default settings are fine). The only thing you need to add is the **Sitemap page slug**; I've simply called it 'sitemap' (remember to click **Update options**):

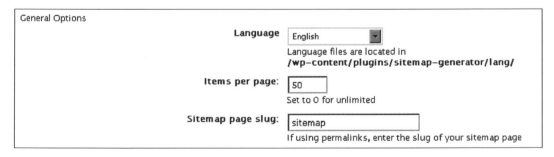

Now create a new page for the blog (**Write | Page**). Give it the title **Sitemap**. Click on the **HTML** tab and add `<!-- ddsitemapgen -->`. **Publish** the page.

Now view the site. The **Sitemap** page will have been added to the menu and it should look like this:

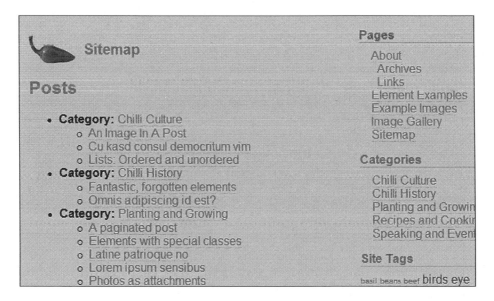

Adding a Google Sitemap

When you submit your blog to Google, you can include a **Google Sitemap**. This is a sitemap in a special XML format and it helps Google to crawl your site more efficiently. It is also recognized by other search engines like Yahoo, MSN, and Ask.

Some may say that it's 'overkill' to use a Google Sitemap when we have already created a regular sitemap, but it won't do any harm so I've included it here for completeness.

Again, there's a great plugin that we can use. It's called **Google XML Sitemaps** by Arne Brachhold: `http://www.arnebrachhold.de/`. Go to `http://wordpress.org/extend/plugins/google-sitemap-generator/` and download the plugin. Once you've installed and activated it, select **XML-Sitemap** under **Settings** in your admin area. At the top of the page, click the link to generate the sitemap for the first time (you don't need to change any of the settings). You should see a success message. You can view the sitemap you just created at `http://localhost/wordpress/sitemap.xml`. The Google Sitemap for the live ChilliGuru blog (`http://blog.chilliguru.com/sitemap.xml`) looks like this:

XML Sitemap

This is a XML Sitemap which is supposed to be processed by search engines like Google, MSN Search and YAHOO. It was generated using the Blogging-Software WordPress and the Google Sitemap Generator Plugin by Arne Brachhold.
You can find more information about XML sitemaps on sitemaps.org and Google's list of sitemap programs.

URL	Priority	Change Frequency	LastChange
http://blog.chilliguru.com/	100%	Daily	2008-03-25 01:32
http://blog.chilliguru.com/sitemap/	60%	Weekly	2008-03-25 01:32
http://blog.chilliguru.com/recipes/27/	20%	Monthly	2008-03-24 21:03
http://blog.chilliguru.com/growing/photos-as-attachments/	20%	Monthly	2008-03-24 20:58
http://blog.chilliguru.com/growing/writing-about-code/	20%	Monthly	2008-03-24 20:52
http://blog.chilliguru.com/culture/an-image-in-a-post/	20%	Monthly	2008-03-24 20:48
http://blog.chilliguru.com/recipes/the-worlds-best-salsa-recipe/	20%	Monthly	2008-03-24 20:42
http://blog.chilliguru.com/growing/latine-patrioque-no/	20%	Monthly	2008-03-23 16:40

You can now go back to the **DDSitemapGen** plugin and add the URL of your newly created Google Sitemap (under the **Miscellaneous** section), which adds a **View XML Sitemap** link at the bottom of your sitemap page:

Miscellaneous

Full path to XML sitemap:	http://localhost/wordpress/sitemap.xml

If you are also using an XML sitemap plugin, you can enter the path to the XML file here, and a link to it will be added to your sitemap page

Where to show XML sitemap link: ● At the end of the last page
○ At the end of every page

Sitemap links open in new window: ☐

Inbound Links

Having plenty of good quality inbound links to your blog will improve your ranking in the search engines. Google started life as a student project to rank the importance of websites based on the number of incoming links; link popularity is still at the heart of Google's ranking process.

But for many people link building seems like a daunting task. How do you get other people to link to you? It's actually not as difficult as it first seems—once you get into it, you'll see there are plenty of strategies to use. The point is to stick at it and treat link building as an integral part of your blogging routine.

You can check how many inbound links Google has found for your blog by using the **link:** command. Enter **link:http://www.packtpub.com** into the Google search box to see all the inbound links for the Packt website. You can do the same for your blog.

Google™ | link:http://www.packtpub.com | Search | Advanced Search / Preferences

Web   Results **1 - 10** of about **654** linking to **http://www.packtpub.com**. (0.29 seconds)

Infrae News http://www.infrae.com/viewer/rss Main site of the ...
Infrae News http://www.infrae.com/viewer/rss Main site of the Infrae software development
company, located in Rotterdam, the Netherlands. ...
www.infrae.com/viewer/rss - 40k - Cached - Similar pages

AJAX and the Future of Web Applications - a free chapter from AJAX ...
AJAX and PHP: Building Responsive Web Applications Free Online Edition. Chapter 1.
ajaxphp.packtpub.com/chapter1.htm - 12k - Cached - Similar pages

Many of the techniques for building links, such as using social bookmarking, social
networking, and getting listed in the blog search engines, will be covered in the
next chapter. There will be some more discussed in Chapter 8. But there is a more
'organic' technique that we'll discuss here.

It's often referred to by SEO pros as **link baiting**. It's basically creating content that
other bloggers and webmasters just can't resist linking to. Obviously, you should
always be trying to create interesting and exciting content, but every now and then
it pays to come up with a killer post that is intended purely to attract links. There are
several methods to achieve this. Here are a few suggestions to get you thinking:

1. Write something controversial that other people will just have to disagree
    with. Be careful not to upset anyone and don't be offensive, but come up with
    something that goes against the grain and makes your opinion on an issue
    stand out.

2. Disagree with a renowned expert. A post title like *Seth Godin Is Plain Wrong
    About XYZ*, backed up with a reasoned argument, could attract plenty of
    attention and encourage backlinks to the post.

3. Provide a really useful resource. This could be something like a 'Top 10' list
    or a how-to guide.

4. Run a contest, competition, or some other event that is likely to
    attract attention.

5. Give away a useful 'freebie'. For example, a PDF e-book, a piece of software
    (that you own the rights to), or a free sample of one of your products.

These are the kind of posts that are likely to attract attention and links back to your
blog. Try brainstorming a few ideas along these lines and you'll be surprised how
many you come up with.

As well as link baiting you can also simply ask other people to link to you. This is a fairly straightforward approach, but you need to be careful not to come across as a spammer. It may be worth restricting this to people you know or people who regularly leave comments on your blog. Some people may be annoyed about receiving an email out of the blue requesting a backlink, so exercise some discretion here. Definitely don't send out a **broadcast** email to lots of addresses requesting links.

Warning

Don't be tempted to buy inbound links. There are many unscrupulous dealers on the Web who will sell you quantities of inbound links. Google and the other search engines regard this practice as 'cheating' and severely frown upon anyone involved. *If you buy links, you will be banned from the search engines.*

Robots.txt Optimization

A **robots.txt** file is read by search engine robots when they crawl your blog. You can use it to tell them which pages should be indexed. There are a couple of reasons why using a robots.txt file is good for SEO. First, Google and other search engines recommend you use one and it's generally a good idea to do what they say. Second, it can help you to cut down on duplicated content.

Search engines do not like duplicated content (that is the same content appearing at two different URLs within a website) because they suspect it might be spam. One minor drawback with WordPress is that it can create a lot of duplicate content. For example, http://blog.chilliguru.com/category/recipes points to exactly the same content as http://blog.chilliguru.com/recipes. Also, the same content is repeated on different pages. For example, most of the posts listed at http://blog.chilliguru.com/category/recipes are also listed on http://blog.chilliguru.com/tag/receipe. We can tell the search engines to ignore any duplicate content by giving instructions in the robots.txt file. Here is the robots.txt file for ChilliGuru:

```
Sitemap: http://blog.chilliguru.com/sitemap.xml

User-agent: *
Disallow: /cgi-bin/
Disallow: /wp-admin/
Disallow: /wp-includes/
Disallow: /wp-content/plugins/
Disallow: /wp-content/cache/
Disallow: /wp-content/themes/
```

```
Disallow: /wp-
Disallow: /category/
Disallow: /comments/
Disallow: /tag/
Disallow: /author/
Disallow: /trackback/
```

The first line is a big signpost to your Google Sitemap. `User-agent: *` means that the file is intended for all robots to read. It is possible to target the different search engine robots with specific instructions, for example, `User-agent: Googlebot` would just apply to the Google robot; however, you don't need to do this with your blog.

The lines that begin with `Disallow:` tell the robots not to visit those files and folders. This is how you tell them to ignore certain parts of your site. For example, we don't need any of the content in the **wp-** directories to be indexed because it's mainly just PHP code. The one exception is **/wp-content/uploads/**. We haven't included this one in the `robots.txt` file, because we *do* want the search engines to crawl its contents. There may be images in there that should be indexed. `Disallow: /category/` should cure the duplicate content problem we outlined above.

You can use a simple text editor (for example, Notepad or Crimson Editor) to create your `robots.txt` file (you can go to `http://blog.chilliguru.com/robots.txt` and use that file as a starting point). Then it's simply a matter of using your FTP client to upload it to the **root** directory of your blog.

Using Excerpts on the Home Page

Another way to cut down on duplicated content is to display just excerpts of the posts on your home page instead of showing them in full. Obviously, each post is displayed in full on its own single post page, so having them in full on the home page may be regarded as duplicate content by the search engines. In fact, it's not just the home page, as the posts slip down to pages 2, 3, 4, and so on; they are still displayed in full.

Using excerpts is not only a great SEO strategy; it is also becoming popular amongst bloggers in its own right. Some people prefer it as it makes the home page more concise and there is less vertical scrolling required to get an overview of all the posts. It makes it easier for readers to scan the posts and pick the ones they are really interested in. Also, forcing readers to click through to the single post page means they see the comments in full for each post and so may be more inclined to make a contribution to the discussion.

It should still be OK to display the most recent post in full as it can take up to a week for a new post to be indexed by the search engines. By then, the post will have moved down the list and become excerpted, thus removing the risk of duplicate content.

I'm noticing home page excerpts more and more. I just did a very quick (and un-scientific) survey of the current top-10 blogs on `technorati.com` and seven of them used excerpts on their home page (these are big names like Gizmodo, The Huffington Post, Lifehacker, and so on).

However, there will always be some traditionalists who prefer to see the full posts on the home page. You need to balance the SEO and usability benefits against the possibility of alienating some of your readers. Personally, I think the benefits of using excerpts outweigh any drawbacks, so we'll go ahead and set them up on ChilliGuru.

You could go through and edit each post adding a `<!--more-->` tag where appropriate. However, there is a plugin we can use that will do this automatically. It's called **Excerpt Editor** by Andrew Ozz of `http://www.laptoptips.ca/`. Go to `http://wordpress.org/extend/plugins/excerpt-editor/`, download, install, and activate it in the usual way on you local development server.

Select the plugin (it's under the **Manage** tab). First, select **Auto-Generate** from the menu and enter the following settings:

Click **Save Auto-Generate Options**.

Now select **Replace Posts** from the menu and enter the following settings:

Replace Posts

Replace the Posts displayed on the Home Page ☑   all Archive Pages ☑ (Category, Author, Day, Month, Year) and all Tags Pages ☑ with excerpts, but show the latest Post in full ☑

 Hide the comments count ☐ from the "Read More" link (if selected in the Auto–Generate options).

· Displaying excerpts instead of full content on all Archive pages, as well as on the Home page and all Tags pages will eliminate content duplication and is one of the main SEO improvements in WordPress.

· Excerpts will be generated according to the Auto–Generate options.

 Save the Replace Posts options

Click **Save the Replace Posts options** and view your home page. You will see that the latest post is shown in full but all the others have been excerpted and now have a **Continue reading** link. The same thing has been applied on all the Archive pages (Category, Author, Day, Month, and Year).

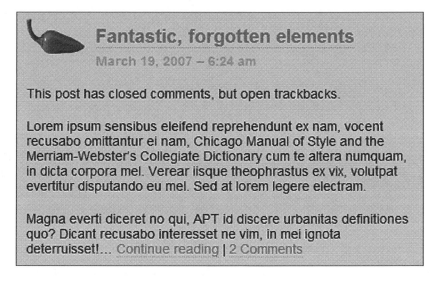

The default settings in the plugin mean that the first 70 words are used in the excerpts. On the **Auto-Generate** page of the plugin, you can change the number of words to be included in the excerpts. Or, if you don't like having the post cut-off in the middle of a sentence, you can use the **Editor** to select each post and then manually set the content you want to appear in the excerpt.

Having set the **Auto-Generate** options, every new post you publish will be excerpted accordingly. Simply deactivate the plugin if you ever want to revert to full posts.

Search Engine Submissions

We've now highlighted some of the most important SEO strategies. Once you've spent some time implementing these on your blog, it's time to submit it to the search engines.

The Big Four

If your blog has been around for some time, then most likely it has already been crawled and indexed by the big four search engines (Google, Yahoo, MSN, and Ask). You can check if they already have it indexed by searching for your home page URL in each of the big four. If you get results in return, they already have it and there is no need to submit it.

If there are no results returned for your URL, it means the search engines have not found it yet. In which case, you can submit it to Google, Yahoo, and MSN (Ask does not have a facility for submitting your URL). If your blog is new, make sure there is a fair amount of content to be indexed—I suggest you wait until you have at least ten posts before submitting. At the time of writing, the submission pages for Google, Yahoo, and MSN are as follows (the URLs for these pages have changed in the past, so you may have to search for them):

- Google: `http://www.google.com/addurl/`
- Yahoo: `https://siteexplorer.search.yahoo.com/submit`
- MSN: `http://search.msn.com.sg/docs/submit.aspx`

For Google and MSN it's simply a case of entering your home page URL. At Yahoo you can also add the URL for your main RSS feed. Yahoo also offers a range of paid-for submission services that guarantee quicker indexing, which you might like to consider.

Although Ask does not have a page where you can submit your URL, you can ping Ask with details of your XML sitemap URL. Simply enter the following URL in your browser address bar, replacing the ChilliGuru XML sitemap URL with your own:

`http://submissions.ask.com/ping?sitemap=http%3A//blog. chilliguru.com/sitemap.xml`

DMOZ.org

DMOZ, or the **Open Directory Project**, is the most important directory on the Web. Its content is licensed in a similar fashion to open-source software, so it is widely syndicated. In fact, almost all of the major search engines use its directory in some way or another. Therefore, it's vitally important to submit your blog to DMOZ. Go to `http://www.dmoz.org/add.html` for full details about submitting.

Minor Search Engines and Directories

Along with the big four search engines and DMOZ, there are thousands of other minor search engines and directories out there. Some of these are general, whilst others operate within a specific niche. For an idea of the sheer quantity take a look at the list at `http://www.searchengineguide.com/searchengines.html`.

Not all of these are worth bothering with as they don't attract very much traffic. However, it's worth doing some research into the ones that serve your particular niche. By looking around a bit, you will identify those that appear to be well used and popular. Ways of spotting decent directories are to look at the number of websites they have listed and check out their ranking at Alexa.com (`http://www. alexa.com/site/ds/top_500`). If they have plenty of websites listed and a decent Alexa ranking, they are probably worth submitting your URL to. Remember, the more good-quality inbound links you can get, the better your ranking will be on Google and the other majors.

If you intend to submit to the smaller search engines and directories, it will be more productive if you log what you're doing. Set aside some time each month to research and submit to the minor search engines. Use a spreadsheet to log which ones you are submitting to and follow up by seeing how much traffic (if any) you are receiving from them. You'll find out how to monitor your traffic sources in Chapter 9.

SEO Software and Tools

There are many tools and applications that claim to help you optimize your site and/or submit it to the search engines. These vary greatly in their usefulness and value for money. If you decide you need some automated help with your SEO (and there's no denying, some of these tools can save hours) I recommend you research the market carefully before you part with any of your marketing budget. SEO products and services are big business and there are plenty of charlatans out there who have jumped on the bandwagon just to make a quick buck. Having said that, there are some excellent tools from reputable vendors. A few of the better ones are mentioned here.

Web CEO

This is one I strongly suggest you take a look at. **Web CEO** (`http://www.webceo.com`) is probably the most complete tool of its kind, and it comes highly recommended by many online marketers and SEO pros. It can help you with several aspects of SEO, including:

- Keyword research
- Optimizing your content
- Submitting to the minor search engines and directories
- Building inbound links

Although it's a paid-for product, there is a free version with plenty of useful features. I suggest you download it, if only to submit your blog to the dozens of minor search engines it supports. The free version allows you to automatically submit your URL to over 100 search engines. It's also very useful for doing keyword research (similar to the Google tool we discussed earlier in this chapter).

Google Webmaster Tools

This collection of tools is indispensable for SEO. It provides you with the information you need to fine-tune your blog to make it more Google-friendly. It gives you some insight into how Google views and ranks your pages, which is a great way of learning about SEO in more detail. Google Webmaster Tools are completely free to use.

It's easy to get started. You just need to sign up for a Google account (if you don't already have one). Then go to `http://www.google.com/webmasters/tools/`, login, and submit your blog's URL. Before you can access any detailed information about your blog, you need to verify that you are the site owner. One of the verification methods is to add a Meta Tag to your home page.

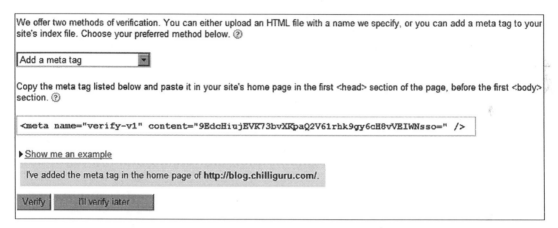

We can use our **All in One SEO** plugin to do this. In your WordPress admin area, go to the plugin page, and copy and paste the Meta Tag that Google gives you into the **Additional Home Headers** box, then click **Update Options**:

Additional Page Headers:	
Additional Home Headers:	`<meta name="verify-v1" content="9EdcHiujEVK73bvXKpaQ2V61rhk9gy6cH8vVEIWNsso=" />`
Log important events:	☐

Now go back to Google Webmaster Tools and click the **Verify** button. You should see a success message:

Google Webmaster Tools is very intuitive with good help files and documentation, so I won't go into detailed instructions here. Use the menu to see what tools are on offer and read the recommendations Google gives you. For example, under **Statistics** you can see the top search queries in which your blog appears — this is very useful for your keyword research. You can also use the **Links** option to see which websites are linking to you.

If your blog is new, some of the data may not be available yet. Keep checking over the coming days and weeks — the data will appear as Google re-indexes your blog. You can see in the **Overview** the last time Googlebot visited your home page.

The first recommendation for ChilliGuru is to add a sitemap. Since we've already created a Google Sitemap, it's simply a matter of telling Google the URL:

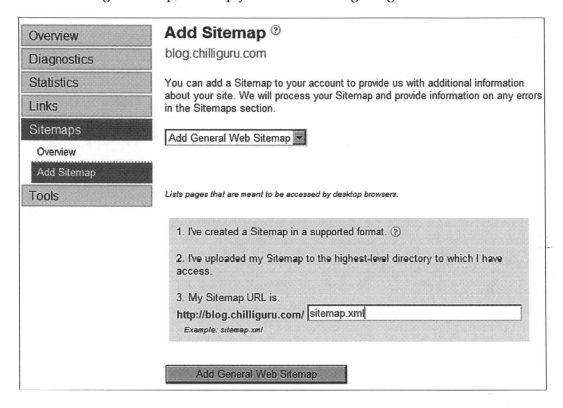

Firefox SEO Extensions

There are several extensions for the Firefox browser that have been developed to help with SEO. My favorite is **SEOQuake** (`https://addons.mozilla.org/en-US/firefox/addon/303`). Its main benefit is to help you evaluate your SEO efforts and track your blog's progress in the major search engines. At a glance you can see a variety of useful SEO parameters like Google Page Rank, Alexa Ranking, Yahoo and Google links data, Del.icio.us and Digg links, and more. Keeping track of this kind of data is really useful to determine how successful your SEO work has been.

The following is a screenshot from the Google results page showing SEOQuake data for `http://www.packtpub.com`:

Packt Publishing Book Store
Packt is a unique publishing company specializing in highly focused books on specific technologies and solutions.
www.**packt**pub.com/ - 36k - Cached - Similar pages

Titles	Joomla
Search	Bookstore
Award	Your Account
Support	PHP/MySQL

More results from packtpub.com »

SeoQuake: | PR: 8 | I: 3,510 | L: 11,400 | LD: 152,000 | I: 16300 | Rank: 30214 | Age: Apr 09, 2004 | I: 157 | whois | source | ?

SEOQuake Data

Seeing Results

SEO should always be seen as an ongoing process. If you've just applied the strategies from this chapter to your blog, don't expect to see big improvements in your search engine rankings overnight. The search engine bots crawl the Web relatively infrequently (usually about once a month) so it will take time for your SEO work to have a visible impact. It will also take time to build links and tweak your keyword list, so it's just right. SEO is not a one-off activity; it's something you should do on a regular basis. Adopt an organized approach and keep records of the SEO work you do and carefully monitor your progress through the rankings. If you put in the effort, you will see results over time.

Summary

In this chapter, we have examined some of the most important SEO strategies and how to apply them. We also looked at submitting your blog to the search engines and introduced some tools and software to make life easier. If you've followed these guidelines, your blog should already be on its way up the search engine rankings.

Next, we'll look at a whole host of other promotion techniques to boost your blog's popularity and send your traffic figures even higher.

7
Supercharged Promotion

You can't rely solely on search engines to spread the word about your blog. In order to supercharge your promotion campaign, you need to get creative.

Promoting your blog and steadily growing your traffic volume is a long, hard job. In fact, it's never ending. A large part of your time should be spent on your promotional work. Indeed, you'll probably need to spend much more time on this than actually writing posts. The key to success is getting to know how the blogosphere works and learning about the tools, websites, and social networks that can help you along the way.

In this chapter, we will examine some of the options available to build up your promotional arsenal. It's by no means an exhaustive reference, but it should get you going. Hopefully, the tips and tricks here will get you thinking more creatively about your promotion work.

Syndication

One of the most powerful promotional tools available to bloggers is RSS. It's a technology that allows your visitors to 'subscribe' to your content using feed-reading software and then receive your latest posts and comments without having to visit your blog. Your new content automatically appears in their **feed reader**.

RSS and blogging have always been intimately related. RSS has been available for many years, but no one really found a mass application for it until blogging arrived on the scene. The two are a perfect match. RSS is just what bloggers need to keep their readers updated with the latest content from their blogs. Pretty much all blogging software (including WordPress) has native support for RSS syndication.

Some may argue that the uptake of RSS by the Web surfing masses has been a relatively 'slow burn'. It's true that it's taken several years for RSS to become mainstream, and there are still many Web surfers who are yet to appreciate its benefits, but take-up remains steady. It will continue to grow as the world's most popular web browsers now ship with integrated feed readers, while more and more high profile websites (for example Yahoo!, Facebook, BBC, and so on) promote RSS to their users. The following screenshots show the built-in feed readers in Internet Explorer 8 and Mozilla Firefox.

WordPress Feeds

There are several different formats of RSS feeds, such as RSS 0.91, RSS 1.0, RSS 2.0, and Atom. The differences between these are in the XML code that makes them work. WordPress supports all of these different formats, which means anyone can subscribe to your feed.

WordPress has an excellent built-in feed generator, which makes your main posts feed auto-discoverable. So, virtually all RSS feed readers and the most popular web browsers will automatically detect your main feed just from your blog's URL. For example, **Google Reader** will find the ChilliGuru feed just from the main URL:

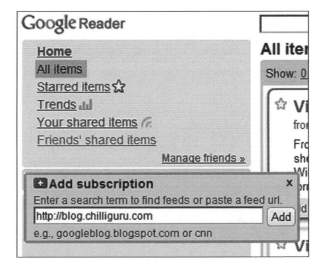

There are specific URLs for accessing each of the different feed formats:

`http://blog.chilliguru.com/wp-rss.php`—RDF/RSS1.0 feed

`http://blog.chilliguru.com/wp-rss2.php`—RSS 2.0 feed

`http://blog.chilliguru.com/wp-atom.php`—Atom feed

However, because ChilliGuru is using **custom permalinks**, the URLs are much simpler:

`http://blog.chilliguru.com/feed`—The main posts feed

`http://blog.chilliguru.com/comments/feed`—The comments feed

`http://blog.chilliguru.com/category/culture/feed`—The 'Chilli Culture' category feed (this uses the culture slug, but you can substitute it with the slug for any category)

`http://blog.chilliguru.com/tag/recipe/feed`—The 'recipe' tag feed (again, you can substitute **recipe** for any tag)

In fact, if you add **/feed** to the end of any URL on the blog, you will see the feed for that page.

Excerpts or Full Posts

You can tell WordPress to display either the full post or an excerpt in your main RSS feed. There are advantages and disadvantages to both and, as with the debate in Chapter 6 over full posts or excerpts on the homepage, it's largely a matter of personal choice.

Full posts may be more useful for your subscribers as they won't have to leave their feed readers to see your content in full. It can be annoying having to click through from the feed reader in order to see the whole post. The downside for you is that it may lose traffic to your blog (if people are reading your posts in their feed readers, they won't be visiting your pages). This is really only a problem if you rely on pay-per-click adverts for revenue (more on this in Chapter 10). A decrease in traffic will probably mean less ad revenues. However, the small amount of revenue you lose may be a price worth paying. At the end of the day, the whole point of your blog is to have it read by as many people as possible. Whether they do that at your blog's URL or in their feed readers doesn't really matter.

I prefer to display full posts in the RSS feed because of the extra convenience it offers to subscribers. However, you can change the settings for this under **Settings | Reading** in the WordPress admin area. You can also change the number of posts to be shown in the feed.

FeedBurner

As we've just seen, WordPress does a pretty good job of handling RSS syndication. However, there's a third-party service that offers better functionality.

FeedBurner (http://www.feedburner.com) provides a great range of feed management tools, and since it was acquired by Google in June 2007, it's completely free to use. It works particularly well with the **FeedSmith** plugin (also owned by Google). FeedBurner gives the following advantages to your RSS feeds:

- The **PingShot** tool automatically updates (or pings) a wide range of search engines, indices, and aggregators as soon as it detects new content in your feed.

- There is a sophisticated email subscription system, which allows people to receive your RSS feed by email. This system is great for people who are still slow to adopt RSS.

- You have the ability to add interactive links into your feed. For example, at the end of each post you can add links that allow users to email the content direct to their friends or add it to social bookmarking sites such as del.icio.us.

- FeedBurner automatically serves the correct format of your feed (RSS 1.0, Atom, RDF, or whatever) to the reader.

- There is a whole host of analytical tools so that you can tell how many people are subscribing to your feed (more on this in Chapter 9).

- The FeedSmith plugin ensures that all the analytic and feed forwarding features offered by FeedBurner work in WordPress without you having to configure them.

Setting Up FeedBurner

We'll run through the process of setting up FeedBurner and take a look at some of its most useful features by applying it to the ChilliGuru blog. As FeedBurner requires a publicly accessible URL in order to work properly, we can't set it up for our local development server, but you can work through the following example on your own live blog.

Begin by downloading the **FeedSmith** plugin from (`http://www.feedburner.com/fb/products/feedburner_feedsmith_plugin_2.3.zip`). Unzip the package and upload the **FeedBurner_FeedSmith_Plugin.php** file to your WordPress **plugins** folder. Log in to the admin area and activate the plugin. Then click **Settings** followed by **FeedBurner** to access the configuration page.

Click on the **create a FeedBurner feed for [yourblogname]** link.

Set Up Your FeedBurner Feed

This plugin makes it easy to redirect 100% of traffic for your feeds to a FeedBurner feed you have created. FeedBurner can then track all of your feed subscriber traffic and usage and apply a variety of features you choose to improve and enhance your original WordPress feed.

1. To get started, create a FeedBurner feed for ChilliGuru. This feed will handle all traffic for your posts.

2. Once you have created your FeedBurner feed, enter its address into the field below (http://feeds.feedburner.com/yourfeed):

3. Optional: If you also want to handle your WordPress comments feed using FeedBurner, create a FeedBurner comments feed and then enter its address below:

Save

You will be taken to the FeedBurner website to sign up (it should open in a new window). Select the Posts feed for your blog (we'll do the Comments feed shortly) and click on **Next**.

On the next screen, enter a **Username**, **Password**, and **Email address**. You can also change the **Feed Title** and **Feed Address**, but the defaults should be fine.

On the next page, you should see a success message. Before we return to WordPress, we'll activate the FeedBurner stats tools. At the bottom of the success page, click on **Next**. On the next page, check all the boxes and click on **Next**.

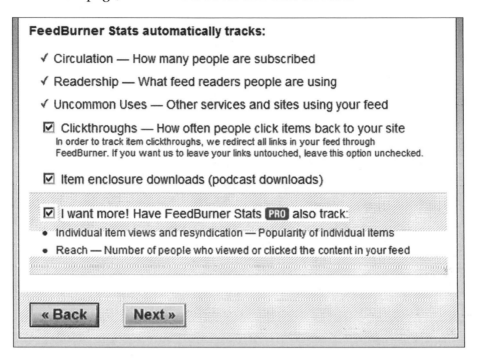

The sign-up process is now complete and you will be taken to your FeedBurner dashboard page.

Now, return to the FeedSmith plugin page in your WordPress admin area and enter your FeedBurner feed URL into the appropriate box (the URL will be something like `http://feeds.feedburner.com/Chilliguru`):

1. To get started, <u>create a FeedBurner feed for ChilliGuru</u>. This feed will handle all traffic for your posts.

2. Once you have created your FeedBurner feed, enter its address into the field below
   (http://feeds.feedburner.com/yourfeed):

   http://feeds.feedburner.com/Chilliguru

3. Optional: If you also want to handle your WordPress comments feed using FeedBurner, <u>create a FeedBurner comments feed</u> and then enter its address below:

   Save

Now, we'll set up our Comments feed. Click on the **create a FeedBurner comments feed** link and you will once again be taken to the FeedBurner website. Work through the sign-up wizard as we did for the Posts feed.

Return to the FeedSmith plugin and enter your FeedBurner comments feed URL:

3. Optional: If you also want to handle your WordPress comments feed using FeedBurner, create a FeedBurner comments feed and then enter its address below:

> http://feeds.feedburner.com/CommentsForChilligu

Click on **Save**.

We have now set up our FeedBurner feeds and configured the FeedSmith plugin. Next we'll take a quick look at some of FeedBurner's most important features.

Using FeedBurner

First, you need to check that your new FeedBurner feed is working. View your blog's homepage and click on the RSS link. As we have installed the FeedSmith plugin, you should now be forwarded to your new FeedBurner feed:

Now, let's take a look at the FeedBurner admin area. You probably still have it open in a browser window, but if not, you can log in at http://www.feedburner.com using the username and password we created earlier.

You'll notice five tabs near the top of the dashboard (**Analyze, Optimize, Publicize, Monetize,** and **Troubleshootize**), which enable you to access all of FeedBurner's features. You need to first activate **SmartFeed** so that your feed has maximum compatibility with the widest range of feed readers and browsers. Click on the **Optimize** tab and then choose **SmartFeed** from the left-hand menu. It's then simply a matter of clicking the **Activate** button to set-up this feature.

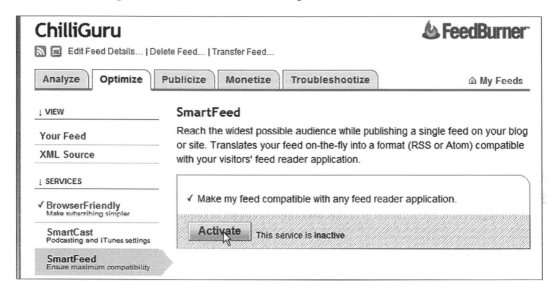

Another cool feature is **FeedFlare**. This allows you to add some interactive links to the bottom of each post in your feed. Click on **FeedFlare** in the left-hand menu to set it up. You're presented with a list of services to add to your feed and there are many more available by clicking the **Browse the Catalog** link.

I wouldn't go overboard by selecting too many as they will clutter up your feed (maybe choose three or four to begin with). Remember to click the **Activate** button at the bottom of the page once you have selected your services. For ChilliGuru, I've chosen **Email This, Add a Comment, Add to del.icio.us**, and **Digg This!**.

This is how they look in the feed:

You can take your time to examine most of the other features under the **Optimize** tab as they are mostly self-explanatory. The only other one I will flag up here is the **Title/ Description Burner**, which enables you to turn your feed's title and description into something more interesting that matches the branding of your blog:

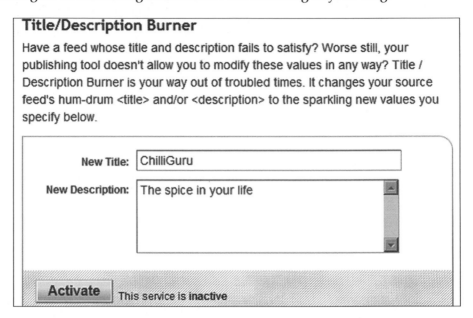

As we move on to the **Publicize** tab, we will see the FeedBurner features that will really help supercharge your blog promotion.

FeedBurner Email is easy to set up. It allows you to provide an alternative method for your readers to subscribe to your RSS feed. Once you have activated the service, you add a small subscription form to your blog where readers can sign up. Your subscribers will receive an email containing your new posts once a day. Obviously, they will only receive an email if you add new posts every day. No emails are sent on days that you don't post.

You have full access to the email addresses of all the subscribers and you can export them for use in other applications. We'll run through the process of setting this up using the ChilliGuru blog **on our local development server**.

Under the **Publicize** tab, choose **Email Subscriptions** from the left-hand menu. Leave FeedBurner selected as the email provider and click the **Activate** button. You will then be taken to a page that contains the HTML code for the sign-up form.

Open up Crimson Editor, then copy and paste the **Subscription Form Code** from FeedBurner into a new Crimson Editor document. Select **View | Word Wrap**. The code is rather messy so we'll tidy it up before inserting it into our WordPress sidebar. Add a few line breaks so that the code is laid out as it appears in the following screenshot:

 We'll use a feature in WordPress called **Text Widgets** to insert the subscription form. Text Widgets allow you to add your own code into an 'empty' widget.

In your local WordPress admin area, go to **Design | Widgets**. We'll place the email subscription form just under the RSS feeds in the secondary toolbar. We'll also move the RSS feed up so that it's just underneath the search box. Select **Sidebar 2** from the drop-down box underneath **Current Widgets**, then click the **Show** button. Add the following widgets, by clicking the **Add** links in the **Available Widgets** list, in this order:

Click on **Save Changes**. Now, click on the **Edit** link for the **Text** widget. Go back to Crimson Editor and copy all of the subscription form code, then paste it into the widget text box. Click **Change** to save and close the text box.

I also changed the title in the **RSS Links** widget. Click on the **Edit** link for the **RSS Links** widget and enter **RSS Feeds** in the **Title** box, then click **Change**.

Click the **Save Changes** button.

If you preview the blog, you will see that the sign-up form appears in the RSS section of the sidebar:

The form doesn't look too bad, but the sign-up instructions aren't very informative and it would be nice if it matched the style of the rest of the blog. We need to edit the code to achieve this. Here is the subscription form code after it's been edited (this is included in the code bundle for this chapter (**email_form.txt**), which you can download from the Packt website):

```
<form action="http://www.feedburner.com/fb/a/emailverify"
      method="post" target="popupwindow"
      onsubmit="window.open('http://www.feedburner.com/fb/a/
      emailverifySubmit?feedId=1872312', 'popupwindow',
      'scrollbars=yes,width=550,height=520');return true">
    <p style="color: #DF5E37; font-size: 12px;
            font-weight:bold;">To receive our main feed by email,
            enter your email address:</p>
    <input type="text" name="email" id="s"/>
    <input type="hidden"
          value="http://feeds.feedburner.com/~e?ffid=1872312"
          name="url"/>
    <input type="hidden" value="ChilliGuru" name="title"/>
    <input type="hidden" name="loc" value="en_US"/>
    <input type="submit" value="Go" name="submit"
            id="searchsubmit"/>
</form>
<p style="color: #DF5E37; font-size: 12px; font-weight:bold;">You
will be taken to the FeedBurner website (in a pop-up) to complete the
subscription process.</p>
<p></br></p>
```

Go back to the **Text** widget and replace the original subscription form code with the improved, edited version. Save your changes. The form looks much better now:

When a user enters their email address, a FeedBurner pop-up will open for them to complete the sign-up process. They will then receive an email containing a confirmation link, which they must click to start their subscription. This protects you from any unwanted sign-ups.

Once you have added the sign-up form to your blog, you can change some of the other settings for email subscriptions from the FeedBurner dashboard. For example, if you select **Email Branding** in the left-hand menu, you can change the subject line for your emails and also add a logo:

Email Branding

HTML Email Appearance

Email Subject/Title: | ChilliGuru - Latest updates |

This line will appear as both the Subject of update emails and as the main title in the body of the message.

Logo URL: | http://blog.chilliguru.com/wp-content/uploads/200 |

Logo URL is optional and it requires that you host an image on a server FeedBurner can access. Only JPEG, GIF and PNG graphic files will work. The recommended size is no larger than 200 pixels by 200 pixels.

You should now have a pretty good idea of what FeedBurner can do for your blog. Spend some time exploring all the services on offer. We will be discussing the **PingShot** feature later in this chapter, in the section on blog indexes and search engines.

Web Slices for Internet Explorer 8

Web Slices are a new feature in Internet Explorer 8. They offer another method for Web publishers to syndicate their content. This may be particularly useful in encouraging the **hitherto** slow adopters of RSS to subscribe to your syndicated content. You can turn a section of your blog into a **Web Slice**, to which readers can easily subscribe with one click. When a user visits a page that contains a Web Slice, the orange feed icon in the Internet Explorer toolbar changes its color to purple. The user can click on it and subscribe to the Web Slice.

Also, when the user hovers his or her mouse cursor over the Web Slice itself, it is highlighted. There is also another purple button that allows them to subscribe:

When they click on either of the subscribe buttons, a dialog box appears to confirm the subscription process:

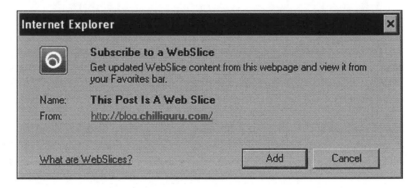

The Web Slices are stored in the **Favorites** folder along with the other RSS feeds:

The link to the Web Slice is also added to Internet Explorer's toolbar. When the user clicks on it, she or he can see a preview of the Web Slice displayed using the styles of the website it is taken from (even when she or he is browsing another website):

 At the time of writing, Internet Explorer 8 is still in Beta. All the preceding screenshots were taken using the Beta version. By the time the final version of IE8 is released, there may be some minor changes in the functionality. You should check the Internet Explorer website (http://www.microsoft.com/windows/products/winfamily/ ie/) for up-to-date information.

Creating a Web Slice

Theoretically, you can make a Web Slice out of any section of a web page. However, in a standard WordPress blog the most obvious place for a Web Slice is the first post on the home page as this is the most frequently updated part of the site. When a new post is added, the Web Slice will be updated.

Creating a Web Slice is a fairly straightforward process but it requires editing one of the WordPress template files. We'll go through the process on our local development server.

We'll use Crimson Editor to make the changes in the template file. You could use the built-in Template Editor in WordPress, but for the purposes of this tutorial, it's easier to see line numbers in Crimson Editor.

In the Sandbox theme folder (**C:\xampp\htdocs\wordpress\wp-content\themes\ sandbox**) open up the **index.php** file in Crimson Editor:

Find the following line of code (it should be around Line 11):

```
<?php while ( have_posts() ) : the_post() ?>
```

Create a new line directly below it and add this code:

```
<div class="hslice" id="FirstPost">
```

What's going on in the code?

The `hslice` class tells Internet Explorer 8 that this is a Web Slice. The `id` is for your reference and can be anything you like, for example, if you had several slices on the same page, you might use `slice01`, `slice02`; `slice03`, and so on. Web Slice syntax is based on the **hAtom** micro-format (you don't need to understand what that means, suffice to say that `entry-title` is specified as part of the hAtom schema). You'll notice that there is already an `entry-title` class in **index.php** (around Line 14) — Internet Explorer 8 will use it as the 'Name' of the Web Slice. In our case the `entry-title` class is the post title.

Now add a closing `</div>` tag just before `<!-- .post -->` (around Line 30), and save the file. (There are already two `</div>` tags at this point — you need to add another one.)

That's it. We've now added a Web Slice to our template file, which encloses the first post on the home page. If you have Internet Explorer 8 installed, you can test it by viewing the blog.

At the time of writing, because Internet Explorer 8 is still in Beta, there is no WordPress plugin currently available for adding Web Slices. There may well be one by the time you read this, so check the plugins database on the WordPress website (`http://wordpress.org/extend/ plugins/`).

Blog Indexes and Search Engines

In the last chapter, we discussed methods of optimizing your blog for the major search engines. However, there is a whole host of other search engines and indexes that are specifically for blogs. One of the most popular of these is Technorati (`http://www.technorati.com`). These search engines represent another great way of promoting your blog by getting it in front of another group of web searchers.

Ping-O-Matic

Luckily, WordPress makes it easy to get listed on the most popular blog indexes and search engines. These search engines compile their indexes from blogs **pinging** them.

 Ping is a mechanism by which blogs notify external servers (in this case, the search engines) that their content has been updated.

By default, WordPress is automatically set up to ping your new content to the most popular blog search engines via a service called **Ping-O-Matic**. You can see the settings for this under **Settings | Writing**:

Update Services

When you publish a new post, WordPress automatically notifies the following site update services. For more about this, see Update Services on the Codex. Separate multiple service URLs with line breaks.

http://rpc.pingomatic.com/

FeedBurner's Pingshot

Ping-O-Matic covers most of the blog search engines, but we can also use FeedBurner's pinging service, **Pingshot**, to add even more. Log into your FeedBurner account. Choose to manage your main content feed (as opposed to the comments feed), click the **Publicize** tab in the dashboard and then **Pinghsot** from the left-hand menu.

On the Pingshot page, you can select which services you want FeedBurner to ping for you. The first four in the list are set up by default, but you should also choose **Google Blog Search Pinging Service** and five of the additional services. Do not select **Ping-o-matic** as we already have that set up in WordPress. Also, some of the options in the list of additional services are covered by Ping-O-Matic (at the time of writing these are: **icerocket**, **Weblogs.Com**, **Blogdigger**, **Syndic8**, and **Moreover**). Therefore, you should choose five different ones, or simply go with the options shown in the following screenshot. Once you have chosen them, click the **Activate** button.

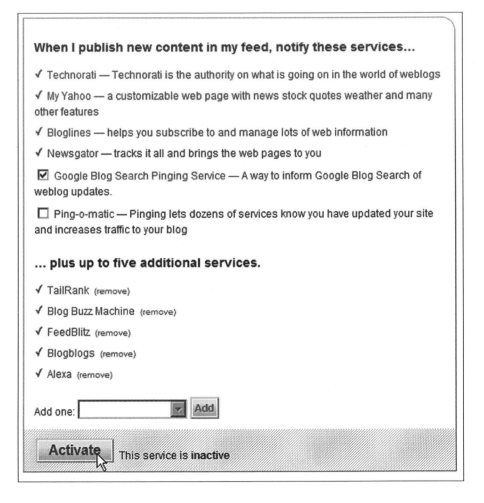

Now we've set-up most of the ping services, but if you find any service that is not covered by Ping-O-Matic or Pingshot, you can add it via **Settings | Writing** under **Update Services**. Place each ping URL on a separate line underneath the Ping-O-Matic URL.

Technorati

We've seen that WordPress will automatically ping your blog updates to Technorati via Ping-O-Matic. However, you should also sign up to Technorati to claim your blog and set up a profile. You can sign up using the **Join** link on the Technorati home page. Once you've signed up, you can edit your profile and claim your blogs:

From the **My Account** page you can upload a photo, add a bio, and claim your blog. In order to claim your blog, you will need to verify it. The best way to do this is to use the **Post Claim** option, which involves creating a new post that includes a special code (Technorati gives full instructions and steps you through the process):

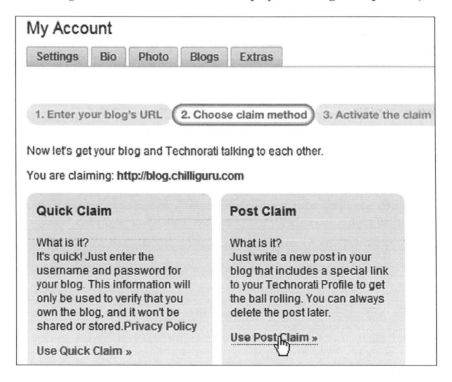

Once your claim has been verified, you can add a short description of your blog and some tags. You should pick some of the most popular tags that appear in your blog's tag cloud.

When you have set-up your profile, people who find your blog on Technorati will get a little bit more information about you (see the ChilliGuru profile page at `http://technorati.com/people/technorati/ChilliGuru`):

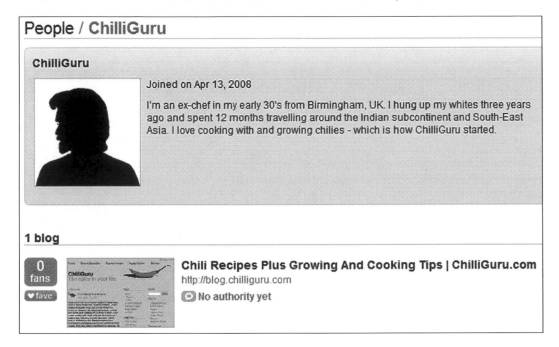

You can also add a Technorati favorites button to your blog, so that people can add it to their Technorati favorites list with just one click. Let's go through the process using the ChilliGuru case study blog.

On the Technorati **My Account** page, under the **Blogs** tab, you can use the **Edit Settings** button to retrieve the HTML code needed for the favorites button:

For this example, you can use the ChilliGuru code, as follows (it's also included in the code bundle for this chapter in the **technorati.txt** file):

```
<a href="http://technorati.com/faves?sub=addfavbtn&amp;
    add=http://blog.chilliguru.com"><img src=
    "http://static.technorati.com/pix/fave/tech-fav-1.png"
    alt="Add to Technorati Favorites" /></a>
```

Once again, we'll use a Text Widget to insert the button. In your ChilliGuru admin area, go back to the **Widgets** page.

Select **Sidebar 1** from the drop-down box under **Current Widgets** and click on **Show**. Add a **Text** widget and click **Save Changes**. Click the **Edit** link for your new **Text** widget and paste the Technorati favorites button code into the text box. Click **Change** and then the **Save Changes** button. View the blog and you will see that the button has been added to the bottom of the primary sidebar, but it has an ugly blue border. We can get rid of the border by adding this CSS rule to the bottom of the blog's style sheet (from WordPress admin, use **Design | Theme Editor** and select **style.css** to edit it):

```
div.sidebar a img {border style:none;}
```

The blue border should now have gone from the button:

Minor Blog Indexes

We've covered most of the major blog search engines by setting up our automatic pings. However, there are plenty of minor blog indexes that don't use the pinging system. These have less traffic, but it may still be worth submitting your URL to them. I won't give a list of these here as many of them cover specific niches. You can find them by searching on Google. A couple of examples are: `http://www.poweredbywp.com/`, which lists blogs that run on WordPress, and `http://www.britblog.com/`, which covers British bloggers.

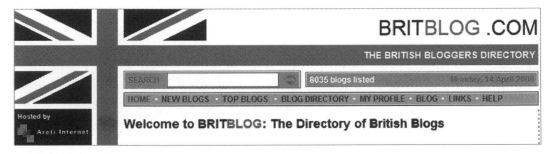

Using Social Networks

In recent years, the social networking phenomenon has swept the Web. Sites like Facebook, MySpace, and Bebo now have millions of users worldwide. Businesses have been hard at work figuring out how to leverage the power of social networks in their marketing activities. Social networks can be useful to you as a business blogger, but it will very much depend on your type of business and you need to know what you are getting into.

Social networks will probably be more useful to you if your business is quite personal in nature. For example, if you are a sole trader, consultant, or freelancer, your personal profile page on Facebook can be a useful place to help build your brand and find new prospects. If, however, you run a larger company and have a more 'corporate' identity, social networking can be more difficult to harness.

The main thing to bear in mind with social networks is that most people tend to use them in a 'social' context, rather than a 'business' context. People use Facebook to stay connected with their friends, see photos of last weekend's parties, talk about vacations, weddings, sports, and so on. This means the content tends to be very informal. This is why social networks are not necessarily a great place to do business. If you frequently post risqué images of your wild weekend escapades, it's probably a good idea to keep your business totally separate. However, if you're a little more restrained about what you post on Facebook and the tone of your profile page is a good match with the tone of your blog, there may be an opportunity for some cross-promotion. But remember that many Facebook users don't like business encroaching onto the network. If you use a 'hard sell' approach, you're likely to lose a lot of friends.

If you have a Facebook profile, you could try using a third-party plugin to get your blog content into your Facebook Mini-Feed. One such plugin is called **Wordbook**. We can install this for our ChilliGuru case study blog. Download the plugin from `http://wordpress.org/extend/plugins/wordbook/`. Unzip the package and place the entire **wordbook** directory into the **plugins** folder on your local development server. Activate the plugin in your WordPress admin area. Now click on **Settings | Wordbook** to complete the configuration process. First, click on the Facebook icon to log into Facebook and generate a one-time code for the plugin.

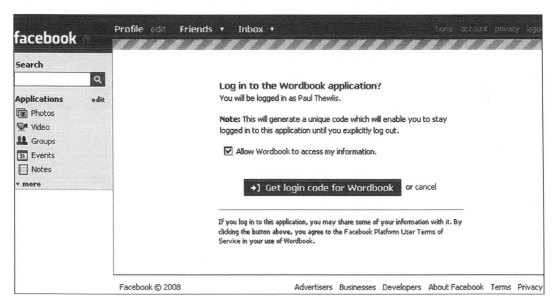

Copy the generated code and return to the Wordbook plugin, enter the code in the box on the configuration page, and then click the **Submit** button. On the next page, you will be prompted to add the Wordbook plugin to your Facebook profile page. Click the Facebook icon and you will be taken to Facebook to complete this step—click the **Add Wordbook** button. The plugin is now set-up, and all your new posts will appear in your Facebook Mini-Feed and in your friend's news feeds.

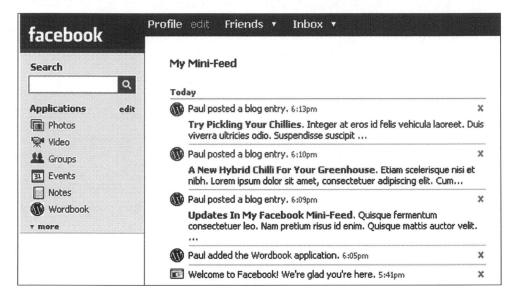

This could be a useful technique for driving some traffic to your blog posts. Remember, however, not to overload your Facebook profile with too much business-related content (keep things informal and bear in mind that the majority of people on Facebook are there for fun).

 If you have a slightly larger business or feel that your personal profile isn't an appropriate place for content from your business blog, you can set up a **Facebook Page**. To set one up, click on the **Businesses** link in the Facebook footer, and then select **Facebook Pages**. The set-up process is straightforward—just follow the on-screen prompts.

Using Twitter

Twitter (http://www.twitter.com) is a micro-blogging platform available via the Web, IM, and mobile devices. It allows you to publish short quick-fire messages, called **Tweets**, up to 140 characters in length, aimed at answering a simple question: 'What are you doing?'. You can invite people to follow your Tweets and in turn, you follow theirs. It's a very social medium, which is one of its major attractions to bloggers.

At the time of writing, Twitter is on the cusp of being 'the next big thing'. There are already over 1 million users and it's well poised to go mainstream. Already, the likes of Hillary Clinton (`http://twitter.com/hillaryclinton`), Barack Obama (`http://twitter.com/barackobama`), and Prime Minister Gordon Brown (`http://twitter.com/DowningStreet`) are using it to get their message out there.

So, what can it do for your blog? Well, as with many Web 2.0 applications, people are still figuring out exactly how they can use it to best effect. At its simplest level, it's just a way of keeping in touch with your friends, family, and colleagues. But it could be used as another channel to publicize your blog.

The most obvious way of putting it to work on your blog is to supplement your RSS feed. Each time you publish a new post, you can announce it via Twitter:

All your followers on Twitter will be instantly notified when a new post is published on your blog.

Likewise, you can display your latest Tweets on your blog, either as posts or in a sidebar widget:

Twitter is great for breaking news fast. If you're unable to write a full blog post, you can Twitter it and follow-up with a full post later. You could also Twitter previews or teasers for your posts. If you are attending a conference or event, you can use Twitter to update your blog with the latest news from the event in real-time using your cell phone or PDA.

Twitter is a great way to get instant feedback, which makes it a useful research tool:

Once you have signed up to Twitter, you will find that you add new followers relatively quickly, which makes it a great networking tool. Having a presence on Twitter adds to your online brand and could bring your blog and your business to the attention of a whole new audience.

Setting Up Twitter in WordPress

It's easy to integrate Twitter into your WordPress blog thanks to a plugin called **Twitter Tools**. We'll run through the process using the ChilliGuru case study. First, you'll need to register for a Twitter account at `http://www.twitter.com`.

Download the plugin at `http://wordpress.org/extend/plugins/twitter-tools/`. Unzip the package and place the **twitter-tools.php** file in the **plugins** directory on your local development server for the ChilliGuru case study. Login to WordPress and activate the plugin in the usual way. Go to **Settings | Twitter Tools** to complete the configuration. Begin by entering your Twitter login details, then click on **Test Login Info**.

Twitter Tools Options

Twitter Username: chilliguru

Twitter Password: ●●●●●●

Test Login Info   Login succeeded, you're good to go.

The other configuration options are fairly straightforward. I used the following settings to begin with:

Create a tweet when you post in your blog? Yes

Create a blog post from each of your tweets? No

Create a daily digest blog post from your tweets? No

Title for digest posts: Twitter Updates for %s
Include %s where you want the date. Example: Tweets on %s

Select a category for your tweet posts: Uncategorized

Select an author for your tweet posts: admin

Tweets to show in sidebar: 3
Numbers only please.

Create tweets from your sidebar? No

Give Twitter Tools credit? No

Click the **Update Twitter Tools Options** button.

Next we can add the Twitter Tools widget to the sidebar, which will display our most recent Tweets. Go to **Design | Widgets**. Add the **Twitter Tools** widget into **Sidebar 1** just above the **Archives** widget, and save the changes. Click the **Edit** link for the **Twitter Tools** widget and change the title to **Twitter Updates**, then save your changes. Your latest Tweets will now be displayed as shown in the following screenshot:

We can improve the styling of our sidebar Tweets by adding a couple of CSS rules to the bottom of the blog's style sheet (from WordPress admin, use **Design | Theme Editor** and select **style.css** to edit it):

```
div.sidebar .aktt_tweets li {padding-bottom:10px; color: #DF5E37;
                             display:block;}
div.sidebar .aktt_tweets li a {border-style:none; font-size: 12px;
                               font-weight:bold; display:block;}
```

The sidebar should now look like this:

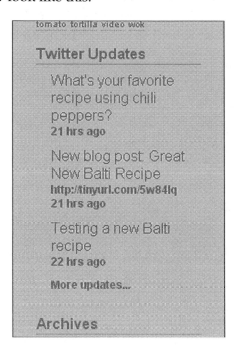

Social Bookmarking

Websites like Digg, del.icio.us, StumbleUpon, Reddit, and Furl list URLs or 'bookmarks' that have been submitted by Web users all over the world. The idea is that if somebody comes across an article or blog post they like, they can submit it as a bookmark and, in doing so, recommend it to other people. The more people who bookmark a particular blog post or article, the higher up the listing pages it will appear. Having one of your posts appear on the front page of Digg or one of the other social bookmarking sites, could send an avalanche of traffic to your blog.

Adding the Links

Before we discuss some tips and tricks to improve your chances of getting your posts bookmarked, we need to make it as easy as possible for your readers to do so. We can use a great plugin called **ShareThis**, which adds social bookmarking links at the end of each of your posts. Readers just click on these links to bookmark your post or email it to their friends. We'll install this plugin on the ChilliGuru case study blog.

Go to `http://wordpress.org/extend/plugins/share-this/` and download the plugin. Unzip the package and place the **sharethis.php** file in the **plugins** folder on your local development server. Login to WordPress and activate the plugin. We've now added the ShareThis button at the end of each of our posts:

When a user clicks on the button, they are presented with a neat widget with three tabs. The **Social Web** tab allows them to bookmark the post at the most popular bookmarking sites; the **Post** tab allows them to add the post to their own blog or social network profile; and the **Send** tab allows them to email the permalink for the post to their friends.

 When you install ShareThis on your live blog, you should register for a free account at `http://sharethis.com/wordpress`. This gives you access to the **Customization Tool**, which allows you to change the settings for the widget and view stats about the usage of your ShareThis button.

Bookmarking Tips

Simply adding the bookmarking links to your blog posts isn't quite enough to get a good placement in the bookmark listings. In fact, getting anywhere near the front page of the big bookmarking sites like Digg and del.icio.us is quite a challenge. If you're serious about social bookmarking as a promotion tool, be warned that it takes time and perseverance to crack it.

The good news is that the big bookmarking sites are just the tip of the iceberg. There are hundreds of smaller sites, many aimed towards a specific niche, which may be much easier to break into. The volume of traffic on these smaller sites may not be as great, but it is likely to be better quality if the niche fits your blog.

You should start by researching these websites. Monitor them for several days and see what kind of posts regularly appear on their front pages. You will soon realize that different sites appeal to different users and this is reflected in the content that gets bookmarked. There is a good list of social bookmarking sites at `http://traffikd.com/social-media-websites/`. Research a selection of these and see which are likely to work well with your content. Choose no more than half a dozen upon which to target your efforts.

You should also focus your efforts on selected posts. There is no point trying to get each and every post you publish into a good position on the bookmarking sites. Wait until you have a really special post that you think will do well on the sites you are targeting.

You should register with the bookmarking sites you are targeting and start bookmarking other people's content. This grows your profile and enables you to build up a group of friends. Networking with other users is the key element of social media. If possible, try to befriend high-profile users on the sites and bookmark their content. Eventually they may notice you and bookmark one of your posts. On some networks (for example Digg), these 'power users' carry more weight than regular users. It's a real boost to have them bookmark your content as they have so many friends who follow their bookmarks and vote them up (it's a snowball effect).

When you have written a good post that you think has a chance on the bookmarking sites, ask your friends and colleagues to bookmark it. On the larger sites you need at least 15 votes before an article even gets noticed. Take some time to come up with a really catchy title for the post.

Examples of the types of posts that might do well include:

- Top-10 lists
- How-To's and 'Ultimate Guides'
- Posts offering free resources and gifts
- Controversial or funny articles about famous personalities
- Interesting or amusing videos

As you can see, these are similar to some of the link-baiting ideas we discussed in Chapter 6.

On the big bookmarking sites, you are not only competing with other bloggers but with some of the biggest media organizations in the world. Therefore, high quality content is a must. If you combine that with diligent research into the networks you're targeting and take time to build up your profile, you could have some great success with social bookmarking.

Beware the 'Digg Effect'

It's fantastic to have a big success on Digg or del.icio.us and get one of your posts at the top of the list. However, the tidal wave of traffic it could bring may totally overload your blog's server and bring it to a complete stop. This is known as the 'Digg Effect'. If you're lucky enough to do well on the social bookmarking networks, make sure your blog can cope with the strain (we look at ways of managing high traffic in Chapter 11).

Summary

In this chapter, we've looked at some of the more advanced techniques for promoting your blog and growing traffic. We began by examining the RSS capabilities of WordPress and how they can be enhanced with FeedBurner. We looked at Internet Explorer's latest syndication technology: **Web Slices**. We also discussed how to use blog search engines like Technorati, as well as a variety of social media like Facebook, Twitter, and bookmarking sites.

In the next chapter, we stay on the theme of promotion and traffic building by examining how your interaction in the blogosphere can create a mutually beneficial relationship with other bloggers.

8
Connecting with the Blogosphere

Blogging should never be regarded as a solitary activity. As a blogger, you are part of the 'social web'. You should always regard your blog as a piece of something bigger — the blogosphere. Interaction with other blogs will be a linchpin in your success.

Defining the Blogosphere

Wikipedia gives this definition:

> **Blogosphere** *is a collective term encompassing all blogs and their interconnections. It is the perception that blogs exist together as a connected community (or as a collection of connected communities) or as a social network.*

The key idea is **connectivity**. The Wikipedia definition is concerned with the connectivity between blogs, which is something we will be exploring here. However, I would also widen this definition to include the connectivity between blogs and their readers. They are as much a part of the blogosphere as the bloggers themselves. The readers are the 'glue' that holds together all the connections in the blogosphere. This is particularly true of the avid blog readers, who probably subscribe to, and regularly read, dozens of different blogs. Readers often discover new blogs thanks to the links that bloggers make to each other. So, as well as connecting with other bloggers, we'll also be looking at ways of connecting with your regular readers.

Why it's so Important to be Connected

The social element of blogs and the connectedness of the blogosphere is a defining characteristic of blogging as a communication platform. It is how blogging began and how it has evolved into what it is today. Blogs feed off each other and are dependent on each other for their existence. Readers are tuned into this sense of connectedness and have come to expect it from the blogs they follow. The relationships between blogs are an intrinsic part of the reader experience (this is how they link to new content and become habitual consumers of the blogging medium).

You need to be part of this in order to truly call yourself a blogger. A blog isn't a blog unless it's a fully connected part of the blogosphere. No blog is an island.

How to Engage with the Blogosphere

You shouldn't view other bloggers as a threat or competition—in fact, they are your friends. Blogging is about mutually beneficial relationships.

Having said that, bloggers are notoriously distrustful and skeptical about any approaches they receive from traditional PR or marketing professionals. If you're going to make friends in the blogosphere you need to engage bloggers on their own terms. Most successful bloggers become a target for PR pros. To them, a blog is just another media outlet to pitch their message to. However, too many people in the PR industry don't understand how to connect with the blogosphere. Bloggers will take a very dim view of approaches made via press releases or unsolicited emails from PR firms. They will (rightly) regard this kind of communication as spam. One blogger has become so annoyed by the constant barrage of PR spam, that he has set up a wiki, which lists the PR companies who have spammed him (http://prspammers.pbwiki.com/):

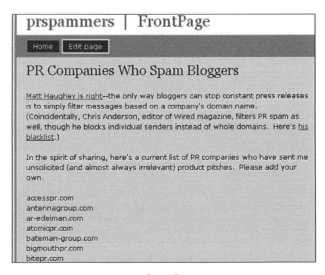

If you're involved with business blogging, you may well be a PR pro and may have experienced this kind of response from angry bloggers. However, the majority of people reading this are not PR pros—so what has this got to do with you, the average business blogger? Well, the fact that you're blogging for a business, particularly if it's a corporate entity, places you in a group alongside PR and marketing pros, in the eyes of many bloggers. They're almost as distrustful of 'corporate' blogging as they are of PR spammers. These are the people you need to befriend, so how do you get them on your side?

Well, we've already established that press releases and unsolicited emails are out. The best way to engage with other bloggers is on their blogs. You need to take the time to read their posts, leave comments, and write posts that link back to them. Here is an outline strategy for becoming a more connected blogger:

- Research the blogs in your market niche or specific arena. Take time to identify the key players. Analyze their content and try to figure out what their readers like.

- Come up with a list of bloggers you intend to target for relationship building. You can start small, just five would be enough to get you going (you can always expand your list as time goes by).

- Begin leaving comments at your target blogs. Try to make them as relevant and 'on topic' as possible. You need to genuinely engage with the issues they raise.

- Write posts on your own blog that expand on the topics raised by those on your target list. Link back to their posts.

- Continue doing this consistently and regularly; soon some of the bloggers you are targeting will notice you. They will begin to comment on your blog and write posts about the issues you are raising.

- Keep expanding your list of target blogs and keep working on this strategy for building new relationships.

In the rest of this chapter, we will examine some of the practical steps you need to take to make this strategy work and improve your connectedness with the blogosphere.

Link Building

We touched on the idea of link building in Chapter 6, where I gave you a fairly organic method of encouraging other people to link to you. Hopefully, you can understand how your blossoming relationships with other bloggers will be a great help in your link-building efforts. This is a more proactive approach to building links, but it is just as useful for search engine optimization.

The Blogroll

A **blogroll** is a list of links to other blogs that you read and wish to recommend to your readers. It's a great way to declare that you belong to the blogosphere. It can also be great for generating traffic. How can that be the case when it's you sending traffic to other blogs? Well, the benefit comes to you from something called **link reciprocity**.

Bloggers are pretty keen when it comes to checking their stats and tracking their referrals (more details on this in the next chapter). When they notice a blog (that is, yours) sending traffic their way, they will most likely check it out. If they like what they see, there's a very good chance they will add you to their own blogroll, and you get the chance of receiving traffic from them. Even if you don't make it onto their blogroll, you will certainly be on their 'radar', and they may link to you in one of their posts.

Managing Your Blogroll

Some bloggers adopt the policy to blogroll anyone who blogrolls them. This may be a useful approach, particularly when your blog is in its infancy. However, you may have to be a little more selective as your popularity grows. Excessively long blogrolls can look messy. Having a fairly indiscriminate list of blogs also defeats the object of the blogroll. The idea is to recommend blogs that you like and think will be of use to your readers. The closer they are to your own topic or area of interest, the more relevant the links will be to your readers. Having a load of dull or dormant blogs in your blogroll may reflect badly on you. As your blogroll grows, you need to be selective. You may also find it useful to organize the links in your blogroll under categories. Not only will this make it easier for you to manage the blogroll, it will also be much more usable for your readers.

Adding Categories and Links

Adding categories is straightforward—we'll run through the process for ChilliGuru. Log into the admin area and click on the **Manage** tab, followed by the **Link Categories** sub-tab. Scroll down to the **Add Category** area and enter the details of your new category, then click the **Add Category** button:

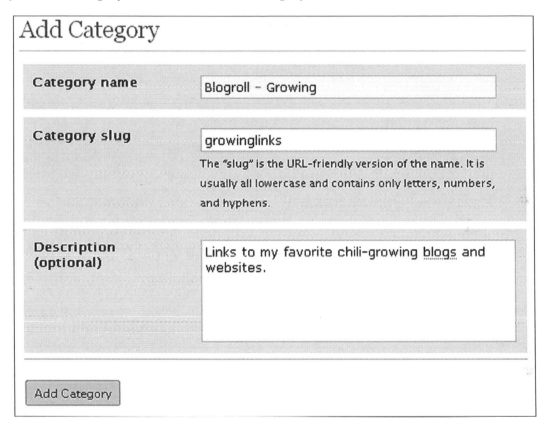

Now you have added new categories, you can add and remove links. Click the **Links** sub-tab under the **Manage** tab:

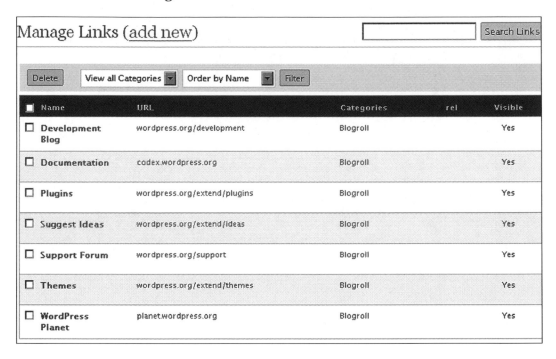

Let's begin by deleting the links that were included in the default installation of WordPress. Simply check the boxes next to the links you want to delete and hit the **Delete** button.

To add links, click on **add new**. Enter the name of the link in the **Name** box and the URL in the **Address** box. The text you enter in the **Description** box will be shown when someone hovers the cursor over the link in the blogroll. You can also select whether the link should be visible or not (invisible links remain in the database, but don't appear in the blogroll—they are like your own private bookmarks):

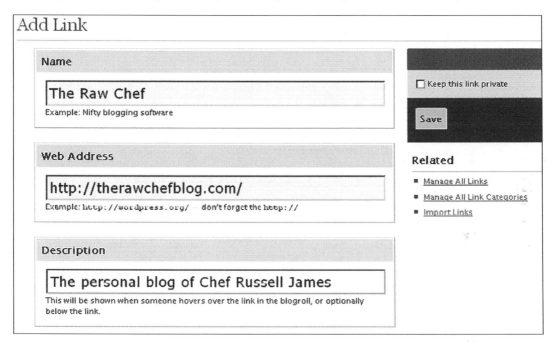

On the second half of the page, choose the category you want the link to appear in. You should also select a target for your link, which tells the user's browser how the link should be opened:

- **_blank** opens the link in a new window.
- **_top** opens the link in the top frame, if your blog is using frames.
- **none** opens the link in the same browser window.

I always select **none** and leave the user to decide whether they want to open the link in a new window (by right clicking it).

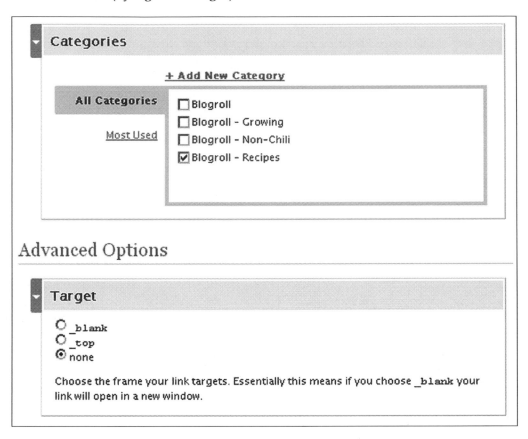

The other options on the **Add Links** page are not as important, and you don't have to use them. The **Link Relationship (XFN)** option allows you to define your relationship to the person you are linking to. It is used by some web applications such as RSS feed readers and search engines. The options under **Advanced** allow you to add an image to the link (this is displayed next to the link in some themes); include the RSS feed for the blog you are linking to (again, used by some themes); add notes (these are not displayed in your blog, they are just for your own reference); and give a rating for the link (some themes display the highest rated links first). Once you have finished, click the **Save** button and view the blog to see your new blogroll. In the following screenshot, you can see the new categories and links I have added to ChilliGuru:

Feeding Off the Blogosphere

Blogrolls have been around for a long time. Many people regard them as a standard feature on any blog. I tend to agree with that point of view. Generally, I find blogrolls useful and they give me an extra insight into the mind of the blogger by showing me his or her favorite links. However, more and more blogs are choosing not to display a blogroll. Probably the main reason for this decision is the difficulty in maintaining a long list of links and the 'politics' that may arise as decisions have to be made about which to add and which to remove.

As an alternative (or even in addition) to a blogroll, some bloggers now include headlines from other blogs using the RSS feeds from those blogs. Usually they only do this for a handful of their most favorite blogs, maybe no more than five—far fewer than the number of links that normally appears in a blogroll. This is easier to manage as the number of links is smaller, but it still demonstrates the blogger's connectedness to the blogosphere.

[If you run more than one blog, you can use this method to display the latest headlines from your other blog(s).]

There is a widget in WordPress that makes it easy to set this up—we'll run through it for ChilliGuru. In the admin area, click the **Design** tab, then the **Widgets** sub-tab. We'll set up two RSS widgets. Under **Current Widgets**, select **Sidebar 2** from the drop-down box and click **Show**. In the **Available Widgets** list, find the **RSS** widget and click **Add** twice to place two instances of the widget in **Sidebar 2**. Move the two new widgets up the list so they are just above the **Links** widget:

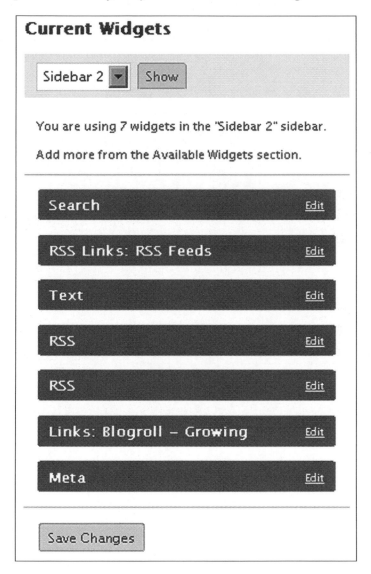

Click on **Edit** for the first **RSS** widget and enter the RSS feed URL for the blog you want to link to, a title for the feed, and the number of posts you wish to display. Leave the checkboxes empty, as we just want to display the headlines for the items in the feed. Click the **Change** button:

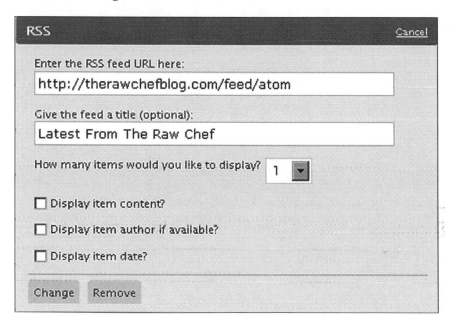

Repeat the configuration process for the second **RSS** widget by entering the details for the second blog you would like to link to. Click the **Save Changes** button.

If you view the blog, you will see the latest posts being pulled from the blogs you linked to:

We need to fix the styling for the titles. To do this, click the **Theme Editor** sub-tab and add the following CSS rule at the bottom of **style.css**:

```
.widget_rss h3 a{text-decoration:none;color:#DF5E37;}
```

Click the **Update File** button. The titles should now match the rest of the sidebar:

The Importance of Comments

Comments are probably one of the most important elements of blogging. They allow a high level of interactivity and really connect the blogger to his or her readership. It's all about being part of a **conversation**; a principle that forms the bedrock of the live Web.

The conversational dimension of comments allows the business blogger to open a dialog with their customers, stakeholders, investors, or whomever their blog is aimed at. Comments also provide a great connection with the rest of the blogosphere. A good blogger should also be an active commenter on other people's blogs. Again, it demonstrates being part of an ongoing and far-reaching conversation. Commenting on other people's blogs also offers an opportunity for you to present yourself to their readership, which may entice new readers to your own blog.

Fishing for Comments

There are several strategies that can be employed to increase the chances of people leaving comments for your posts. The first is simply to ensure that your content is engaging, interesting, and raises some tangible issues or opinions. A dull post that doesn't really say anything of interest is not going to inspire commenters.

The second is a technique we mentioned in Chapter 5—ask questions. There's no more direct and straightforward approach for soliciting some kind of response than asking a question. Make the questions quite direct and focused so that they are easy to answer in a fairly short comment. If the question is too complicated or ethereal, it will be unlikely to inspire readers to hit the comment button.

Another approach is to set tasks or assignments for your readers. Of course, this should not be anything too difficult or time consuming, but something fun or interesting. It may not be appropriate for all types of blogs. However, many bloggers who are experts or 'gurus' in their field use their blogs to impart knowledge to their readers; they're teachers. For example, ChilliGuru may write a post about a new recipe that's a variation on the traditional *Thai Green Curry*. He could then ask his readers to come up with their own versions of the recipe and post them as comments. This approach could spark a lively thread of comments as readers submit recipes and critique each others' recipes. Another example could be asking your readers to come up with the slogan for your next advertising campaign. You could even run this type of thing as a contest, rewarding the best suggestion with a prize.

Another approach to encourage comments and feedback is to involve your readers in the research and development of new products and services. Get them involved in the early days of R&D. Not only does this encourage interactivity on your blog, it's a great form of market research. Your readers are likely to be potential customers for your product or service, so if they have been involved in the development of your products they may well feel a sense of 'ownership' for them, which is likely to reflect positively in your sales figures.

Managing the Conversation

You should assume the role of **facilitator** or **moderator** in any discussions that arise in the comments section of your blog. This means being active in the comment threads. Don't think that just because you did all the work in writing the original post, you can hand it over to your readers and let them run with it. You should always try to steer the debate in the direction you would like it to go.

This involves responding to comments as much as possible. By doing so, you demonstrate that you are listening to the people who take the time to leave comments, which will encourage them and others, to respond some more. Obviously, your time restraints may make it difficult to give in-depth responses to every comment, but do ensure you set aside some time to get involved. At the very least try to engage with new commenters, those who are frequent contributors, and those who leave negative comments (more on this later). Remember, it's a conversation.

Moderation

Some staunch 'old-school' bloggers may balk at the notion of moderating or censoring comments. They may argue that it stifles the debate and erodes the free-speech ethos of social media. These may be worthy values for a personal blogger, but for any business, reputation management is extremely important. No profit-making organization can allow complete openness on what is, essentially, its own communication channel.

WordPress gives you the tools to moderate comments on your blog. I suggest you use these and ensure you have a system in place that allows you to control what's published. You can set this up in the WordPress admin area. Select the **Settings** tab and the **Discussion** sub-tab. I recommend that you approve every comment. This can be done by checking all the boxes in the top half of the page:

Discussion Settings

Default article settings	☑ Attempt to notify any blogs linked to from the article (slows down posting.)
	☑ Allow link notifications from other blogs (pingbacks and trackbacks.)
	☑ Allow people to post comments on the article
	(These settings may be overridden for individual articles.)
E-mail me whenever	☑ Anyone posts a comment
	☑ A comment is held for moderation
Before a comment appears	☑ An administrator must always approve the comment
	☑ Comment author must fill out name and e-mail
	☑ Comment author must have a previously approved comment

You will receive an email every time someone leaves a comment and the comment will not be published until you have approved it. Approving every comment will obviously take more time, but it does give you complete control over what appears on your blog. As your blog becomes more popular and more comments are being left, you may consider reducing your workload by lowering the moderation level for comments. For example, remove the requirement for an administrator to always approve each comment, but keep the requirement that the comment author must have a previously approved comment. Continue monitoring your comments and see if this level of moderation works for you. However, unless you *really* can't find the time to moderate every comment, I would recommend keeping the moderation levels at their highest setting.

I also recommend displaying a **comments policy** on your blog. This clearly lays out the 'rules of engagement' for commenters. It may also help readers who are staunchly 'anti-moderation' to understand why, as a business, you need to moderate comments. Remember, you may be held legally responsible for any content that appears on your blog. This means there is a certain amount of risk, which any business must seek to mitigate. Making this clear in your comments policy may help readers understand why you moderate all comments. I have placed a sample comments policy on ChilliGuru. It's a static page under the **About** section: `http://blog.chilliguru.com/about/commentspolicy/`.

Comments Policy

We welcome comments from our readers and value your contributions. We do moderate all comments to ensure our legal obligations as a responsible publisher are met. We reserve the right to edit or remove any comment that we believe is inappropriate. We will not publish any of the following:

- Potentially libelous comments
- Obscene or sexually explicit comments
- Hateful or mean-spirited comments
- Plagiarized material or material that violates intellectual property rights
- Commercial promotions or spam
- Comments that are off topic or that link to material that is off topic
- Comments that violate any law

We ask for your co-operation by ensuring any comments you post meet the above guidelines.

Dealing with Negative Comments

At some point you're going to come across a certain amount of negativity from commenters. This may take the form of constructive criticism and reasoned argument against your post, or it may be random insults and seemingly off-topic **flaming**.

If you're not familiar with the term, this is how Wikipedia defines flaming:

> **Flaming** *is the hostile and insulting interaction between Internet users. [...] An Internet user typically generates a flame response to other posts or users posting on a site, and such a response is usually not constructive as it does not clarify a discussion, and does not persuade others. Sometimes, flamers attempt to assert their authority, or establish a position of superiority over other users. Other times, a flamer is simply an individual who believes he or she carries the only valid opinion. This leads him or her to personally attack those who disagree. Occasionally, flamers wish to upset and offend other members of the forum, in which case they can be called* **trolls**. *Most often, however, flames are angry or insulting messages transmitted by people who have strong feelings about a subject.*

Dealing with flame comments is simple—hit **Delete**; don't give them the time of day. You should also block persistent offenders by using the **Comment Blacklist** at the bottom of the **Discussion Settings** page:

Comment Blacklist

When a comment contains any of these words in its content, name, URL, e-mail, or IP, it will be marked as spam. One word or IP per line. It will match inside words, so "press" will match "WordPress".

```
jollyrodger@hatemail.com
125.10.80.650
http://WeHateChilies.com
```

Dealing with constructive criticism is a slightly more delicate issue. The fact is that this kind of 'negativity' could actually be a good thing. Not only does it bring your shortcomings to your attention, but the fact that it's happening on your territory (that is, your blog) and on your terms make it easier for you to deal with this.

Resist the temptation to delete comments that contain this kind of constructive criticism, instead adopt a cool, calm, and honest approach to answer the issues straightforwardly. Reassure your readers that you have taken the comments on board and either present your argument to show that the comments are not true, or if they are true, explain how you are going to put things right. It's important not to be combative or aloof as this may make matters worse.

The beauty of blogging is that it provides you with a platform to turn these potentially 'negative' opinions into something positive. You have the ability to demonstrate to your readers and customers that you are listening to their constructive criticism and you are constantly working to put things right.

If you have successfully built up and nurtured a loyal community of readers on your blog, you may find that they do some of the work of answering constructive criticism for you. If this is the case, it may not always be necessary for you to immediately jump in on a negative comment. See if any commenter comes to your defense. If they do, there is probably no need to get involved.

Trackbacks

Trackbacks provide a simple way for bloggers to comment on each others' posts via their own blogs. In WordPress, you can leave a trackback to another blogger's post simply by including the permalink for their post in your own post. We have already set up the automatic pinging feature that makes this happen, on the **Discussion Settings** page (highlighted in the following screenshot):

So let's imagine ChilliGuru wants to comment on another blogger's post by using a trackback.

The permalink for the post he wants to comment on is: `http://paulthewlis.com/blog/uncategorized/hello-world/`.

So, ChilliGuru writes a new post and includes the permalink:

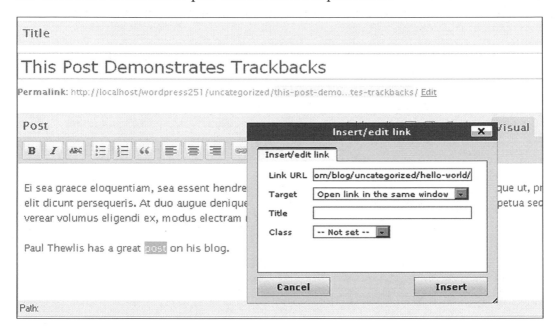

A trackback will be sent to the blog he is linking to, which will appear in the comments for the post:

Likewise, if someone links to a ChilliGuru post from their blog, the trackback will appear in the comments (of course, because of the moderation settings, ChilliGuru has to approve the comment first):

> « This Post Is A Web Slice
>
> ## One Trackback
>
> 1. By Paul Thewlis » Blog Archive » ChilliGuru Is Right On The Money on May 10, 2008 at 10:20 am
>
>   [...] I just read a great post by ChilliGuru. [...]

Readers can view the post by clicking on the link that appears in the trackback.

Comment and Trackback Spam

Sadly, we live in a world plagued by spam. Blogs are now a target for spammers, as the comment and trackback facilities that feature on most blogs provide spammers with a mechanism to get their message published.

The developers of WordPress have worked hard to free their users from the frustration and inconvenience of spam by providing a service called **Akismet**. The Akismet plugin is provided by default in all WordPress installations. If you haven't done so already, you should activate Aksimet now.

In the WordPress admin area, choose the **Plugins** tab and activate **Akismet**. WordPress will tell you that the plugin has been activated, but you need to enter your WordPress API key:

> **Akismet is almost ready.** You must enter your WordPress.com API key for it to work.
>
> Plugin **activated.**

To get an API key, you need to sign up for an account at WordPress.com. If you already have a WordPress account, head over there and log in. If you don't have one, go to `http://wordpress.com/signup/` and sign up (use a new browser window or tab). You don't need a WordPress.com blog (unless you really want one!), so at the bottom of the sign up page, check **Just a username, please**:

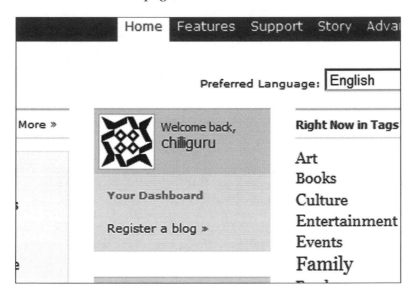

Once you've clicked the confirmation link in the email they send you, log in to your account.

From the WordPress.com home page, click the **Your Dashboard** link:

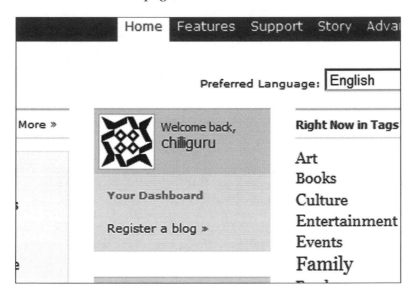

Then, in your dashboard, click the **Profile** link, which is way over on the right-hand side of the page.

You will see your API key as part of your profile information (in the following screenshot, I've hidden mine, for security reasons):

Your Profile and Personal Options

Your WordPress.com API key is: e⁻ ⁻ ⁻˙⁻˙ ⁻˙ ⁻˙ ⁻ ic. Don't share your API key, it's like a password.

Personal Options

Now copy the API key and go back to your blog's admin area.

Click on **enter your WordPress.com API key** link. You will be taken to the **Akismet Configuration** page, where you need to enter your API key:

Akismet Configuration

For many people, Akismet will greatly reduce or even completely eliminate the comment and trackback spam you get on your site. If one does happen to get through, simply mark it as "spam" on the moderation screen and Akismet will learn from the mistakes. If you don't have a WordPress.com account yet, you can get one at WordPress.com.

WordPress.com API Key

Please enter an API key. (Get your key.)

[   ] (What is this?)

☐ Automatically discard spam comments on posts older than a month.

Update options »

Now, Akismet is activated; it will automatically intercept comments it believes to be spam. Akismet holds these spam comments for 15 days before permanently deleting them. Therefore, you should check your Aksimet spam at least once a week to ensure that no genuine comments have been mistaken for spam. You can access Akismet from the **Comments** tab in your WordPress admin area:

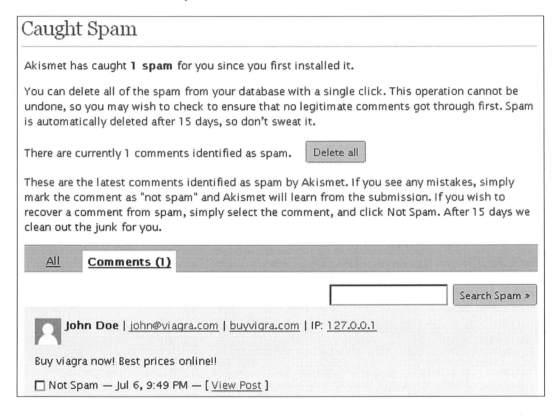

If any genuine comments have been intercepted, you can release them by checking the **Not Spam** box and clicking the **De-spam marked comments** button. You can also delete all the comments by using the **Delete all** button.

Akismet learns from its users, so by 'de-spamming' genuine comments in Akismet, you're helping it to get smarter and doing the whole WordPress community a favor.

By moderating all comments and using Akismet, you shouldn't have the problem of spam comments appearing on your blog. However, if you get to the enviable position of receiving hundreds of comments per day, you may not be able to moderate them all and decide to loosen your moderation settings. If this is the case, you will find that Akismet does a pretty good job. But if you do notice a large amount of spam comments slipping through the net, there are some even tougher anti-spam precautions you can take.

For example, you may decide to add a **Captcha** to your comments form. Captcha is an anti-spam technology that requires a random code to be entered before a form can be submitted. The code is displayed as an image, so it cannot be read by non-human users. This prevents spam bots from using the form. Captcha is an effective anti-spam technology, but it does have drawbacks. It can cause accessibility issues for users who have vision impairment, and users who choose to browse with images turned off in their browser will not be able to see the code image. Therefore, you should consider carefully whether or not to use Captcha. It should be a last resort only to be used if spam is a real problem for you.

If you feel that you really must use Captcha on your comment form, there is a plugin called **Simple Captcha**. You can download it at `http://wordpress.org/extend/plugins/simple-captcha/`. Unzip the file, place the **simple_captcha** folder in your **plugins** directory, log in to WordPress and activate the plugin. You will now have a Captcha image at the end of your comment form:

Installing a Contact Form

Comments provide a great platform for a public discussion on your blog. However, some readers may prefer to contact you privately. You could simply provide an email address on your **About** page or on a dedicated **Contact** page, but you can present a far more professional image for your blog by providing a contact form. It also provides an easy and obvious way of making yourself contactable by other bloggers and the wider blogosphere, enforcing your image as a 'connected' blogger who is open to feedback and discussion.

Using cforms II to Build a Contact Form

We'll set up a contact form for ChilliGuru. To do this we'll use an excellent plugin called **cforms II**, provided by Oliver Seidel (`http://www.deliciousdays.com/plugins/`). First, download the plugin from `http://wordpress.org/extend/plugins/cforms/`. Unzip the package and place the entire **cforms** folder into the ChilliGuru **plugins** directory. Log in to WordPress and activate the plugin.

cforms II is probably the biggest and most flexible plugin that we've installed so far. Click on the **cformsII** tab in the admin area to access the configuration page. As you can see, there are lots of options for cforms, which give you plenty of flexibility. There is also very good documentation, which takes you through all of the features—there is a link to the help files on the configuration page:

You can browse the full documentation at your own pace, but in the meantime, we'll dive right in and create a very simple contact form.

There is a default form already set up, which we can modify to create our own. I have made a couple of changes to the settings. First, I have renamed the default form to **Contact form**. Second, I have changed the top field name to **Email ChilliGuru**. I have left everything else unchanged. Once you've made these changes, click the **Update Settings** button:

Next, we need to check that the email settings are correct.

 Remember, that we do not have email set up on our local development server, so the form will not actually work on our local case study blog, but this step is important when you install cforms II on your live blog.

Expand the **Core Form Admin / Email Options** section on the configuration page by clicking on the plus symbol next to the section heading. Check that the email addresses that appear in the **FROM: email address** and **Admin email address(es)** fields are correct. The **FROM: email address** should be the default email for your blog and you shouldn't change this. You can add more admin emails, separated by commas. You can also have a **BCC** email address. When you're happy with the email addresses, click the **Update Settings** button:

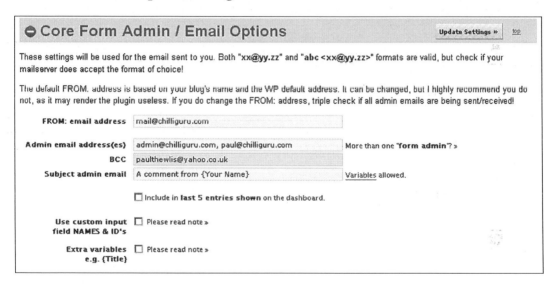

Our basic contact form is now set up and ready for us to embed in a new page. First, we need to enable button support, which makes embedding the form into the page much easier. In the menu at the top of the configuration page, click the **Global Settings** sub-tab. Then, on the **Global Settings** page expand the **WP Editor Button support** section. Mark the checkbox and click the **Update Settings** button:

Now click the main WordPress **Write** tab, followed by the **Page** sub-tab.

 Check that the cforms II button appears on the editor toolbar (as shown in the following screenshot—it's the last button on the right). If not, refresh your browser and it should appear.

I've called the new page **Contact**. In the first part of the page I've put a selection of contact methods:

 It's important to include 'bricks and mortar' contact details whenever possible. This gives your blog a higher level of legitimacy. Research has shown that web users are far more trusting of the websites that display real-world contact details.

Place your cursor on the line below the contact details, and click on the cforms button.

Select the form you would like to insert (in our case, there is only one in the list, but you can create multiple forms using cforms and place different ones on different pages):

The form has now been embedded in the page.

I've placed the **Contact** page under the **About** section of the blog:

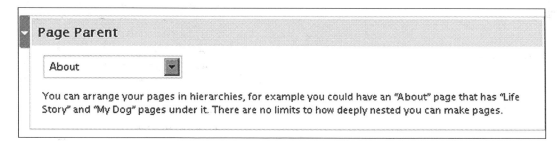

Now click the **Publish** button and view the blog:

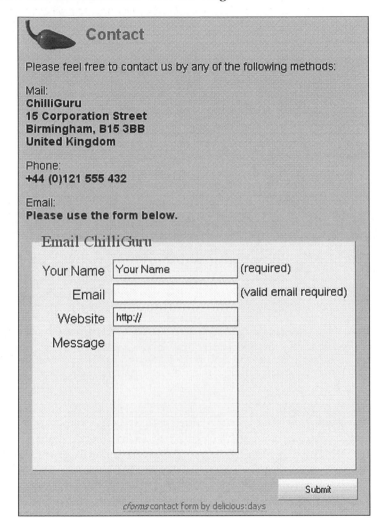

The form looks OK, but it could be improved if the styling matched the rest of the blog.

Styling the Contact Form

The developer of cforms has provided a useful styling configuration page, which is a great help in changing the styling for our forms. Back in the WordPress admin area, select the **cformsII** tab followed by the **Styling** sub-tab. We won't go through a complete re-style of the form, but I will give you a few pointers to get you started. These should be useful when you want to install a contact form on your own blog.

At the top of the **Styling** page, you will see there is a drop-down menu, which provides several ready-made styles. The quickest approach for styling your form is to select the ready-made style that best matches the look you want to achieve and then make minor changes to the CSS to get it just right.

I have chosen the **minimal.css** style as the basis for our ChilliGuru form. Select **minimal.css** from the drop-down and click on the **Select Style** button:

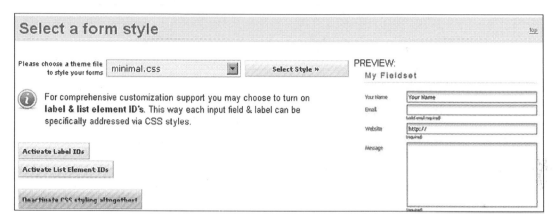

The minimal form style is a pretty good fit for any blog design because it's so simple. All we really need to do is change the color scheme and make sure the font families and font sizes match the overall ChilliGuru style.

The lower half of the cforms **Styling** configuration page contains a CSS editor, similar to the one we've seen in the WordPress **Theme Editor**. We'll use it to edit the CSS rules we need to change.

> I have included the new version of **minimal.css** in the code bundle for this chapter, which you can download from the Packt website. I recommend you follow the steps below, to see all the changes one by one. However, you can place the new **minimal.css** file in the following folder on your local development server (overwriting the old file): **C:\xampp\htdocs\wordpress\wp-content\plugins\cforms\styling**. You will then see the changes in full when you refresh the **Contact** page on the ChilliGuru blog.

The first rule to edit is this one:

```
.cform legend {
  margin:0;
  padding:0;
  font:normal 18px Helvetica;
  color: #aaa;
  letter-spacing:3px;
}
```

Locate the rule in the CSS editor and change the color as follows:

```
.cform legend {
  margin:0;
  padding:0;
  font:normal 18px Helvetica;
  color: #DF5E37;
  letter-spacing:3px;
}
```

The next rule to edit is:

```
ol.cf-ol {
  margin:0!important;
  padding:15px 0 0 0!important;
  border-top:1px solid #f2f2f2;
}
```

Change the border color, as follows:

```
ol.cf-ol {
  margin:0!important;
  padding:15px 0 0 0!important;
  border-top:1px solid #F5AD61;
}
```

The next rule to edit is:

```
.cform label {
  width:90px;
  margin:4px 10px 0 0;
  display:-moz-inline-box; /*for mozilla*/
  display:inline-block; /*for Opera and IE*/
  text-align:left;
  vertical-align:top;
  color: #aaa;
  font:0.9em Trebuchet MS, sans-serif;
}
```

Change the color and font, as follows:

```
.cform label {
  width:90px;
  margin:4px 10px 0 0;
  display:-moz-inline-box; /*for mozilla*/
  display:inline-block; /*for Opera & IE*/
  text-align:left;
  vertical-align:top;
  color: #DF5E37;
  font: 100% Arial, Helvetica, sans-serif;
}
```

The next three rules to edit appear one after the other in the style sheet:

```
.cform input,
.cform textarea,
.cform select {
  padding:3px;
  border:1px solid #aaa;
  font:0.9em Trebuchet MS,sans-serif;
  color:#888;
  background:#ffffff url(../images/field-bg-top.gif)
             repeat-x top left;
  vertical-align:top;
}

.cform input:hover,
.cform textarea:hover,
.cform select:hover  {
  border: 1px solid #FFCC00;
  background:#ffffff url(../images/field-bg-bottom.gif)
             repeat-x bottom left;
}
```

```
.cform input:focus,
.cform textarea:focus,
.cform select:focus   {
  color:#666;
  background:#ffffff url(../images/field-bg-bottom.gif)
            repeat-x bottom left;
}
```

Make the following changes:

```
.cform input,
.cform textarea,
.cform select {
  padding:3px;
  border:1px solid #F5AD61;
  font:0.9em Arial, Helvetica, sans-serif;
  color:#800000;
  background:#ffffff;
  vertical-align:top;
}

.cform input:hover,
.cform textarea:hover,
.cform select:hover   {
  border: 1px solid #DF5E37;
  background:#ffffff;
}

.cform input:focus,
.cform textarea:focus,
.cform select:focus   {
  color: #DF5E37;
  background:#ffffff;
}
```

The next rule to edit is this one:

```
span.reqtxt,
span.emailreqtxt {
  margin:0px 5px 7px 98px;
  display: block;
  vertical-align:top;
  color: #aaa;
  font-size:0.7em;
  line-height:1.2em;
}
```

Change the color, as follows:

```
span.reqtxt,
span.emailreqtxt {
  margin:0px 5px 7px 98px;
  display: block;
  vertical-align:top;
  color: #800000;
  font-size:0.7em;
  line-height:1.2em;
}
```

We're almost done—we just need to edit the CSS for the **Submit** button:

```
.cform input.sendbutton {
  width:100px;
  padding:2px;
  margin: 0 0 0 100px;
  font-size:0.8em;
  background:url(../images/button-bg.gif) repeat-x;
  border:1px solid #adadad!important;
  border-left-color:#ececec!important;
  border-top-color:#ececec!important;
}
```

Make the following changes (note that I've added two new declarations at the end of the rule):

```
.cform input.sendbutton  {
  width:100px;
  padding:2px;
  margin: 0 0 0 100px;
  font-size:12px;
  background:#F5AD61;
  border: 1px solid #DF5E37;
  border-left-color: 1px solid #DF5E37;
  border-top-color: 1px solid #DF5E37;
   color: #DF5E37;
   font-weight: bold;
}
```

And finally, add the following new rule straight after the one we just edited:

```
.cform input.sendbutton:hover {
       background: #800000;
       border: 1px solid #F5AD61;
       color: #F5AD61;
       font-weight: bold;
}
```

Now click the **Update Changes** button for the CSS editor and view the blog. You will see that the contact form now matches the search box and the FeedBurner subscription box in the sidebar. Hover the cursor over the input boxes to see the full effect:

Preventing Contact Form Spam

We saw earlier in the chapter that comment forms can cause a spam problem. Unfortunately, the same is true for contact forms. Spam bots trawl the web looking for unprotected forms and then use them to send spam. There's a chance they could find the contact form on your blog.

Luckily cforms provides a couple of features to help prevent spamming via your contact form. You can use a Captcha image or a verification question. As we discussed earlier, Captcha images can cause accessibility and usability issues. However, the verification question approach is less prone to accessibility problems. The person using the contact form is asked a very simple question; they cannot submit the form unless they answer it correctly. The questions are so easy that no human user is likely to get them wrong, but a spam bot is unlikely to get the answer right as it's not smart enough to understand the question.

No anti-spam protection can be guaranteed 100% effective. The verification question method is fairly sound, but spammers are constantly improving their techniques and re-programming their evil bots. Some people suggest that it may be possible to programme a spam bot and increase its chances of answering verification questions correctly. So far this doesn't seem to have caused any major problems, but it's always a possibility that your spam guards could be breached. Sadly, that's the world we live in.

If your contact form begins to generate large amounts of spam, you can add one of the security measures provided by cforms. We'll run through the process of setting up the verification questions.

Go back to the cforms configuration page in your WordPress admin area. At the end of the list of fields for our contact form, there is an icon that enables you to add a new field. Go ahead and click it:

In the new **Field Name** box, enter the text: **Verification question**. In the **Type** drop-down select **Visitor verification (Q&A)** and then click the **Update Settings** button:

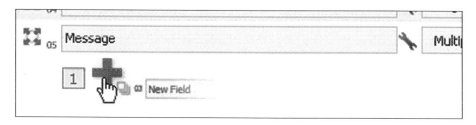

When you view the blog you will see that the verification question has been added at the end of the contact form:

By default, cforms has three different verification questions, but you can add more to make the form even more secure. When devising new questions, make sure they are simple enough for anyone to answer. They must also be completely unambiguous so that there is only one possible answer. Simple math questions are good as they are so unambiguous. For example, "Twelve minus two equals".

You can add more questions by clicking the **Global Settings** sub-tab and then expanding the **Visitor Verification Settings (Q&A)** section. Enter the questions in the format: **Twelve minus two equals=10**:

Summary

In this chapter, we discussed the importance of connecting with the blogosphere. We began by defining what the blogosphere is and why you need to be an active part of it. We then discussed a simple strategy for engaging with other bloggers. We also looked at the practical steps you need to take in becoming a well-connected blogger, including managing your blogroll, using RSS feeds to display content from other blogs, how to manage comments, and how to make yourself as approachable as possible by using a contact form.

In the next chapter, we will look at the important subject of web analytics. You will learn how to measure the success of your blog by analyzing the visitor data.

9
Analyzing Your Blog Stats

How do you know if anyone's reading your blog? Is the time and effort you put in showing any results? These are some questions you should be able to answer. The whole point of blogging is to help your business, so you need to be sure you're reaching your target audience. In this chapter, we will look at statistics that are essential for measuring your success and the tools that can help you gather them.

Key Performance Indicators

As with any other aspect of business, measuring the performance of your blog is the key to understanding its value and success. There are many different metrics that can inform you about the progress of your blog. Some bloggers look at many indicators and aggregate them to give a very detailed analysis of their blog. Others prefer to focus on a smaller set of metrics.

The information you choose to measure the success of your blog will be largely dependent on your blogging goals, which you decided in Chapter 2. For example, if you see your blog as a vehicle for building your company brand, then the number of unique visitors may be relevant. If the main aim of your blog is to improve communications and open a dialog with your existing customer base, then the number of comments may be more important to you.

Broadly speaking there are five groups of **KPIs (key performance indicators)** that can be applied to a blog:

- Traffic
- Subscribers
- Number (and quality) of comments and feedback
- Search engine results
- Inbound links

In this section, we'll take a look at each of these in turn, before moving on to examine the tools we can use to measure them.

Traffic

Raw traffic is probably one of the simplest metrics for measuring the success of any website, including your blog. However, even this seemingly simple indicator has several facets, as there are different ways of measuring it. Different people will prefer different methods.

Hits

These days, **hits** are pretty much obsolete as a method of measuring traffic. A 'hit' is a request sent to a web server for a file. In the early days of the Web, hits were regarded as an important statistic. However, as web analytics became more sophisticated, people began to realize that server hits are a fairly meaningless way of measuring traffic. This is because a web page can contain several links to files on the server. For example, if a page has six images, there will be seven hits on the server when the page is requested (one for the page itself, and then one for each of the images). So you could increase your hits simply by adding more images to the page!

The term 'hits' has slipped into common usage over the years; people use it (wrongly) when they are talking about traffic in general.

Unique Visitors

The number of **unique visitors** is one of the most important metrics for measuring a blog's traffic. It is particularly favored by potential advertisers, so if you ever decide to sell advertising on your blog, you will need to have this statistic available. It's basically the number of different people who visit a website.

It can be difficult to measure unique visitors. The only way any website owner could be certain about the number of unique visitors would be to have every visitor register for a user account and log in each time they use the site. Obviously, this isn't practical! Unfortunately, each of the two main ways of measuring unique visitors has pitfalls.

The first approach is to log the IP address of each visitor. Every device that connects to the internet has an IP address, but the accuracy of this approach can't be guaranteed. This is because some ISPs and company networks issue their users with dynamic IP addresses. This means that each time a user connects to the internet they have a different IP address. In this situation, the same person visiting a website at different times would be counted as a different unique visitor each time. A second problem arises because users on some large networks are all connected to the internet via the *same* IP address. So, if there were 20 people on such a network, all accessing the same website independently, it would only be counted as one unique visitor.

The second approach for measuring unique visitors is to use **cookies**. A cookie is a snippet of text, usually containing a unique reference code, which is saved by the user's browser when they visit a website. Each web page that uses this approach also contains a small piece of JavaScript (usually in the page footer), which detects the cookie (or installs it, if it's the user's first visit) and sends information back to the analytics software. This avoids the problems that may arise with the IP address logging approach, but has its own limitations. The problem is that some people delete cookies or choose not to accept them, as they believe they pose a security and/or privacy threat. They may also disable JavaScript in their browsers, for similar reasons.

Visits

Hopefully, each unique visitor will visit your blog more than once. This is measured simply as **visits**. It is a more reliable statistic than unique visitors because it is easier to measure. However, most analytics software packages add a little more depth to the measurement of visits than simply the headline number. For example, it's also useful to know how long each visit lasted. This gives you a good indication of how well your readers are engaging with your content, and whether or not they find it interesting. Obviously, if a visit only lasts a few seconds, you know the visitor was not impressed and clicked away from your blog very quickly.

Different analytics software has different ways of defining what a visit is. A **visit** is usually classed as a continuous series of page views, uninterrupted by any period of inactivity.

Page Views

Page views are the total number of pages read by all your visitors. Basically, this statistic tells you how many of your blog's pages have been opened on a daily, weekly, or monthly basis. It's also useful to know the average page views per visit. This tells you how many pages, on average, a visitor looks at each time they visit your blog. It gives a good indication of how engaged users are and how 'sticky' your content is. Low average page views show that visitors soon get bored of your content and are not motivated to read another post.

You should also pay attention to the number of views for individual pages. From this data, you can identify which of your posts are popular with your readership. This helps you to create content that your readers are more likely to enjoy.

Subscribers

Blogging adds another dimension to web analytics—it's not just about traffic to web pages. As most of the blog content is syndicated via RSS feeds, bloggers need to measure how many subscribers they have.

Subscriber data seems particularly important when you consider who your subscribers are. Quite simply, they're your biggest fans, your loyal supporters (the people who are waiting for your next post). They have taken the effort to subscribe to your blog and in doing so, are making it clear they are interested in what you're saying on a long-term basis. These people are far more valuable than the casual readers who just stop by your blog now and again, or those who may only ever visit once. As we discussed in Chapter 7, subscription is extremely important in blogging. Therefore, it's essential you know the levels of subscription for your blog. As you already know, there are two types of subscription: **RSS** and **email**.

RSS Subscriptions

RSS feeds are notoriously difficult to track and measure. However, **FeedBurner** provides statistics about how many people are subscribed to your feed. This is one of the main attractions of FeedBurner and has made it very popular with bloggers. The problem is that counting the number of feed readers is not an exact science. This means you are likely to see anomalies and inconsistencies in your FeedBurner stats. Even so, the stats are better than nothing and will at least give you a good indication of the progress of your feed subscriptions, even if the numbers are not exact.

Email Subscriptions

Measuring the number of people who are subscribing to your feed by email can be done much more accurately than for RSS readers. It's simply a matter of counting up the email addresses in your subscription list. Again, FeedBurner is a useful tool for providing email subscription options to your readers (as we saw in Chapter 7). We will be looking at FeedBurner stats in more detail later in this chapter.

Comments and Feedback

The number of comments that your blog receives is another statistic that helps you measure your success. Watching the number of commenters increase as your blog gains popularity is not only satisfying, but should be regarded as a key indicator of your performance.

By admin | Posted in Planting and Growing | Tagged fertilizer, pruning, seeds | Comments (11)

However, along with the simple number of comments, it's also important to consider the quality of the comments that people are leaving. Carefully considered, on-topic comments that, in themselves, are good content for your blog are far more valuable than short one-liners that don't really say very much. You will receive many comments that simply say, 'Great post! ☺'. They're nice to have, but they have most likely been left so that the commenter gets a link back to his or her own blog.

Along with the comments, you should also take note and count the amount of feedback you receive by email or through your contact form. Again, as these will increase in volume, it will give a fairly good indication that your blog is becoming more widely read and is making an impact in the blogosphere. As with comments, you should also take note of the quality of the feedback you receive and whether it is negative or positive.

Search Engine Results

Another important performance indicator is how well you rank in the search engines for certain keywords. Along with your regular web analytics, this is something that you should constantly monitor. We touched on this topic in Chapter 6, but I raise it again here to remind you that monitoring your SEO performance should be a routine part of your blog analysis.

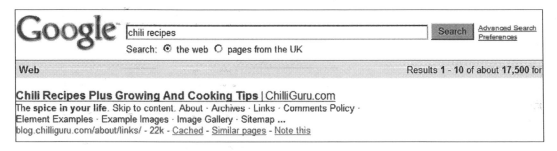

Inbound Links

Again, we mentioned this in Chapter 6, but as with search engine results, it's something you need to constantly monitor and treat as part of your web stats analysis. Having plenty of inbound links is not only good for your search engine rankings, but it also demonstrates how well you are connecting with the blogosphere. There are several ways you can measure how many inbounds links there are to your blog.

The first is simply to count the number of trackbacks coming in to your blog. Remember, a trackback is a link from another blogger when they refer to one of your posts.

You can also use search engines to check your incoming links. By typing `links:blog.chilliguru.com` into Google, you will see a list of all the incoming links that Google has indexed for ChilliGuru. You can do this for any domain. Your Google Page Rank is also largely based on incoming links, so periodically checking it can give a good indication of your blog's performance. To check the Page Rank for any web page, you can use the SEOQuake Firefox plugin that we installed in Chapter 6 or download the **Google Toolbar** from `http://toolbar.google.com`. The following screenshot shows the Google Page Rank for `http://www.packtpub.com` using the Google Toolbar:

Technorati provides another way of monitoring your incoming links. Each blog listed on Technorati has something they call **authority**. The authority of a blog is based on the number of incoming links to that blog — the higher the authority, the more incoming links the blog has. The following screenshot shows the authority for `http://scobleizer.com`:

Web Analytics Tools

Now you know the kind of things you need to be monitoring, let's take a look at some of the tools that can help you do this.

There are dozens of web analytics tools available. They have varying degrees of complexity and widely varying costs—some of the high-end solutions require expensive licenses. However, the good news for bloggers is that there are some great solutions that don't cost a penny. We'll take a look at two, here: WordPress.com stats and Google Analytics.

WordPress.com Stats

The hosted version of WordPress includes a great stats system. Many self-hosted WordPress users were green with envy when they saw what WordPress.com bloggers got to play with. So the WordPress.org community (specifically, Andy Skelton) came up with a plugin that makes WordPress.com stats available to anyone with a self-hosted blog.

We'll run through the process for installing the plugin. Go to `http://wordpress.org/extend/plugins/stats/` and download the plugin. Unzip the package and upload the **stats.php** file to your blog's **plugins** directory. (There's no point installing this on your ChilliGuru local development server as no one else can visit that blog except you.)

As with the Akismet plugin we looked at in the last chapter, you need your WordPress.com API key in order to make the stats plugin work. Log in to your admin area and activate the plugin. You will be asked to enter your API key. Once you've done so, the plugin is ready to start collecting your blog's stats.

To access your stats page, click on the **Blog Stats** sub-tab below the main **Dashboard** tab.

 When you first install the plugin, it will take a while for any stats to come through, so for the time being your stats page probably has a message telling you to wait patiently.

The beauty of the WordPress.com Stats system is its simplicity. It doesn't over-complicate things by providing too much information. In fact, for many bloggers WordPress.com Stats provides all the information they need (or want) to know.

I'll run through a few of the major features. When you click on the **Blog Stats** sub-tab, you will be asked to log in to WordPress.com—you need to use your WordPress.com login details, not the login for your blog.

 At the time of writing, ChilliGuru was still 'in development' and had not been released as a live blog. This means that visitor numbers you see in the following screenshots are very small, but they still illustrate how WordPress.com stats work.

At the top of the stats page you will notice a large graph, which gives you an overview of page visits by **Days**, **Weeks**, or **Months**:

The points on the graph are clickable. When you click on one you will be shown more details for that particular day:

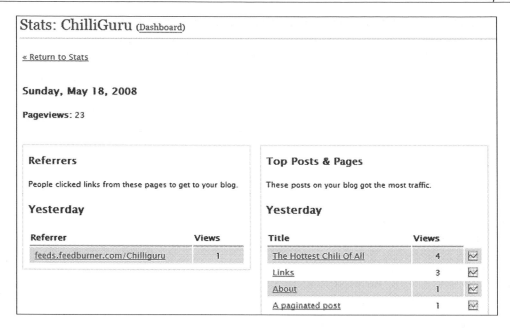

Below the graph on the main stats dashboard page, you will see more information about your blog. One of the good things about WordPress.com stats is that everything appears on one page.

The first stat you can see is **Referrers**. This tells you where your visitors are coming from. It's extremely important to know who your best referrers are as this tells you which of your relationships with other bloggers and websites are more important. As we discussed in Chapter 8, building relationships with the rest of the blogosphere is the key to your success, so being able to monitor your progress in this respect is very useful:

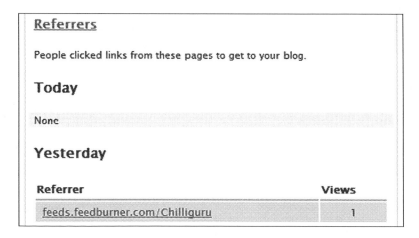

The dashboard gives you an overview of your most recent stats. You can get more historical information for each statistic by clicking on the headings. This is the information you can see by clicking on the **Referrers** heading:

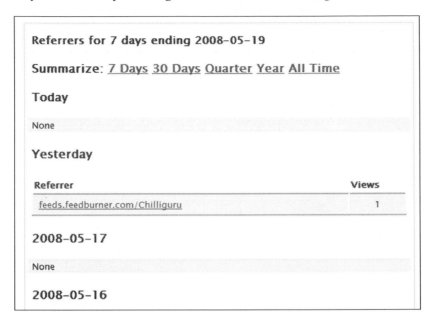

As you can see from the preceding screenshot, you can see data for different periods by clicking on the **Summarize** links. The data in the preceding screenshot is for the last seven days.

Next to the **Referrers** data is another very important piece of information for bloggers. **Top Posts & Pages** tells you what is the most popular content on your blog. This will really help you to tailor your posts for your readers. You can easily see which posts work well and which don't, and therefore give them more of the kind of content they really like:

Along with the **Referrers** data, **Top Posts & Pages** can also help you monitor the effect of other bloggers linking to one of your posts. For example, if a well-known blogger decides to link to one of your posts, there is a good chance you will see an increase in the number of people viewing that post on the day he or she links to you.

Search Engine Terms tell you what people are searching for in order to find your blog via the search engines. This is very useful for your keyword research that we discussed in Chapter 6. Hopefully, as time goes by, you will see patterns emerging in the search engine terms people are using. This will tell you the best keywords to use in your posts and post titles.

Clicks tell you which links to external blogs and websites are most popular on your blog. This is useful information for building up a profile of your readers. It helps you to understand what they find interesting, and the types of blogs and websites they want to visit. This will help you to create content your readers are likely to enjoy and engage with. It also allows you to monitor the blogs and websites they are visiting. By doing so, you may be able to identify opportunities for cross-promotion. You're sending traffic to them, so it may be that they could send traffic to you.

The **Blog Stats** box displays a cumulative total of all the page views for your blog, as well as your best ever day and today's running total:

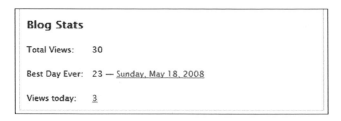

And finally, the **Incoming Links** section lists the most popular links to your blog that have been detected by **Google Blog Search** (http://blogsearch.google.com). You can see more incoming links by clicking on **More>>**. Again, this is useful in tracking your referrals and also monitoring the information that Google has indexed for your blog:

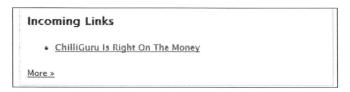

You can make your blog stats available to any other WordPress.com user simply by entering their registered email address in the **Stats Access** section:

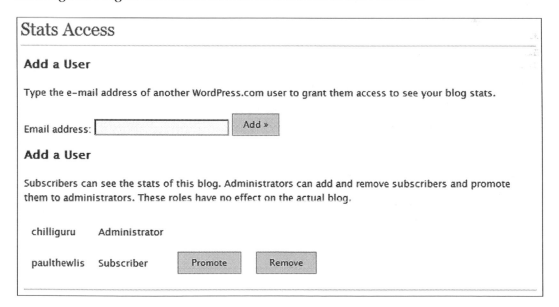

Any users you add under **Stats Access** can view your blog stats either from their WordPress.com dashboard or from the admin area in their own blog (if they have a self-hosted WordPress blog with the WordPress.com Stats plugin installed). You can, of course, view your own blog stats via your WordPress.com dashboard.

Google Analytics

For many bloggers WordPress.com stats provide all the information they need. However, if you want to analyze your blog in more detail then you might want to use Google Analytics.

 Google Analytics works perfectly well alongside WordPress.com stats, so you can have both installed at the same time.

Google Analytics is a free service, which provides some pretty powerful features. Before we go through the process of signing up for a Google Analytics account, we will install a WordPress plugin that makes it easy to integrate Google Analytics into your blog.

The plugin is called **WP Google Analytics**, by Aaron D. Campbell. Go to `http://wordpress.org/extend/plugins/wp-google-analytics/` and download it. Unzip the package and place the **wp-google-analytics.php** file in your blog's `plugins` directory. Log in to your admin area and activate the plugin. Then click the **Settings** tab followed by the **Google Analytics** sub-tab—you'll see the plugin's configuration page. At this point, we need to sign up for a Google Analytics account, so open up another browser window and go to Google's home page.

To get started with Google Analytics you need a Google account. If you don't already have a Google account, click the **Sign in** link in the top right-hand corner of Google home page, then follow the **Create an account now** link.

Once you have a Google account, go to `http://www.google.com/analytics/` and sign in with your Google account details.

On the next page, click the **Sign Up** button:

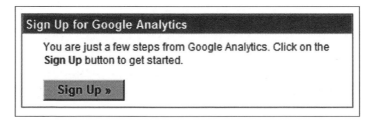

On the following page, enter the details for your blog:

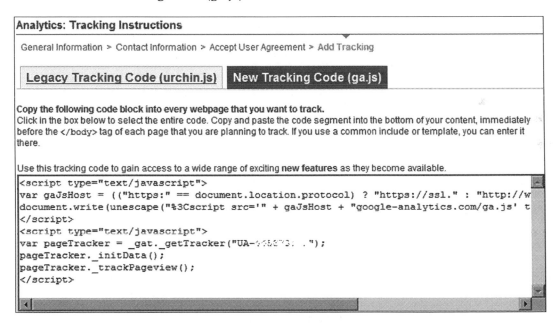

On the next page, enter your contact information, and then on the final page, accept the terms and conditions.

You will then be taken to a page that contains your Google Analytics tracking code. Click the **New Tracking Code (ga.js)** tab:

> The legacy code is there for people who are old users of Urchin. Google acquired the Urchin software company in 2005 and it then became Google Analytics.

Select all of the code in the text area and copy it to your computer's clipboard. Now return to your WordPress admin area. On the Google Analytics plugin configuration page, paste your code into the box. You should also select the four checkboxes shown in the following screenshot, and then click the **Update Options** button:

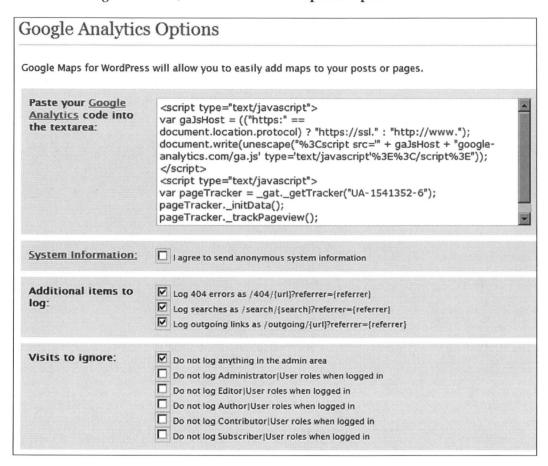

You now have Google Analytics installed on your WordPress blog. Unfortunately, it will take up to 24 hours before any data is available in your Google Analytics account. You may want to return to the next section tomorrow, when you have some data to look at.

Using Google Analytics

You can log in to Google Analytics at http://www.google.com/analytics. The first page you see shows the **Analytics Settings** for your accounts. This is basically a list of all the websites you are tracking.

You can track several websites using the same Google Analytics account. So if you have other websites besides your blog, you can add them too.

The Dashboard

Click on the **View Reports** link to go to the **Dashboard**. From here you can access all the data for your blog. The **Dashboard** page gives a general overview of the headline numbers, while the menu on the left-hand side gives you options to drill down deeper. As you can see, there are quite a lot more features than in WordPress.com stats; we'll run through some of the more useful ones for bloggers.

The top half of the dashboard shows a graph and some of the most important statistics:

By default, the graph shows visits but you can have it display different metrics, and even compare two by clicking the drop-down arrow next to **Visits**:

You will then be taken to the page as shown in the following screenshot:

You can also select the date range you want to display by clicking on the date:

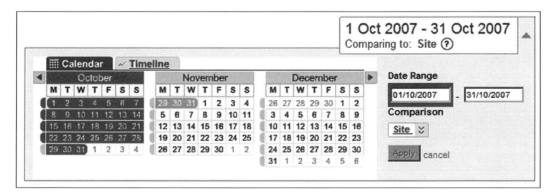

Most of the stats under the **Site Usage** heading are self explanatory, with one exception: **Bounce Rate**. The bounce rate is the percentage of visits in which the visitor left your blog from the page they entered—it was the only page they visited. A high bounce rate means that visitors are not clicking around your blog; they're leaving virtually straightaway. You can lower the bounce rate by making sure that your content (particularly on the home page) is engaging and tailored to the readers you are targeting.

The second half of the dashboard gives you an overview of the three other reporting categories: **Visitors**, **Traffic Sources**, and **Content**. It also shows the **Map Overlay** overview. We will be looking at each of these in more detail, but we will access them from the left-hand menu.

Visitors

Click on **Visitors** in the left-hand menu. The menu expands and you are taken to the **Visitors Overview**. Now click on **Map Overlay** in the menu:

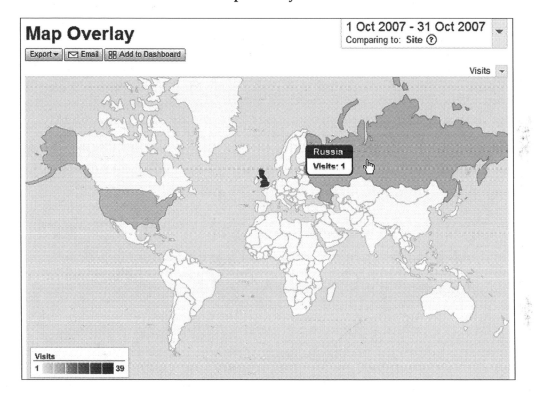

You can hover over individual countries to see the number of visitors from there.

This is an interesting feature that gives you geographic data about the visitors to your site. It could be very useful in helping you to tailor your content for the countries from which you receive the most visitors. For example, you may be a blogger-based in the UK and notice that the majority of your readers are from the US. Maybe you should consider adapting your writing so that you are using US spelling. Or consider including cultural references that an American audience is more likely to appreciate. Of course, you need to monitor this carefully. Maybe your US readers like your blog precisely because of the quirky British spellings and its UK cultural bias—changing things might drive them away.

Below the map there is a tabulated break down of the map data. If you click on a country name you are presented with a larger scale map of that country. In the table below the country map, you are presented with data by state, province, or city. Again, clicking on one of the place names will drill down more finely until you come to the most precise location available. The following screenshot shows there were three visitors from Grand Rapids, MI:

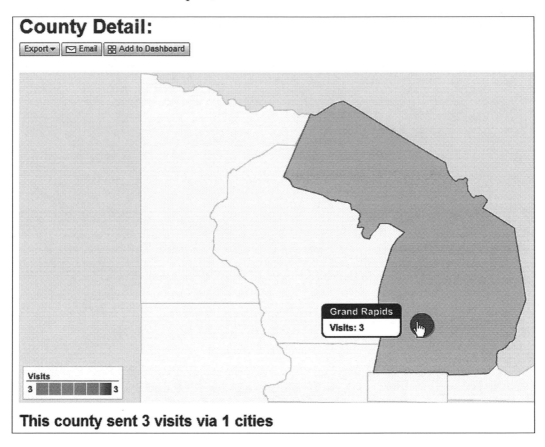

Clicking around on the map is not only useful for your blog stats, but it can also be good fun seeing where in the world your visitors are coming from. You may be surprised by the far-flung destinations!

Also, under the **Visitors** menu is the rather self-explanatory **New vs. Returning**. It's good to have a high percentage of returning visitors, particularly for a blog. It shows you are providing interesting content that people want to come back for time and time again.

Languages is also an interesting statistic. If you are receiving a high proportion of visitors who are non-English speakers, maybe you should consider providing some of your posts translated into their own languages. However, as we saw with the idea of making content country-specific, monitor things carefully—maybe they are reading your blog to improve their English skills and don't want content in their own language!

The **Visitor Trending** menu provides more detailed information on a range of metrics.

The **Visitor Loyalty** menu is fairly self-explanatory. It includes **Recency**, **Length of Visit**, and **Depth of Visit**. This data is another good indication of how 'sticky' your blog's content is. The more engaging and interesting your posts, the more loyal your visitors are likely to be.

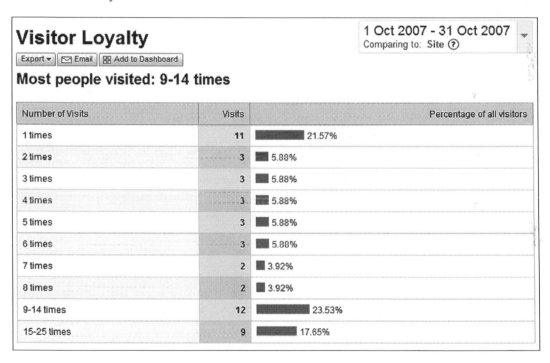

The rest of the data under the **Visitors** menu is mainly concerned with technical information about the people visiting your site. You can see which browsers and operating systems are most used by your readers. Browser type, in particular, is important. It can give an indication of how 'tech-aware' your readers are. For example, older versions of Internet Explorer are likely to be used by less technically aware visitors as opposed to the latest version of Firefox.

It's important to know browser types if you are re-designing your blog or adding new features. You should try to test your blog in the most common browsers used by your visitors as different browsers render some CSS features differently. You need to be sure that your blog looks right in the browsers used by the majority of your readers.

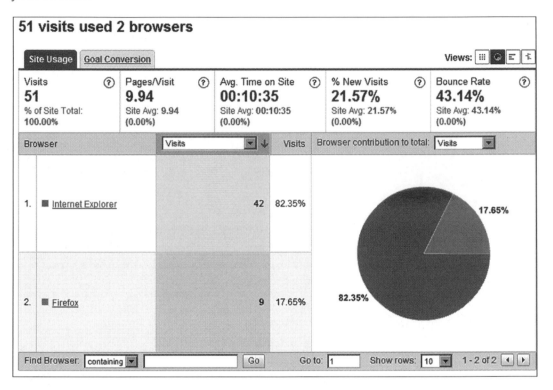

Traffic Sources

Click on **Traffic Sources** in the left-hand menu. The menu expands and you are taken to the **Traffic Sources Overview**.

If you select **Direct Traffic**, you will be shown how many visitors arrived at your blog directly. This means they came to you either by using a bookmark in their browser or by typing your URL into their browser address bar. This can be a useful statistic if you have recently done any offline promotion. For example, people who saw your blog's URL in a newspaper article, on your company letterhead, or in an advert will be direct visitors.

The data under **Referring Sites** is the same as the information we saw for **Referrers** in WordPress.com stats. Again, it's useful for analyzing your connectedness with other bloggers and websites.

The **Search Engines** and **Keywords** data is useful for monitoring your search engine optimization work. Combined with the similar data you receive in WordPress.com stats, it should help you to hone your list of keywords and fine-tune how you are using them in your posts.

The **AdWords** menu allows you to monitor any **AdWords** campaigns you may have running.

Google AdWords

Google AdWords is the search giant's advertising platform—it's how they generate the vast majority of their revenue. I didn't include AdWords in Chapter 7 because, frankly, it's rather beyond the scope of this book. But it does deserve a quick mention here as it is closely integrated with Google Analytics.

As you may be aware, the principle of AdWords is that advertisers bid against each other for certain keywords. The advertisers who place the highest bids get their adverts to appear above all the others. AdWords ads are the sponsored links you see down the right-hand side and at the top of Google search results pages:

)0,000 for **recipes** [definition]. **(0.05 seconds)**

Sponsored Links

Easy **Recipes**
Nutritious & delicious **recipes**
Tefal makes healthy eating easy
www.tefal.co.uk/Tefal

BBC Good Food **Recipes**
Search hundreds of **recipes** and get
top tips from the top chefs.
www.bbcgoodfood.com

Recipe Finder
1000's of **recipes** at the tips of

It's not a promotion technique that's particularly popular with bloggers, for a couple of reasons. First, it can require a fairly substantial budget in order to see any consistent results. Second, bloggers prefer the more 'organic' promotion methods like the ones we covered in Chapter 7. However, if you have a fairly healthy marketing budget for your blog, it might be something you want to try. It's likely to be particularly useful when you first launch your blog as it may provide an early boost in your efforts to build an audience. You can find out more at `http://www.google.com/adwords`.

Content

Much of the data you find here is similar to what's available in WordPress.com stats. However, there are a couple of extra features that are interesting. The information under **Top Exit Pages** tells you from which pages your readers are leaving your blog. If a pattern emerges with a few pages having a particularly high exit rate, it may mean that the posts on those pages are not relevant or interesting to your readers. However, it may just be the case that there is a particularly interesting external link within those posts.

The **Site Overlay** is a very interesting feature that gives you a visual representation of which links on your blog are most popular. For example, you can see at a glance which links people are clicking on your home page. Again, this helps you to build a picture of the kind of content your readers want. The following screenshot shows the site overlay for a post on the ChilliGuru home page—the bars show the percentage of visitors who clicked on each link:

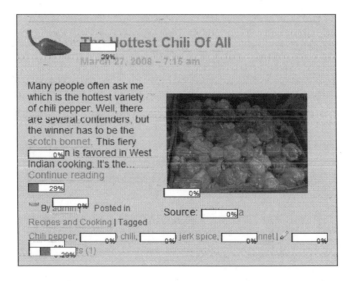

That concludes our very quick introduction to Google Analytics. As you can see, there are a few other features you may wish to explore in more depth. There is detailed documentation about Google Analytics at `http://www.google.com/support/googleanalytics/`.

Not an Exact Science

As you use WordPress.com stats and Google Analytics, you will probably notice some discrepancies between what you think ought to be identical data in both tools. This is largely due to the technical difficulties associated with tracking visitors, some of which were mentioned earlier in the chapter (for example, people deleting cookies or switching off JavaScript in their browsers). It's also down to the fact that they are two different pieces of software developed by different programmers, so each will have its own idiosyncrasies.

The point to bear in mind is that no web analytics software is ever going to be 100% accurate, so it's important not to get too hung up on the exact numbers of visits, page views, unique visitors, or whatever. Instead, use tools like Google Analytics and WordPress.com stats to identify trends and monitor your progress over time as your blog grows. Are the graphs heading North or South?

FeedBurner Stats

As I mentioned earlier in the chapter, counting your subscribers is very important for measuring the success of your blog. FeedBurner provides you with the means to do this. You should be aware that the data it provides is unlikely to be completely accurate because it's very difficult to track RSS subscriptions, but it will give you an idea as to how your feed is performing.

When you log in to FeedBurner you can view your stats under the **Analyze** tab. The **Feed Stats Dashboard** gives you an overview; you can then drill down for more detail using the left-hand menu. There is a drop-down menu on the right that allows you to specify a time period for analysis.

Subscribers

This section gives you two main statistics: **subscribers** and **reach**. The subscriber count is based on an approximation of how many times your feed has been requested in a 24-hour period. It is the approximate number of people who are currently subscribed to your feed. The reach measurement assumes that a certain percentage of your subscribers will be actively engaging in your feed content. It also assumes that there are people engaging with your feed content beyond your known subscriber base (for example on a feed search engine or news filter site). The reach measurement aggregates these two groups to provide an indication of your true audience.

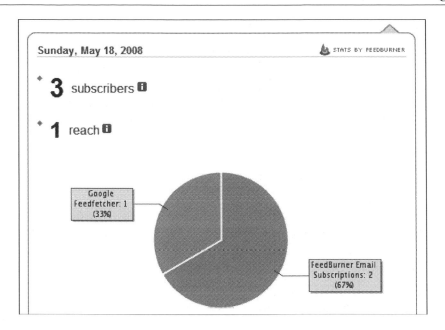

Live Hits

A **Live Hit** is recorded each time your feed is requested by a web browser, feed reader, bot, or other automated service. These are not necessarily subscribers. In fact, most of them probably aren't even subscribers. However, the live hits measurement gives you an idea of the level of exposure of your feed.

Live Feed Hits

Last 41 and a half hours (We're live and on the scene!)

* **18 hits** in the last **41 and a half hours** 🛈

All times are translated to your local time zone.

TIME	USER AGENT	COUNTRY
23:49:10 (2008-5-19)	Google Feedfetcher ▼	United States
20:44:58 (2008-5-19)	Google Feedfetcher ▼	United States
17:44:56 (2008-5-19)	Google Feedfetcher ▼	United States
14:44:54 (2008-5-19)	Google Feedfetcher ▼	United States
12:05:32 (2008-5-19)	Windows RSS Platform ▼	United Kingdom

Item Use

This simply tells you how many items in your feed have been viewed and how many clicks back to your blog there have been.

Uncommon Uses

This measurement tells you about any other uses your feed is being put to, in addition to normal views and subscriptions in web browsers, feed readers, and the like. FeedBurner says that uses like these could be "…a neat little news filter somebody wrote, a blog somebody assembled from feeds, or even blog spam". Obviously, it's useful to know who is using your feed in this way. You should monitor this and if you feel any of these uses are inappropriate, contact the owner of the domain that's listed.

Alexa Rankings

As well as monitoring your blog stats you may also want to keep an eye on your Alexa ranking. Don't get too hung up on the exact ranking, but use it as a way to track your progress. Maybe check your Alexa ranking once a month and make sure it's heading in the right direction. To see your ranking, go to `http://www.alexa.com/site/ds/top_500` and enter your full URL into the search box. As you can see from the following screenshot, a new blog like ChilliGuru that has virtually no traffic at present will have a seemingly abysmal ranking—it's way down at 15,17,552. However, you'll soon notice vast improvements even with fairly modest traffic growth.

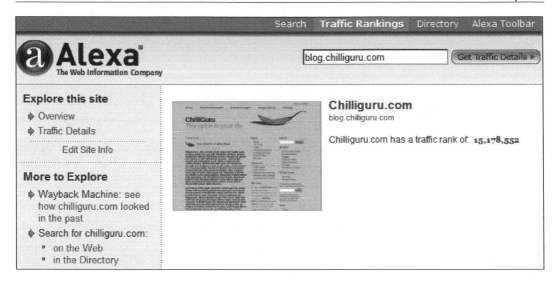

Summary

In this chapter, we examined the data you need to know about your blog and the tools you can use to collect it. We identified five categories or groups of data that comprise your blog statistics: Traffic, Subscribers, Comments, Search Engine Results, and Inbound Links. We looked at WordPress.com stats, Google Analytics, FeedBurner Stats, and how these tools can be used to measure your statistics.

In the next chapter, we will examine a variety of ways to monetize your blog, including advertising revenue and affiliate programs.

10
Monetizing Your Blog

As your blog's traffic levels grow, you may see some potential for revenue generation. Don't expect floods of money—very few bloggers make a fortune from their efforts. But you could reasonably expect to cover your monthly web hosting costs and perhaps a few other expenses, which may at least make your blog self-financing.

Monetization will not be an appropriate option for all business bloggers. This is particularly true for the more corporate blogs. Most cash generating strategies, especially the ones covered in this chapter, involve showing adverts or promoting affiliate programs of some kind. Displaying ads may be completely inappropriate for many corporate blogs; in fact, your company may well have policies that forbid it. However, for smaller, independent operators, selling advertising may be an attractive additional feature for your blog.

You are probably already monetizing your blog, but in indirect ways. Hopefully, you're already seeing the benefits in your business's bottom line. Remember the strategic goals you set for your blog? These may have included things such as, 'building a brand', 'reputation management', and 'improving customer relations'. These are all fairly intangible, but they will certainly add value to your business. If you're achieving those goals, then your blog is already paying you, even if the precise cash amount is hard to quantify.

This chapter is concerned with the direct monetization strategies you can employ. Selling advertising is the most straightforward way of directly monetizing your blog. Advertising, in one form or another, is what this chapter is all about. Whether it's displaying Google AdSense or promoting products as an Amazon associate, we'll discuss some of the best ways of raising revenue through advertising on your blog.

Google AdSense

This is one of the largest advertising programs available to web publishers. In Google's own words:

> *Google AdSense matches ads to your site's content and you earn money whenever your visitors click on them.*

It really is as simple as that. AdSense is a straightforward way of introducing advertising to your blog. It may not be the most profitable form of advertising, but it can generate a steady income stream.

As with most Google applications, AdSense has plenty of advanced features. Most of these are beyond the scope of this chapter, but we will run through a quick-start guide for getting AdSense on your blog. Once you have it set up, you can explore the more advanced features with the help of Google's excellent documentation.

Getting Started with AdSense

First, you need to sign up for an AdSense account. Go to `http://www.google.com/adsense`, click on the **Sign up now** link, and fill out the registration form. Google will then review your application and contact you within a couple of days to let you know if it has been successful. Your application should be approved. The reasons why Google may reject it could be if your blog content breaches their terms of service (for example spam, pornography, and so on), or if they have reason to believe the account may be used for fraudulent activity.

Once you have your account approved, go to the AdSense home page and log in.

The first page you see is the **Reports** page. Obviously, there's nothing to report yet, but when you start using AdSense, you will see information about the number of times your ads are viewed, how many clicks they have attracted, and what your earnings are.

Creating AdSense Ad Units

To set up an ad, click on the **AdSense Setup** tab. You will see that there are several different AdSense products to choose from. To begin with, we'll start with the simplest; click the **AdSense for Content** link. On the next page you can choose the type of ad you want to display. These can be image ads, text ads, or a combination of both. Again, we'll keep it simple, so choose **Text ads only** and click **Continue**.

Next you can choose the format of your ads. We'll be placing our AdSense unit in the sidebar, so we need a vertical format. I think it's also a good idea to begin with a relatively small AdSense unit, so as not to clutter your sidebar too much. If you feel that a small size isn't getting good enough results, you can always experiment with larger formats later. Select **120 x 240 Vertical Banner** from the drop-down menu. For the time being, we'll leave all the other format options (**Colors, Corner Styles**, and **More Options**) to their default settings. Just below the **Colors** section, you'll see there is a **Preview this AdSense unit** link. Click on it to see what the ads will look like:

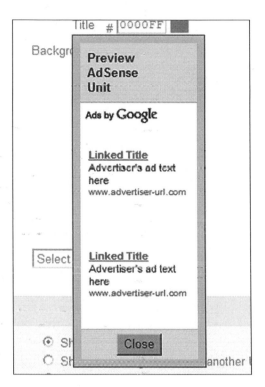

Close the preview window and then click **Continue**. The next page allows you to select channels to track your ads. We'll skip this feature for now; it's something you may want to explore later, when you're more used to the basic functionality of AdSense. Click on **Continue**.

On the next page, you can choose a name for the AdSense unit to help you identify it amongst others in your account (call it something like **Adsense1**). Click on **Submit and Get Code**. The code for the AdSense unit appears in the text area. Now, we need to get this code into WordPress.

Your AdSense unit code:

```
<script type="text/javascript"><!--
google_ad_client = "pub-5346607943336104";
/* Adsense1 */
google_ad_slot = "7305070722";
google_ad_width = 120;
google_ad_height = 240;
//-->
</script>
<script type="text/javascript"
src="http://pagead2.googlesyndication.com/pagead/show_ads.js">
```

Using AdSense in WordPress

You could simply copy and paste the code into a text widget. However, we'll install a plugin that allows more advanced management of your AdSense units. It's called **AdSense Manager**, by Martin Fitzpatrick. The plugin allows you to create and edit AdSense ads from within the WordPress admin area—you don't need to log in to the Google website. It also gives a lot of flexibility for the placement of your ads either in posts and pages, or in widgets. We'll install it for ChilliGuru.

Go to `http://wordpress.org/extend/plugins/adsense-manager/` and download the plugin. Unzip the package and place the **adsense-manger** folder in the **plugins** directory for your ChilliGuru blog. Log in and activate the plugin.

Click the **Settings** tab, and then the **AdSense Manager** sub-tab.

On the **AdSense Manager Options** page, click on the **Manage Ad Units** link from within the **Getting Started** section.

You'll notice the **Be Nice!** section on the options page. This allows you to support the development of the plugin by donating a percentage of your ad space. By default it's set at 3%, which means 3% of your ad space will show ads on behalf of the developer. You can set this to zero, if you wish (the plugin will still work). But in keeping with the spirit of the open-source movement, you might want to make a small donation.

On the **Create Ads** page, paste your Google AdSense unit code into the box and click the **Import to New Ad Unit** button.

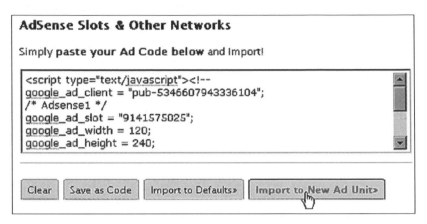

You'll now be taken to a page that allows you to edit your ad. There are three sections: **Basic**, **Appearance**, and **Advanced**. We won't make any alterations at this time, so just click the **Save changes** button.

Now you're on the **Manage Ad Units** page and you can see that AdSense Manager has created a network, Google AdSense, and within that network is our first ad, **ad-1**.

We can now place **ad-1** in the sidebar. Click on the **Design** tab, then the **Widgets** sub-tab. In the **Available Widgets** list, you can see that AdSense Manager has generated a widget called **ad-1**. Add it to **Sidebar 2** below the **Meta** widget and click on **Save Changes**. Now view the blog and you will see the AdSense unit at the bottom of Sidebar 2:

The default AdSense style isn't a great fit with the overall look of ChilliGuru. We could go back to AdSense and edit the colors there. But now you have AdSense set up as a network in AdSense Manager, you can create customized ad units right from your WordPress admin area. So, go back to the admin area and select **Manage Ad Units**.

Click the **Create New Ad** link. On the **Create Ads** page, click the **AdSense Ad Unit** button in the **AdSense Classic** section:

On the next page, in the **Basic** section, enter **ad-2** in the **Name** box:

Leave the **Display Options** at their default settings. Under the **Appearance** section, enter the following settings (note: **Channel**, **Text**, and **Corner Style** will remain unchanged):

- **Ad Type**: Text Only
- **Format**: 120 x 240 Vertical Banner
- **Border**: #F8DC9E
- **Title**: #DF5E37
- **Background**: #F8DC9E
- **URL**: #DF5E37

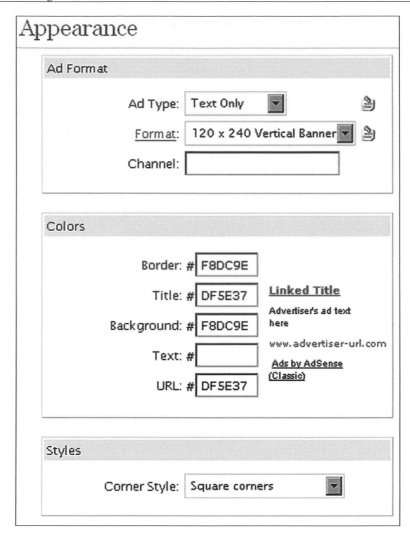

We don't need to change any settings in the **Advanced** section, so click **Save changes**.

Now go back to the **Widgets** page (**Design | Widgets**). You'll see that an **ad-2** widget has been generated. Replace the **ad-1** widget in **Sidebar 2** with **ad-2**. This time, we'll add a title for the widget. Click on the **Edit** link for **ad-2** and enter **Sponsored Links** in the title box:

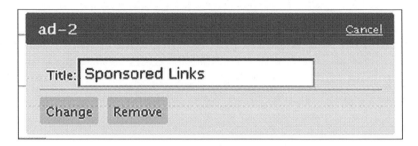

Click on **Change**, and then finally click on **Save Changes**. Now view the blog and you'll see that the new AdSense unit blends in with the ChilliGuru style much better:

You will have realized by now that there are many more features in both Google AdSense and the AdSense Manager plugin that we haven't been able to cover here. Now you understand the basics, take some time to explore the other features and experiment with AdSense to see what works best on your own blog.

Affiliate Programs

Affiliate programs allow web publishers, like bloggers, to earn commission when they refer customers to other businesses' websites. Affiliate marketing offers you the opportunity to earn revenue by generating sales for some of the Web's biggest e-commerce sites.

Amazon Associates

One of the oldest and biggest affiliate programs is **Amazon Associates**, which has been running since 1996. Once you have signed up to be an Amazon Associate (or affiliate), you can place links to Amazon on your blog. These links contain your own unique tracking ID. If one of your referrals makes a purchase, Amazon pays you a percentage of the sale. Your tracking ID tells Amazon that you were the affiliate who generated the sale.

The program offers many features that enable you to target Amazon products that are likely to be of interest to your readers. Think about the massive inventory that Amazon holds across diverse departments like books, electronics, and kitchenware. There is bound to be at least one product on Amazon that your readers might consider buying and therefore, potentially generate some commission for you.

There are several ways you can use your Amazon Affiliate links. For example, you may write a review of a new book or product. You could place an affiliate link within the text that points straight to the product page on Amazon. Some of your readers, who may be interested in the product, may click the link, and hopefully buy it. You can also showcase products on your blog—the sidebar is a good place for this. You can choose a specific product, or use a widget that randomly displays products from a particular department or category. There are many ways to get your Amazon links in front of your readers. You should take time to look around the Amazon Associates members' area to see what's available—the following screenshot shows some of the options:

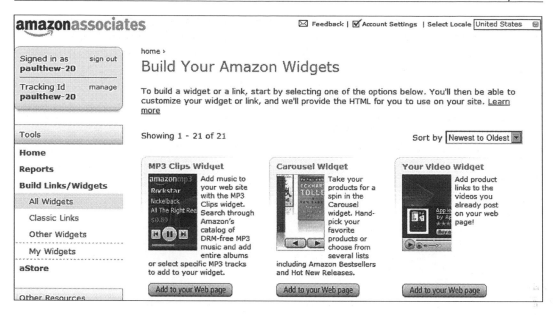

Creating an Amazon Associates Widget

Let's imagine that ChilliGuru has written a chili cookbook. He could place an Amazon advert for this book in his sidebar. We'll work through how to do this, but first you need to sign up for an Amazon Associates account. Go to `http://affiliate-program.amazon.com/join/`, click on the **Apply Now** link, and fill out the registration form.

Log in to the Amazon Associates members' area. Click on the **Build Links/Widgets** link under the **Tools** menu. Find the **Product Links** widget and click the **Add to your Web page** button:

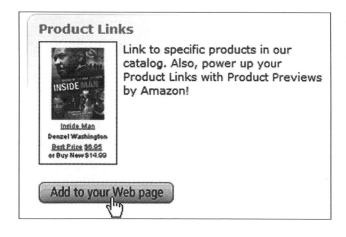

On the next page, you can search for the product you want to display by keyword, the ISBN, or the **ASIN (Amazon Standard Identification Number)**. Of course, ChilliGuru hasn't really written a cookbook (because he doesn't exist!). So, you can use any book (or product) you like. You'll be presented with a list of results for your search. Click the **Get HTML** button next to the book you want.

The next page allows you to customize the widget. If you look at the **Live Preview** of the widget, you'll see it's a fairly simple design. Try selecting different options and see how they look in the preview (I recommend you stick with the **Text and Image** link type; I've also removed the border). Once you're happy with your option choices, we can change the color scheme to match ChilliGuru a little better. Enter the following values in the color fields: **Background Color**: F8DC9E; **Text Color**: 000000; **Link Color**: DF5E37:

Copy the HTML code, which appears in the box below the widget editor.

Using Your Amazon Widget in WordPress

Now we'll paste the HTML code into a text widget in WordPress. Log in to your ChilliGuru blog. Click the **Design** tab, and then the **Widgets** sub-tab.

Add a **Text** widget to **Sidebar 1**; place it between the **Pages** and **Categories** widgets:

Click the **Edit** link for the new **Text** widget and paste the Amazon HTML code into the text area. Give the widget a title: **My Book**. Click the **Change** button.

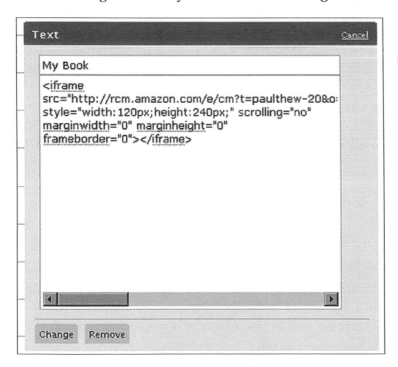

Click the **Save Changes** button and view the blog. You'll see the widget in Sidebar 1. Go ahead and click on the image or one of the other links, and you'll be taken to the product page on Amazon. Your tracking ID is embedded into the link, so if anyone clicks through and buys the book, you earn commission. This is how the widget looks in the sidebar:

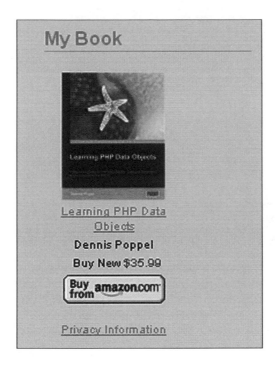

Affiliate Networks

Along with Amazon Associates, there are many other affiliate programmes and networks that you may wish to join. Some companies (for example, Amazon) manage their own affiliate programmes; others use affiliate networks, such as Commission Junction, Share Results, or ClickBank to take care of their affiliates for them. These networks manage affiliate programs on behalf of hundreds of companies from household names to small independents.

If there is a particular company for which your readers may be potential customers, check to see if they have an affiliate program. You should also consider signing up to a couple of affiliate networks and see if they are promoting programs that might earn revenue on your blog.

Direct Ad Sales

AdSense and affiliate programs provide an easy-to-manage, quick-start advertising option for your blog. However, if you're prepared to do some extra work, you may find it more profitable to sell ads directly. This will involve finding your own advertising clients, in other words, **sales**. If you don't have the time or inclination to take on yet another role for your blog, then stick with AdSense and let Google do the selling for you—they seem to be quite good at it!

Don't even think about direct ad sales until your traffic hits a respectable level. There's no point me recommending any precise traffic volumes—it will vary from blog to blog, depending on your industry, and who your readers and potential advertisers are. However, suffice to say that your daily page views will probably need to be in the thousands, or even tens of thousands, before you'll have anything like an attractive proposition to take to potential advertisers.

Banner Sizes

The web advertising industry uses a range of standard banner sizes. This helps advertisers save money on their design costs. They know that once they've had advertising artwork created to industry-standard sizes, it will be acceptable to a wide range of publishers. So, when you're deciding how much room you need for advertising, you should think in units of space that match the standard sizes. The **Interactive Advertising Bureau (IAB)**, a trade body for the online advertising industry, maintains guidelines for the standard ad sizes (see `http://www.iab.net/Ad_Unit` for details).

When it comes to choosing which banner sizes you want to display, there are a few standard sizes that seem to be popular with bloggers. Perhaps, the most common size on blogs at the moment is the `125 x 125` square button. The following screenshot shows this type of ad on TechCrunch (`http://www.techcrunch.com`):

As with most things blog-related, it's difficult to generalize. Yes, `125 x 125` is a popular size, but it's by no means the only one in common usage. Many blogs, particularly the big players, use ads of all sizes. Personally, I think that smaller ads look better and are more appropriate on small business blogs. I recommend you start your banner advertising venture with fairly small banners. If your advertisers suddenly start demanding `160 x 600` skyscrapers, and are prepared to pay for them, you can consider up-sizing then.

Where to Place Banner Ads

There's always a trade-off when it comes to advertising. You can charge more for the most prominent positions on your blog, but then these will be unavailable for your own content. Placing your ads in less prominent positions means they don't get in the way of your content, but they are worth less to advertisers. In fact, you will find it difficult to sell ads that are tucked away below the fold, right at the bottom of the sidebars.

To stand a chance of making any money from banner advertising, you have to be prepared to let go of some of your best screen real estate. This probably means at the top of your sidebars. You don't need to sacrifice a whole load of space to begin with—I suggest you start with maybe two 125 x 125 banners. If your ad sales really start to take off, you can consider devoting more space. Luckily, the widgetized sidebars in WordPress make it fairly easy to move stuff around.

How Much to Charge

The simple answer to this is: Whatever you can get! It's going to be tough to get advertisers on board in the early days of your sales efforts. Making your prices attractive will be a big help in closing those crucial initial deals. You may even consider giving advertisers a free trial as an incentive to sign up.

There are various pricing models used in web advertising. Probably the most attractive to advertisers is pay-per-click, for example, you charge, say, $0.20 each time someone clicks on your advertiser's banner. Advertisers like this model as they are paying for objectified, clearly visible results. Unfortunately, the technology required to operate this pricing model is quite complex and there are no WordPress plugins currently available to make it any easier. Therefore, I suggest you consider two other possible pricing models, which can be managed using the plugin we'll install in the next section. The first is simply time-based—your advertisers pay an agreed price for their banners to be displayed for a certain period; a month, three months, or whatever. The second is based on the number of times their banner is viewed—for example $100 per 5,000 views.

Your prices will also vary depending on the position of the banner. As I already mentioned, the most valuable (and easiest to sell) position is at the top of your sidebar. However, if you were to offer ad positions below the fold at the bottom of the sidebar, your price would have to be adjusted downwards in order to be attractive.

As to the exact dollar amount you should be charging, it really depends on your sales skills and the abundance (or lack) of advertisers in your niche or industry. As a very rough guide, a blog in my home city (Birmingham, UK), aimed at the arts and creative sector with around 32,000 monthly page views, is charging £100 (about $200) for a one-month text ad displayed in the header (see http://www.createdinbirmingham.com). If they were selling graphical banner ads, the price would probably be slightly higher. In working out your prices, do some research—see if you can find out what other bloggers are charging. If your sales drive is not going too well, it could mean your price point is a little high.

Your Media Pack and Rate Card

A **media pack** gives prospective advertisers all the data they need before deciding whether to buy advertising in a publication. If you're intent on selling adverts on your blog, you will be taken far more seriously if you have a detailed proposition for your advertising customers. In the world of offline publications, the media pack is usually a glossy brochure. On the web, publishers often present it as a well designed PDF or fancy online presentation. You don't necessarily need to go to these lengths. Your media pack can be in the form of a static page on your blog. The important thing is to include all the pertinent information. Remember, prospective advertisers want to know the **benefits** they will receive from advertising on your blog—what's in it for them? Your media pack might include:

- Page views and visitors per month (these are essential stats for advertisers)

- Number of subscribers by RSS and email

- Google Page Rank, Technorati 'Authority' Ranking, Alexa Ranking (only include these if they are reasonably good; if your Alexa rank is way down in the millions, omit it)

- The number of links in to your blog

- Average number of comments per month

- A description of your target audience

- Any demographic data you may have about your readers (for example gender, age, income, and so on)

- Any awards your blog may have picked up

- Any testimonials and reviews you can get

- Details about the type and size of adverts you will accept

- Where the ads will appear (use screenshots, if possible)

A rate card is a price list for all the advertising options you're selling. While a rate card can help enhance your professional image, it might not be such a good idea to publish your rates in the early days of your sales efforts. You might find a rate card useful for your reference, but hang fire on publishing it until you've spoken to a few prospective clients. Gauge their reaction to your prices and see if you're in the ballpark. Another reason for not publishing your rates up front is that you may be able to negotiate higher prices for some clients than others. On your media pack page, provide contact details for requesting more information about rates. You might consider setting up a special email address (for example, `advertising@ yourcompany.com`) or a dedicated contact form for advertising enquiries, using **cforms II**.

Rotating Banner Ads

Once you have more than two or three advertising clients, you may decide to rotate their adverts. This means you can display several ads in a much smaller space. Each time the page is reloaded, one of the adverts will be displayed at random.

We'll set this up in ChilliGuru so that there are two advertising spots in Sidebar 2. One will rotate three 125 x 125 ads and the other will rotate three 120 x 240 ads. I've supplied six JPG images in the code bundle for this chapter, which you can use as dummy adverts for testing. They're in a folder called **ads**. Place the entire folder in the **htdocs** directory for your local development server (**C:\xampp\htdocs**).

We will use a plugin called **WPAds**, by Nick Brady, to handle the ad rotation. We will also need a plugin called **Exec-PHP**, by Sören Weber, which enables the WPAds PHP code to execute in a text widget.

Download WPAds from `http://thesandbox.wordpress.com/wpads/` and then download Exec-PHP from `http://wordpress.org/extend/plugins/exec-php/`. Unzip all the files in the **wpads** package into a folder called **wpads**, and then unzip the **exec-php** package. Place both of the unzipped plugin folders into the **plugins** directory for your ChilliGuru test site. Log in to the admin area and activate both plugins.

Exec-PHP does not require any further configuration. So let's begin setting up the ad rotations. Click the **Settings** tab and then the **WPAds** sub-tab. In WPAds you create **banners**—which are the ads you want to display, and **zones**—which are the positions on the page where you want the banners to be displayed. Click the **Add new banner** link. In the **Description** box, enter **banner1**—this is just a label to help you identify the banner; in a live situation you might use the advertiser's name. In the **HTML Code** box you need to enter a **destination URL**, which is the link to open when the advert is clicked. The code is as follows (I'm using the Google home page for this demonstration; in a live situation this would be your advertiser's target page):

```
<a href="http://www.google.com">
```

You also need to specify the **source URL** for the ad image. This can be a link to any server on the Web. Your advertisers may keep their ad graphics on their own server, instead of supplying you with the images. This way they can make changes to the graphics, which will be automatically updated on your blog and anywhere else they have placed the ad. For this demonstration, the ad images are placed in the **ads** folder in the **htdocs** directory of our local server, so this is the URL for the first advert (this goes on the second line in the **HTML Code** box):

```
<img src="http://localhost/ads/ad1.jpg" />
```

You also need the closing `</a>` tag (this goes on the third line in the **HTML Code** box). So the complete code looks like this:

```
<a href="http://www.google.com">
<img src="http://localhost/ads/ad1.jpg" />
</a>
```

In the **Zones** box, enter **sidebar1**. This will create a zone by that name. Leave the default values in all the other fields and click the **Save** button:

WPAds - New banner

Description	banner1
	Any text that helps you identify this banner

HTML Code	`<a href="http://www.google.com">`
	`<img src="http://localhost/ads/ad1.jpg" />`
	`</a>`

	Copy and paste the HTML code to show the ad (for example, the Google AdSense code)
Zones	sidebar1
	Enter names of the zones where this banner will show, separated by commas. Example: *sidebar1, sidebar2*
Active	☑
Weight	1
	Sets how much a banner is displayed in relationship with other banners in the same zone. Default: 1
Max views	0
	Maximum number of times this banner will be shown. Default: 0 (unlimited views)
	Save

You can see that **banner1** and **sidebar1** have been created:

Now we'll create a couple more banners to be rotated in the **sidebar1** zone. So add a new banner called **banner2**, using the image **ad2.jpg**; I've used Yahoo! as the destination, this time. Remember that the zone is **sidebar1**:

Description	banner2
	Any text that helps you identify this banner

HTML Code	`<a href="http://www.yahoo.com">`
	`<img src="http://localhost/ads/ad2.jpg" />`
	`</a>`

	Copy and paste the HTML code to show the ad (for example, the Google AdSense code)
Zones	sidebar1
	Enter names of the zones where this banner will show, separated by commas. Example: *sidebar1, sidebar2*

Repeat the procedure, one more time, to create **banner3** using **ad3.jpg** — use a different destination URL and remember the zone is still **sidebar1**.

You'll now see that sidebar1 contains three banners:

Banners (Add new)

ID	Description	Zones	Active	Weight	Max views	Views served		
1	banner1	sidebar1	Y	1	0	0	Edit	Delete
2	banner2	sidebar1	Y	1	0	0	Edit	Delete
3	banner3	sidebar1	Y	1	0	0	Edit	Delete

Add new banner

We now have three 125 x 125 banners ready to rotate in the **sidebar1** zone. Before we add the zone to the ChilliGuru sidebar, we'll set up a second zone, **sidebar2**, to display our 120 x 240 ads.

Add three new banners (**banner4**, **banner5**, and **banner6**) for images **ad4.jpg**, **ad5.jpg**, and **ad6.jpg**. Place these in a zone called **sidebar2**. You can use different destination URLs, if you like. The following screenshot shows the setup for **banner4**:

Description	banner4
	Any text that helps you identify this banner

HTML Code	`<a href="http://www.bbc.co.uk">`
	`<img src="http://localhost/ads/ad4.jpg" />`
	`</a>`

	Copy and paste the HTML code to show the ad (for example, the Google AdSense code)
Zones	sidebar2
	Enter names of the zones where this banner will show, separated by commas. Example: *sidebar1, sidebar2*

Now we can add our zones, **sidebar1** and **sidebar2**, to the ChilliGuru sidebar. You'll see there is a simple snippet of PHP code for each zone:

Zone	Banners (Probability)	Code in templates	Code in posts
sidebar1	banner1 (33%) banner2 (33%) banner3 (33%)	`<?php wpads('sidebar1'); ?>`	`<!--wpads#sidebar1-->`
sidebar2	banner4 (33%) banner5 (33%) banner6 (33%)	`<?php wpads('sidebar2'); ?>`	`<!--wpads#sidebar2-->`

Copy the code for **sidebar1**: `<?php wpads('sidebar1'); ?>`.

Click the **Design** tab in the main admin menu, followed by the **Widgets** sub-tab.

Now add a **Text** widget to **Sidebar 2**, right above the **Search** widget:

Click the **Edit** link for the new **Text** widget and paste the WPAds code into the text area. Give the widget a title—**Our Sponsors**:

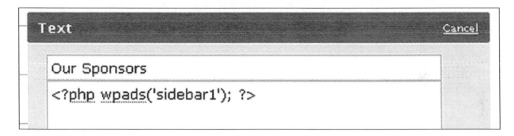

Now, click on the **Change** button. Repeat the same process with another new **Text** widget. Drag it just below the first **Text** widget in **Sidebar 2**, and enter the code for the WPads **sidebar2** zone: `<?php wpads('sidebar2'); ?>`. This time, **don't** use a title.

Click the **Save Changes** button.

Now view the blog. You will see that the ad widgets have been added to Sidebar 2. Go ahead and reload the page a few times and you will see the ads rotating at random. Click on the ads and you will be taken to the corresponding destination URL.

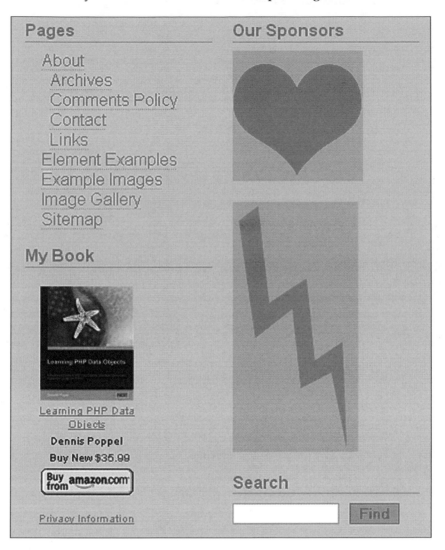

OK, so the dummy images look a bit weird, but you get the idea! Hopefully your advertisers' banners will be a little more attractive. You might also think that the 125 x 125 + 120 x 240 banner configuration takes up too much space. If so, consider just one or two 125 x 125 banners. It's really up to you.

Remember, it's the **Exec-PHP** plugin we installed earlier that makes the WPAds code execute in text widgets.

Now go back to the WPAds configuration page in the admin area and we'll take a look at a couple of the other features.

You'll notice that the **Views served** column in the **Banners** section has recorded the number of times each banner has been viewed. This is useful information to report to your advertisers.

Banners (Add new)

ID	Description	Zones	Active	Weight	Max views	Views served		
1	banner1	sidebar1	Y	1	0	5	Edit	Delete
2	banner2	sidebar1	Y	1	0	5	Edit	Delete
3	banner3	sidebar1	Y	1	0	1	Edit	Delete

You can also set a maximum number of views for each banner. This would allow you to charge your advertisers per 1000 views. Click on the **Edit** link for **banner1**.

If you were to deselect the **Active** checkbox, the banner would no longer be rotated in its zone. Also, you can change the **Weight** (probability) for each banner. Changing it to **2** will make the banner twice as likely to be served in the rotation cycle than a banner with a weight of 1. You can also set the **Max views**. Enter the following settings and click **Save**:

Active	☑
Weight	2
	Sets how much a banner is displayed in relationship with other banners in the same zone. Default: 1
Max views	1000
	Maximum number of times this banner will be shown. Default: 0 (unlimited views)
	Save

Notice that the probability for **banner1** is now twice that for **banner2** and **banner3**:

Zone	Banners (Probability)
sidebar1	banner1 (50%)
	banner2 (25%)
	banner3 (25%)

Rotating Amazon Banners

You may aim to sell three rotating banners per zone, but it can take time for your sales efforts to come to fruition. In the meantime, you could fill the gaps with Amazon Associates banners, or banners from other affiliate programs you have joined.

Log in to your Amazon Associates account, click **Build Links/Widgets** in the **Tools** menu, and select the **Banner** widget:

On the next page, choose an appropriate banner category. Then choose a couple of `125 x 125` banners that you like. Copy the HTML code and use it to create banners in WPAds. I've replaced the dummy images on ChilliGuru with banners from Amazon and the Share Results affiliate network:

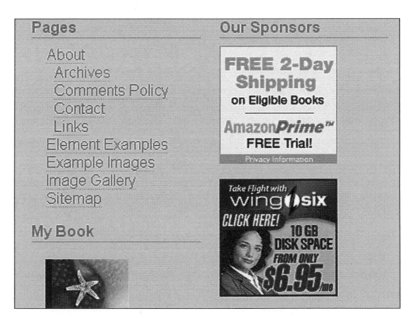

You now know how to set up a system that allows you to rotate ads in your sidebar. WPAds is a fairly simple banner rotation system. If your advertising sales really start to take off, you may find you need something more sophisticated. For example, your advertisers may want more detailed statistics about their ad campaigns, like click-through rates. You may also want to set up a charging model based on click-through rather than ad views. I haven't found a WordPress plugin that can handle this kind of complexity. However, there is a third-party open-source application, which offers an advanced solution for managing your advertisers. It's called **OpenX**. It's a very sophisticated system and is well beyond the scope of this book, but if you think you need something more powerful, check it out at `http://www.openx.org/`.

Paid Reviews

Paid reviews are a contentious issue in the blogosphere. As the name suggests, the practice involves bloggers receiving a payment from a company in exchange for reviewing that company's product or service. Many bloggers have ethical objections because they believe paid reviews can mislead readers, and distort the spirit of blogging, which, in its early days, was not about making money. I mention paid reviews here because they can be a useful source of revenue. But think carefully before using them as you could upset a sizeable proportion of your readers (and other bloggers).

You're the best person to judge the likely reaction of your readers and whether they would appreciate paid reviews. If you're not certain, ask them. Write a post about it to canvass opinion and/or conduct a poll. There are paid review networks that can help match you up with companies who want their products reviewed and are willing to pay—a couple of the biggest are **Pay Per Post** (`http://payperpost.com/`) and **ReviewMe** (`http://www.reviewme.com/`).

WP-Polls Plugin

On the subject of polls, you may be interested in the **WP-Polls Plugin**, by Lester Chan. It's a little off-topic for this chapter, so we won't go through a full installation here. However, it's a very simple plugin to install and use. You can have reader polls up and running in no time. Go to `http://wordpress.org/extend/plugins/wp-polls/` for full details.

Case Study Review

We've now completed all the work on the ChilliGuru blog. I've made one final change and that's to hide the **Element Examples** and **Example Images** pages by changing their status to **Private**—it just makes the top menu a little neater (you may recall these pages were included with the Sandbox dummy content).

I hope the work we've done on the case study has shown you how straightforward it can be to create a feature-rich, professional-looking business blog using WordPress. You should also now realize how easy it is to extend WordPress, thanks to the large and active community of developers who have created so many cool plugins.

Just because the case study is over for the book—that's not to say it's finished. Likewise, you'll discover that your blog is never 'finished'. You will be constantly tweaking it and adding functionality. The beauty of web publishing is that things will always evolve.

I will be adding updates and additional tutorials to my own blog at `http://blog.` `paulthewlis.com`. WordPress is constantly developing with new versions and plugins. I'll try to cover as many of these as possible on my blog, and show you how they can be applied to the ChilliGuru case study.

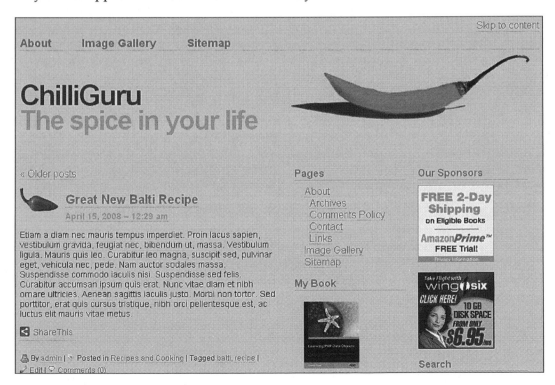

Summary

In this chapter, we looked at how you can place advertisements on your blog to generate revenue. We began with an introduction to Google AdSense and the AdSense Manager plugin, which allows you to mange your ad units in WordPress. Next, you learned about affiliate programs, in particular Amazon Associates. We set up an Amazon book widget and placed it in the sidebar. Finally, we looked at display advertising and how you can set up ad rotation using the WPAds plugin.

In the next chapter, we will look at strategies to help you cope as your blog grows and the number of visitors increases.

11
Managing Growth

If you've applied the tips, techniques, and methods you have learned throughout this book, you should be well on your way to having a successful blog that's attracting lots of visitors. Hopefully, it won't be long until your blog grows into something big. Of course, that's great—it's what every blogger wants. But success can bring with it a whole host of issues you need to deal with. In this chapter, we will explore some of these and discuss how you can address them.

Keeping Up with the Workload

As the number of visitors to your blog increases, so will your workload. You'll notice your inbox filling up with emails from your readers and you'll spend more and more of your time moderating and replying to comments. If your traffic volume really starts to take off, you could soon find yourself snowed under with correspondence from your blog.

If you find yourself in this situation, it may well be worthwhile bringing in some help. Many of the emails and comments you receive will be of relatively low-level importance. You will inevitably receive a high volume of 'Great Post!!' comments that require no response from you and just need to be moderated. You may also receive a lot of emails all asking the same or similar questions. You could easily make a list of stock replies to these FAQs. You may well find that only a small proportion of your correspondence requires your personal attention, in which case, get someone to filter it so you only see the stuff that matters.

You may already have a PA or admin assistant who is good at vetting your emails. You could set them to work moderating simple comments and responding to FAQ emails using your list of stock replies, while only passing on the correspondence which needs your attention. It may be difficult to let go this amount of control of your blog, but it will certainly free up a great deal of your time for more important tasks, like writing new posts.

Going Mobile

As your visitor base grows, there's a good chance that more and more of your readers will want to access your blog on mobile devices such as PDAs and cell phones. Mobile computing is a growth sector and savvy web publishers are doing all they can to ensure their content is compatible with as many devices as possible. You can provide a great service to your expanding readership by giving them a version of your blog that is optimized for mobile viewing.

There is a plug-in called **WordPress Mobile Edition**, by Alex King, which makes mobile optimization a cinch to set up.

Go to `http://wordpress.org/extend/plugins/wordpress-mobile-edition/` and download the plugin. Unzip the package and upload the **wp-mobile.php** file to your **plugins** directory (**/wp-content/plugins/**). Upload the **wp-mobile** folder to your themes directory (**/wp-content/themes/**). Log in to your admin area and activate the plugin. That's all you need to do to optimize your blog for mobile content. As you can see from the following screenshot, the plugin strips out most of the styling and delivers a very simple page that is quick to load on a mobile device.

If your mobile phone has trouble displaying your blog, the developer of the plugin asks that you notify him. You can identify your phone's browser type by opening this page with your phone: `http://alexking.org/who.php`. Then send the results from that page, along with the name of your phone to the developer: `http://alexking.org/contact`.

Managing Increased Traffic

As your traffic increases, there is a chance you could run into technical issues related to your web server. You may well notice your blog running slow. This is a particular risk if your blog is getting 'spikes' of high traffic that place a sudden strain on the server. These spikes can be caused by a number of reasons, for example, one of your posts making it onto the front page of Digg or a couple of major bloggers linking to you. Of course, this is all good, but only if your server can handle it.

If you work in a corporate environment and your blog is hosted on your company's web server, then these performance issues are a problem for your IT department—submit a support ticket.

However, if you're an independent operator or a small company, you may not have the luxury of a dedicated IT team. If you notice your blog slowing down or even crashing completely, and you suspect it may be caused by high traffic volumes, the first remedy to try is installing a great little plugin called **WP Super Cache**. (We'll go over what to do when you've outgrown your web host in the next section of this chapter.)

Installing WP Super Cache

This plugin is designed to reduce the server load for high-traffic blogs. It could be the solution to your slow performance problems. It works by converting your blog's pages into static HTML files and serving them to your visitors instead of the dynamic pages from the database. Static files are quicker and easier for your web server to handle, so it will be able to deal with far greater volumes of traffic before it slows down.

 You need to have **mod_rewrite** enabled on your server for this plugin to work. Check with your hosting company to ensure that it is. If it isn't, most web hosts will enable it for you.

We'll run through the installation process, which is slightly different from most of the other plugins we've used. Go to `http://wordpress.org/extend/plugins/wp-super-cache/` and download the plugin. Unzip the package and use your FTP software to upload the entire folder to your blog's **plugins** folder (**/wp-content/plugins/**). Log in to your admin area and activate the plugin. Click on the **Settings** tab, and then on the **WP Super Cache** sub-tab.

You may see a warning message advising you that **wp-content** is writeable. If this is the case, use your FTP client to change the permissions for your **wp-content** directory to **755**.

Select the **ON** radio button and then click **Update Status**:

Now scroll down the page to the **Mod Rewrite Rules** section and click the **Update mod_rewrite rules** button:

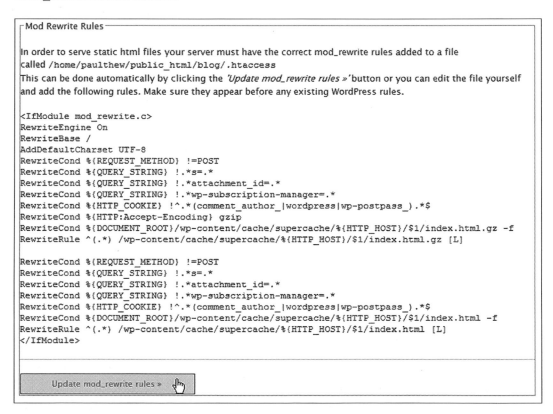

You should now see a message telling you that the **Mod Rewrite rules updated!**

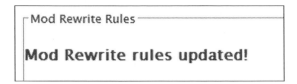

It's a good idea to check that the rules have actually been updated in your blog's **.htaccess** file. Use your FTP software to find the **.htaccess** file, which is in the root directory of your WordPress installation. Download the file to your computer, and open it up in WordPad or Crimson Editor. It should contain the mod_rewrite rules between two comments: `# BEGIN WPSuperCache` and `# END WPSuperCache`. Following is a screenshot of my **.htaccess** file in Crimson Editor:

```
# BEGIN WPSuperCache
<IfModule mod_rewrite.c>
RewriteEngine On
RewriteBase /
AddDefaultCharset UTF-8
RewriteCond %{REQUEST_METHOD} !=POST
RewriteCond %{QUERY_STRING} !.*s=.*
RewriteCond %{QUERY_STRING} !.*attachment_id=.*
RewriteCond %{QUERY_STRING} !.*wp-subscription-manager=.*
RewriteCond %{HTTP_COOKIE} !^.*(comment_author_|wordpress|wp-postpass_).*$
RewriteCond %{HTTP:Accept-Encoding} gzip
RewriteCond %{DOCUMENT_ROOT}/wp-content/cache/supercache/%{HTTP_HOST}/$1/index.html.gz -f
RewriteRule ^(.*) /wp-content/cache/supercache/%{HTTP_HOST}/$1/index.html.gz [L]

RewriteCond %{REQUEST_METHOD} !=POST
RewriteCond %{QUERY_STRING} !.*s=.*
RewriteCond %{QUERY_STRING} !.*attachment_id=.*
RewriteCond %{QUERY_STRING} !.*wp-subscription-manager=.*
RewriteCond %{HTTP_COOKIE} !^.*(comment_author_|wordpress|wp-postpass_).*$
RewriteCond %{DOCUMENT_ROOT}/wp-content/cache/supercache/%{HTTP_HOST}/$1/index.html -f
RewriteRule ^(.*) /wp-content/cache/supercache/%{HTTP_HOST}/$1/index.html [L]
</IfModule>

# END WPSuperCache
# BEGIN WordPress
<IfModule mod_rewrite.c>
RewriteCond %{REQUEST_FILENAME} !-f
RewriteCond %{REQUEST_FILENAME} !-d
RewriteRule . /index.php [L]
</IfModule>

# END WordPress
```

You can check that the plugin is working by viewing your blog and opening a few random pages. Now go back to the **WP Super Cache** configuration page under the **Settings** tab in your admin area and scroll down to the **Cache contents** section. You should see that some pages have been cached:

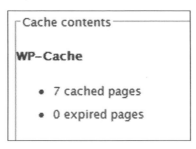

Uninstalling WP Super Cache

WP Super Cache may prevent some plugins from working properly. In particular, plugins that require dynamic data from the database may not update immediately. If you find this to be a problem you can switch the plugin off via the configuration page, or follow these steps to uninstall it completely.

Clear the cache by clicking the **Delete Cache** button under the **Cache Contents** section of the configuration page. Deactivate **WP Super Cache** on the **Plugins** page. Use your FTP software to download the **.htaccess** file, open it up in Crimson Editor, and delete the mod_rewrite rules. Make sure you only delete the WP Super Cache section and leave everything else. My **.htaccess** file looks like this when the WP Super Cache mod_rewrite rules have been deleted:

```
C:\Documents and Settings\Paul Thewlis\Desktop\.htaccess
1 # BEGIN WordPress
2 <IfModule mod_rewrite.c>
3 RewriteCond %{REQUEST_FILENAME} !-f
4 RewriteCond %{REQUEST_FILENAME} !-d
5 RewriteRule . /index.php [L]
6 </IfModule>
7
8 # END WordPress
9
```

Save the **.htaccess** file and FTP it back to your server. Now, use your FTP software to download the **wp-config.php** file from the root directory of your WordPress installation and open it up in Crimson Editor. Delete this line of code: define('WP_CACHE', true); //Added by WP-Cache Manager, save the file, and then FTP it back to the server. Again using your FTP software, open the **/wp-content/** directory, and delete the following files and folders:

- **advanced-cache.php**
- **wp-cache-config.php**
- **cache**

The following is the view in my FTP software (CuteFTP):

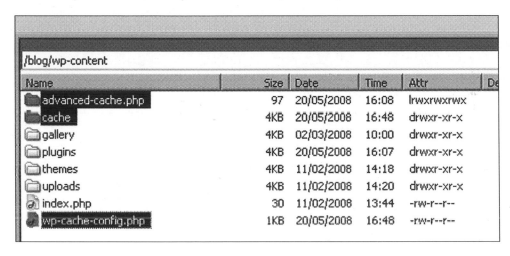

Now open the **plugins** directory and delete the entire **wp-super-cache** directory.

WP Super Cache is now completely uninstalled.

Outgrowing Your Web Host

This won't be a problem for you if your blog is running on your company web server, managed by the IT department. However, many readers will have installed their self-hosted WordPress blog on a shared hosting account. This means it's on a web server alongside lots of other people's websites, all of which have to share the server's resources, such as memory (RAM) and processing power.

Shared hosting accounts have limits set on disk space and bandwidth. As the traffic volumes to your blog increase, you may well start to exceed these limits. You may also experience performance issues (remember you're sharing memory and processor with lots of other websites). There may well come a time when your blog simply outgrows its shared hosting space, and you have to think about upgrading. If this happens, you need to move to a dedicated server.

As its name suggests, a dedicated server is all yours. There will be no more sharing of resources, which should improve performance. Also, the bandwidth limits on dedicated servers are usually much higher. The downside is that you will see a considerable increase in your monthly hosting bills. Unfortunately, that's an unavoidable cost of your new-found success!

As with desktop computers, server specs are constantly improving. Choosing a dedicated server is a bit like choosing a new desktop computer—you should go for the fastest processor and the largest RAM you can afford. For most standard blogs, disk space is less of an issue. These days, even low-end servers come with at least 80 GB hard disks. That should be more than enough, unless you have a lot of media files such as video, audio, and images.

With a dedicated server, you also need to consider server administration. Web servers don't just run themselves; they need to be constantly monitored and maintained. With your shared hosting account, all of the server administration is done by the hosting company. However, for a dedicated server, essential routine tasks such as backups, operating system patches, virus scanning, reboots, and monitoring are not necessarily included in your monthly rental costs. You're probably not a dab hand at server administration via the command line, so you'll need to buy in this expertise. Most hosting companies will offer server admin as an add-on service, or you may be able to find it cheaper if you outsource to a specialist server admin company (you provide them with access to your server and they carry out all the maintenance tasks remotely).

You should also check that your new dedicated server has all the software you need to run WordPress. Many web hosts will provide their dedicated servers pre-configured with a similar setup to their shared hosting plans. But some web hosts might just provide an 'empty box' and you may have to ask them to do the initial setup for you. As a minimum, you need to have installed: a Linux operating system, Apache web server, a control panel (for example cPanel or Plesk), PHP (version 4.3 or higher), and MySQL (version 4.0 or higher) with phpMyAdmin.

The web hosting industry is a very competitive market, so it's well worth shopping around and doing some research. There are literally thousands of hosting companies out there. I've listed a few of the best known and established hosting companies next, all of which offer dedicated servers. This is in no way an endorsement of these companies, nor is it anywhere near an exhaustive list. I've just provided them as a starting point for your own diligent research:

- Rackspace: http://www.rackspace.com
- Media Temple: http://www.mediatemple.net
- GoDaddy: http://www.godaddy.com
- Host Gator: http://www.hostgator.com
- Lunarpages Dedicated: http://www.lpdedicated.com

> Of course, you may decide to remain loyal to your existing hosting company if they offer dedicated servers! In fact, there could be advantages of staying with your existing web host; they may offer to move your WordPress blog and database for you, if you upgrade to one of their dedicated servers.

Moving WordPress to a New Server

Once you've chosen your new dedicated hosting package, you'll need to move your blog to it. Moving WordPress is not a particularly difficult task, but as with any job involving a remote web server, things can go wrong. Check with your new web host and see if they offer any assistance in moving websites for new customers—some companies do offer this service and it's always good to have some personal assistance from experts who have done it before.

If you're taking on the task yourself, here are a few preliminary guidelines before we look at the detailed procedure:

- Make a full backup of your WordPress files and database before you begin moving your blog, just in case things go wrong (see Chapter 5 for backup instructions).

- Try to figure out the time and day of the week when your blog is quietest, in terms of traffic. Use Google Analytics to work this out. Moving your blog to a new server will inevitably mean it's unavailable for a certain amount of time. Doing the work at a quiet time will minimize disruption for your readers. It's worth choosing the slowest time of the week, even if that's 4 a.m. on a Sunday morning!

- Be sure to warn your readers in advance that your blog is likely to be unavailable at the specified time. Try to give as much notice as possible, in a prominent place. Maybe use a text widget in the sidebar to make the announcement, or mention it in a blog post and on Twitter.

- Any delay is most likely to be caused when you change your domain's nameservers to point at your new server. It will take time for these new DNS settings to propagate across the Web. Ask your domain registrar and new web host for advice on how to keep this delay to a minimum.

We'll now run through the process of moving WordPress. These instructions assume that you will be keeping the same domain (and subdomain, if you're using one). They also assume that you have already downloaded your blog's database as part of the backup process.

First, use your FTP client to download your entire WordPress installation to your computer — 'entire' means all the files and folders in the WordPress root directory. This may take quite a long time. The following screenshot shows the entire WordPress installation for ChilliGuru:

Name	Size	Date	Time	Attr
wp-admin	4KB	11/02/2008	15:26	drwxr-xr-x
wp-content	4KB	20/05/2008	19:35	drwxr-xr-x
wp-includes	4KB	11/02/2008	14:53	drwxr-xr-x
.htaccess	204	22/05/2008	17:55	-rw-r--r--
index.php	94	11/02/2008	14:53	-rw-r--r--
robots.txt	351	25/03/2008	10:54	-rw----r--
sitemap.xml	8KB	10/05/2008	10:14	-rw-r--r--
sitemap.xml.gz	1KB	10/05/2008	10:14	-rw-r--r--
wp-app.php	32KB	11/02/2008	14:53	-rw-r--r--
wp-atom.php	129	11/02/2008	14:53	-rw-r--r--
wp-blog-header.php	997	11/02/2008	14:53	-rw-r--r--
wp-comments-post.php	2KB	11/02/2008	14:53	-rw-r--r--
wp-commentsrss2.php	153	11/02/2008	14:53	-rw-r--r--
wp-config-sample.php	942	11/02/2008	14:53	-rw-r--r--
wp-config.php	931	22/05/2008	04:41	-rw-r--r--
wp-cron.php	851	11/02/2008	14:53	-rw-r--r--
wp-feed.php	120	11/02/2008	14:53	-rw-r--r--
wp-links-opml.php	1KB	11/02/2008	14:53	-rw-r--r--
wp-login.php	16KB	11/02/2008	14:53	-rw-r--r--
wp-mail.php	5KB	11/02/2008	14:53	-rw-r--r--
wp-pass.php	296	11/02/2008	14:53	-rw-r--r--
wp-rdf.php	190	11/02/2008	14:53	-rw-r--r--
wp-register.php	251	11/02/2008	14:53	-rw-r--r--
wp-rss.php	127	11/02/2008	14:53	-rw-r--r--
wp-rss2.php	129	11/02/2008	14:53	-rw-r--r--
wp-settings.php	10KB	11/02/2008	14:53	-rw-r--r--
wp-trackback.php	3KB	11/02/2008	14:54	-rw-r--r--
xmlrpc.php	59KB	11/02/2008	14:54	-rw-r--r--

The directory path shown is `/www/blog`.

Once it's all downloaded, you can upload it to the correct directory on your new server (for example, if your blog was installed in a directory called **blog** on your old server, place it in a directory called **blog** on the new server).

Next we need to create a new MySQL database for WordPress. The best way to do this is to use phpMyAdmin. If your new server doesn't have phpMyAdmin installed, ask your web host if they can install it for you. When you create the database, try to use the same database name, username, and password as you had on your old server (this is not always possible, it will depend how your new web host has configured MySQL).

[If you can't use the same database settings on your new server, make sure you change them in the **wp-config.php** file in the root directory of WordPress.]

Once the database is created, you can upload all the WordPress tables using the backup copy of the database from your old server. Again, use phpMyAdmin for this. Select your new database from the list in phpMyAdmin:

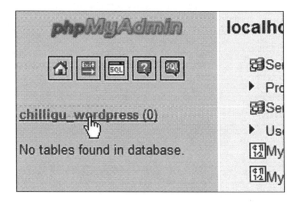

Click on the **Import** tab:

Click on the **Browse** button and locate the backup **.sql** file (remember, this is the file you downloaded when you backed up the database from your old server):

Now click the **Go** button and your database will be populated with all the WordPress tables from your old server:

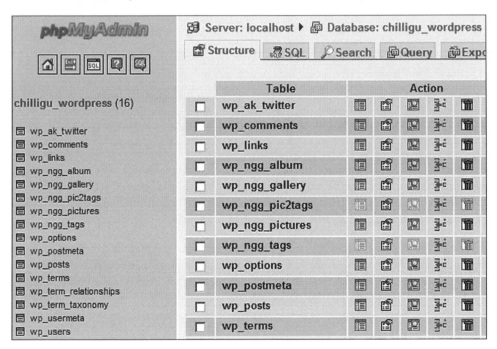

Now all you need to do is change the nameservers for your domain so that it points to your new server. If you're not sure how to do this, seek advice from your domain registrar and web host. This is the point in the process where your blog is likely to be unavailable for a few hours while the new nameservers propagate. If you're using a subdomain, set this up for your new server using the control panel.

Do not delete the WordPress files or database on your old server until you are sure the move to your new server has been successful. Once the nameservers have propagated, view your blog. Make sure the content is all there and that all the permalinks are working. You may need to re-confirm the permalink settings (go to **Options | Permalinks** and click **Update Permalink Structure**).

Bringing In Other Writers

This is a strategy that can bring a number of benefits as your blog grows. As we discussed earlier, as your blog traffic increases, so will your workload with an ever increasing number of comments and emails to answer. You may well find that the time you have for writing new posts diminishes. This is where bringing in guest writers can be a big help. You can use them to create content so you don't have to.

There will also be periods when you can't devote time to your blog, for example, during vacations or when other work activities have to take priority. Again, a guest writer can provide a much-needed break from your blog work.

Unless you are very lucky, you will also experience a common problem faced by most bloggers: writer's block. If you can't think of anything to write about, bring someone else in to plug the gap.

Guest writers will also add variety to your blog, which may help to keep your readers interested and provide them with a new perspective. Working with guest writers will also demonstrate your connectedness with the blogosphere, as most of them are likely to be bloggers themselves. They will undoubtedly tell their readers that they are posting on your blog, which can bring new visitors for you.

How to Find Guest Writers

Often the best people to approach to be guest writers are your most active commenters. These are people who already know your blog and have already taken the time to contribute content. They also enjoy your blog because they keep returning to view your posts and add comments.

You could also approach other bloggers who you follow on a regular basis—maybe ones who you have included in your blogroll. Pay particular attention to bloggers who appear to be keen networkers; these are the ones who are active commenters on several other blogs that you read.

Other possibilities for guest bloggers could be well-known people in your industry. They may not necessarily have their own blogs but could have done some offline writing in industry journals and magazines. Your colleagues, associates, and even clients may also make very good guest writers.

If your blogging budget is big enough, you may even consider hiring a freelance writer. This should guarantee some good copy. However, it's not necessary to pay your guest writers. Most of them will be happy to gain the exposure and links back to their own blog (if they have one). You could also engage them on a 'quid pro quo' basis, where you agree to do some guest writing for them some time.

You stand a better chance of having prospective guest writers accept your invitation if you don't demand too much from them. Don't set them a challenging 'assignment' that requires lots of research and writing time. Help them out by keeping your request fairly open ended so they can choose a topic they feel comfortable with.

Introducing WordPress MU

As your blog grows and you see the benefits it brings to your business, you or your colleagues, may decide to set up other blogs. You may want each member or your team, or each department in your company, to have their own blog. Or maybe your CEO is so impressed he or she wants his or her own blog, too. You could run each of these blogs with their own individual installations of WordPress. However, WordPress has a cousin that allows you to run multiple blogs from a single installation. It's called **WordPress MU**. It's a modified version of WordPress that makes running a network of blogs on a single domain much easier.

WordPress MU allows an unlimited number of blogs to run off one installation. All the blogs on a WordPress MU system operate completely independently of each other. Each can use different themes and settings. The administrator decides which plugins to install, and can give different permissions to different users.

We'll look at the basics of WordPress MU so that you can see just how easy it can be to get multiple blogs up and running for your business.

Installing WordPress MU

The process for installing WordPress MU on a live production server is a little more complicated than a regular WordPress installation. This is because there are some additional server and DNS configurations that need to be done. You can find full details of this at `http://trac.mu.wordpress.org/browser/trunk/README.txt`.

For the purposes of this demonstration, we will install WordPress MU on our local XAMPP development server, which won't require as many additional DNS and Apache configurations.

Switching ON mod_rewrite

However, there is one change we need to make to the configuration of the Apache server in XAMPP. You should do this before you start the server—if the server is already running, stop it now by using the XAMPP control panel:

Go to this folder in your XAMPP installation: **C:\xampp\apache\conf**.

Open the **httpd.conf** file in Crimson Editor. Locate the following line of code (it should be around line 118):

```
#LoadModule rewrite_module modules/mod_rewrite.so
```

Uncomment the line by deleting the #:

Now search for AllowOverride None (from the Crimson Editor menu, select **Search | Find...**):

Change `AllowOverride None` to `AllowOverride All`, then search for the next instance and change it. There should be only two instances of `AllowOverride None` that need to be changed (around lines 188 and 331), but search one more time just to be sure—if you find another instance, change it.

Now save the **httpd.conf** file.

Creating the Database

Start your local XAMPP server and open `http://localhost/phpmyadmin/` in your browser. Create a new database with an appropriate name:

Setting up a Test Domain and Subdomains

WordPress MU cannot be installed on localhost, so we need to set up a test domain. Locate the following directory in Windows: **C:\WINDOWS\system32\drivers\etc**. There should be a file in there called **hosts** (if there isn't, create one—make sure it's just called **hosts** and **not hosts.txt** or anything else). Add this line at the end of the **hosts** file:

```
127.0.0.1 localhost testdomain.com
```

That takes care of the main test domain, but we also need a couple of subdomains to run our test blogs. In a live installation of WordPress MU on a production server, the subdomains would be created automatically, thanks to the configuration settings we would make on a live server. However, those settings won't work on localhost, so we need to add all the subdomains for our test blogs in the Windows **hosts** file. Go ahead and add the following to the **hosts** file:

```
127.0.0.1 localhost firstblog.testdomain.com
127.0.0.1 localhost secondblog.testdomain.com
```

Save and close the **hosts** file.

Installing the WordPress MU Script

Now go to `http://mu.wordpress.org/download/` and download WordPress MU. Unzip the package and rename the extracted folder to **wpmu**. Place the **wpmu** folder in your XAMPP **htdocs** directory (**C:\xampp\htdocs**).

Point your browser at `http://testdomain.com/wpmu`. You will be presented with the installation page:

WordPressµ

Installing WordPress µ

Welcome to WordPress µ. I will help you install this software by asking you a few questions and asking that you change the permissions on a few directories so I can create configuration files and make a directory to store all your uploaded files.

If you have installed the single-blog version of WordPress before, please note that the WordPress µ installer is different and trying to create the configuration file wp-config.php youself may result in a broken site. It's much easier to use this installer to get the job done.

Scroll down to the configuration area and enter the following details. Note that the database username should be **root** and the password is the MySQL root password you set up for XAMPP in Chapter 3.

Blog Addresses

Please choose whether you would like blogs for the WordPress µ install to use sub-domains or sub-directories. You can not change this later. We recommend sub-domains.

- ⦿ Sub-domains (like `blog1.example.com`)
- ○ Sub-directories (like `example.com/blog1`)

Database

Below you should enter your database connection details. If you're not sure about these, contact your host.

Database Name	wpmu
User Name	root
Password	password
Database Host	localhost

Server Address

What is the Internet address of your site? You should enter the shortest address possible. For example, use *example.com* instead of *www.example.com* but if you are going to use an address like *blogs.example.com* then enter that unaltered in the box below.
Server Address: testdomain.com

Site Details

Site Title	Testdomain.com Blogs	What would you like to call your site?
Email	paulthewlis@yahoo.co.uk	Your email address.

Submit

Hit the **Submit** button and you should see a page telling you that the installation was successful:

WordPressμ

Installation Finished!

Congratulations! Your WordPress μ site has been configured.

You can log in using the username "admin" and password 0f4c5defc5b8

Make a note of your admin password (or copy it to your clipboard), click on the log in link, and **log in** to the admin area.

In a live situation you would probably install WordPress MU in the root directory on your web server, so that the domain points directly to it. However, because this is a test installation, and I didn't want to crowd out the root of the XAMPP **htdocs** directory with all the WordPress MU files and folders, we've installed it in a sub-directory. So the URL for our installation is http://testdomain.com/wpmu.

WordPress MU Basics

We'll now run through a few of the basic features of WordPress MU to give you a taste of what can be achieved.

The first thing to do is change your password to something more memorable. Click on the **Users** tab over on the right-hand side of the page. Click on **admin** in the list of users. Scroll down to the bottom of the page and enter a new password, then click the **Update Profile** button.

Now go back to the main **Dashboard** by clicking the **Testdomain.com Blogs** tab right in the top left-hand corner of the page.

You'll notice that the whole environment looks very similar to WordPress, so many of the admin options will be familiar.

Let's take a look at the default blog that has been set up. This is the 'main administrator' blog. Click the **Visit Site** button to view it:

The **Login** link will take you back to the admin area. Try clicking the **Create a new blog** link. You should see a page like this:

This tells you that registration is disabled, which means new blogs can only be created by the main administrator (that is 'you') from within the admin area. We'll enable registration later.

Go back to the admin area and we'll try setting up a new blog.

Click on the **Site Admin** tab, then the **Create a New Blog** button. You'll be taken to the **Blogs** page. At the top of this page is a list of all the existing blogs (just one at the moment). Further down there is the **Add Blogs** section. Enter the following details and click the **Add Blog** button (note that the email functionality isn't working on our local server, so you can enter any email address you like):

You should now see the new blog, **First Blog**, in the blog list. On a live installation, WordPress MU would email a random password to the blog owner. However, because we don't have email functionality on our test server, we'll reset the password.

 When you're logged in as the main administrator you can edit the settings for any blog in your WordPress MU community.

Click on the **firstblog** username:

Domain	Last Updated	Registered	Users
testdomain.com	2008-05-25 4:05:22 pm	2008-05-25 4:05:21 pm	admin (paulthewlis@yahoo.co.uk)
firstblog	2008-05-25 10:13:29 pm	2008-05-25 10:13:26 pm	firstblog (david@mail.com)

Scroll down to the bottom of the page and enter a new password, then click the **Update User** button.

Now click **Log Out,** in the top right-hand corner of the page. Point your browser at `http://firstblog.testdomain.com/wpmu/`. You can now see the new blog we just created:

Click the **Login** link and log in with username, **firstblog**, and the password you just set. You'll notice that the admin area is the same as a regular WordPress blog. The only difference is that the **Plugins** menu is not there. This is because the main administrator of the WordPress MU community can restrict access to plugins for all blogs.

Log out of the first blog and go back to `http://testdomain.com/wpmu` and log in as the main administrator. Click the **Site Admin** tab, and then **Options**. Scroll down to the bottom of the page and select the checkbox next to **Plugins**:

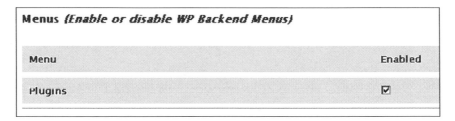

This enables the **Plugins** menu for every blog in the community. WordPress MU handles plugins slightly differently from WordPress. The main administrator can install plugins that are activated and installed on every blog in the community, or they can install plugins that are available to users on a per blog basis. It is up to the individual blog owners to decide if they want to activate those optional plugins.

There are two plugins folders in the **/wp-content/** directory:

- **/mu-plugins/**: Plugins in this folder can only be controlled by the main administrator. Any plugins that are placed in this folder are automatically activated and apply to every blog in the community.

- **/plugins/**: Plugins in this folder can be activated by individual blog owners, if they decide to use them.

To see how this works, let's copy a plugin from the ChilliGuru case study blog. Go to **C:\xampp\htdocs\wordpress\wp-content\plugins** and copy the **subscribe-to-comments.php** file. Now go to **C:\xampp\htdocs\wpmu\wp-content\plugins** and paste the file in there. Log in to the first blog and click the **Plugins** menu. You will see the **Subscribe to Comments** plugin (activate it). The plugin is now working on the first blog comments form. It's only activated on the first blog—if you log in to the main administrator blog and click on the **Plugins** tab, you'll see **Subscribe to Comments** is there, but it is not activated.

A similar principle applies to themes. The main administrator can activate a theme and make it available to every blog in the community. However, themes can also be deactivated globally and then activated on a per blog basis. To see this in action log in to the first blog and click the **Design** tab. You should see **WordPress mu Default** as the **Current Theme** and **WordPress Classic** as an **Available Theme**. Now go back to the main administrator blog. Click on the **Site Admin** tab, and then on **Themes**. Select the **No** radio button for the **WordPress Classic** theme and click the **Update Themes** button:

Site Themes

Disable themes site-wide. You can enable themes on a blog by blog basis.

Active		Theme	Version
○ Yes ◉ No		WordPress Classic	1.5
◉ Yes ○ No		WordPress mu Default	1.6
○ Yes ◉ No		WordPress mu Default/home	1.6

If you go back to the first blog admin area and click the **Design** tab, you will see that the **WordPress Classic** theme is no longer available.

The main administrator can activate the WordPress Classic theme on individual blogs. Back in the main administrator dashboard, click the **Site Admin** tab and the **Blogs** sub-tab. In the blog list, click the **Edit** link for **firstblog**. In the **Blog Themes** section, select the checkbox for **WordPress Classic**, and then click the **Update Options** button.

Blog Themes	
Theme	**Enable**
WordPress Classic	☑
WordPress mu Default/home	☐

The WordPress Classic theme is now available for the first blog but no other blog in the community.

Developing a Blog Network

Hopefully you're beginning to see how easy it is to set up a network of blogs using WordPress MU. You could set up blogs for anyone in your company in no time at all. You could even configure WordPress MU so that your colleagues can register for their own blogs without having to bother you. We'll set this up now.

In the main administrator blog, click on the **Site Admin** tab then the **Options** sub-tab. In the **Allow new registrations** area, select the radio button for **Enabled for all. Blogs and user accounts can be created**:

Allow new registrations	○ Disabled ◉ Enabled for all. Blogs and user accounts can be created. ○ Enabled for users only. Only user account can be created. ○ Enabled for blogs only. Only logged in users can create new blogs. Disable or enable registration and who or what can be registered. (Default=all)

This setting would allow anyone to register their own blog on your network. However, you only want people within your company to be able to do this. So scroll down to the **Limited Email Registrations** area and enter your company's domain:

Limited Email Registrations	mycompany.com
	If you want to limit blog registrations to certain domains. One domain per line.

Click the **Update Options** button. Now registrations are restricted to people who have an email address for your company. No one else will be able to sign up.

We can try this out. Log out from the main administrator blog. Go to `http://testdomain.com/wpmu/` and click on the **Create a new blog** link. You will be taken to the registration page:

Get your own Testdomain.com Blogs account in seconds

Username:

(Must be at least 4 characters, letters and numbers only.)

Email Address:

(We'll send your password to this address, so **triple-check it.**)

⊙ Gimme a blog!
○ Just a username, please.

Next »

In the **Username** box enter **secondblog**. To test the sign-up restriction, enter an email address that does **not** end in **@mycompany.com** and click **Next>>**. You should see a message telling you that the email address is not allowed:

So now enter an email address ending with **@mycompany.com** and click **Next>>** again. You'll be taken to the next page, where you should enter **secondblog** in the **Blog Title** box and click **Signup>>**. You will be taken to the 'success' page:

> ## Congratulations! Your new blog, Second Blog, is almost ready.
>
> But, before you can start using your blog, **you must activate it**.
>
> Check your inbox at **andrea@mycompany.com** and click the link given. It should arrive within 30 minutes.
>
> If you do not activate your blog within two days, you will have to sign up again.

As you can see, WordPress MU will now send a confirmation email, which contains an activation link.

Of course, we don't have email functionality on our local test server. However, we can work around this for the purposes of this demonstration. Go to `http://localhost/phpmyadmin`. Select the **wpmu** database, then the **wp-signups** table, and then click the **Browse** tab. There should be a record for **secondblog.testdomain.com**. Look for the **activation key** and copy it to your clipboard:

The activation link that the new sign-up receives in their confirmation email looks like this:

http://secondblog.testdomain.com/wpmu/wp-activate.php?key=c6786f75912b6361

Replace the activation key with the one you copied from the database and then enter the activation link URL into your browser's address bar. You should see a page telling you that the second blog is now active:

Copy the password and use the **Login** link to access your new blog's admin area.

Note that the **Plugins** menu is available, but **Subscribe to Comments** is not activated. Also, the WordPress Classic theme is not available for this blog.

That was a very quick run through some of the basic features of WordPress MU, but hopefully it has shown you how easy it is to create a network of blogs for your business. You now have a test installation of WordPress MU to experiment with and explore the features in more detail before deciding if you'd like to use it on a live server.

Summary

In this chapter, we have discussed some of the issues that may arise as your blog grows. You learned how to improve your blog's performance by installing WP Super Cache. You should now know how to choose a dedicated server for when you outgrow your shared hosting account and how to move your blog to the new server. You also had an introduction to WordPress MU and saw how it can be used to easily set up a network of blogs for your business. We also looked at how to make your blog 'mobile-friendly'; how to handle the increased levels of correspondence you'll receive; and how to find guest writers.

Index

Thank you for buying
WordPress for Business Bloggers

Packt Open Source Project Royalties

When we sell a book written on an Open Source project, we pay a royalty directly to that project. Therefore by purchasing WordPress for Business Bloggers, Packt will have given some of the money received to the WordPress project.

In the long term, we see ourselves and you—customers and readers of our books—as part of the Open Source ecosystem, providing sustainable revenue for the projects we publish on. Our aim at Packt is to establish publishing royalties as an essential part of the service and support a business model that sustains Open Source.

If you're working with an Open Source project that you would like us to publish on, and subsequently pay royalties to, please get in touch with us.

Writing for Packt

We welcome all inquiries from people who are interested in authoring. Book proposals should be sent to authors@packtpub.com. If your book idea is still at an early stage and you would like to discuss it first before writing a formal book proposal, contact us; one of our commissioning editors will get in touch with you.

We're not just looking for published authors; if you have strong technical skills but no writing experience, our experienced editors can help you develop a writing career, or simply get some additional reward for your expertise.

About Packt Publishing

Packt, pronounced 'packed', published its first book "Mastering phpMyAdmin for Effective MySQL Management" in April 2004 and subsequently continued to specialize in publishing highly focused books on specific technologies and solutions.

Our books and publications share the experiences of your fellow IT professionals in adapting and customizing today's systems, applications, and frameworks. Our solution-based books give you the knowledge and power to customize the software and technologies you're using to get the job done. Packt books are more specific and less general than the IT books you have seen in the past. Our unique business model allows us to bring you more focused information, giving you more of what you need to know, and less of what you don't.

Packt is a modern, yet unique publishing company, which focuses on producing quality, cutting-edge books for communities of developers, administrators, and newbies alike. For more information, please visit our website: www.PacktPub.com.

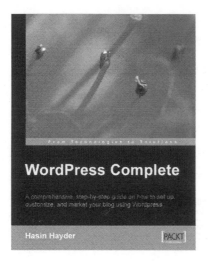

WordPress Complete

ISBN: 1-904811-89-2   Paperback: 272 pages

A comprehensive, step-by-step guide on how to set up, customize, and market your blog using WordPress

1. Clear practical coverage of all aspects of WordPress

2. Concise, clear, and easy to follow, rich with examples

3. In-depth coverage of installation, themes, syndication, and podcastin

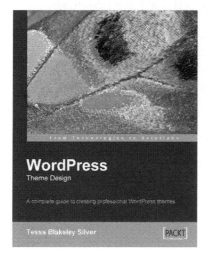

WordPress Theme Design

ISBN: 978-1-847193-09-4   Paperback: 211 pages

A complete guide to creating professional WordPress themes

1. Take control of the look and feel of your WordPress site

2. Simple, clear tutorial to creating Unique and Beautiful themes

3. Expert guidance with practical step-by-step instructions for theme design

4. Design tips, tricks, and troubleshooting ideas

Please check **www.PacktPub.com** for information on our titles

DATE DUE

Made in the USA